'Few are better placed to explore the sinister world of cyber scam operations than Ivan Franceschini, Ling Li, and Mark Bo. Brimming with first-hand accounts and painstakingly sought testimonials from survivors of these brutal compounds, their book stands testament to the chaos these operations have wreaked across Southeast Asia and beyond. The authors make the stakes clear, contextualising it within the rise of Global China and the rise of transnational criminal enterprises that have burgeoned alongside it, but never forgetting the voices of those enslaved inside these compounds. From forced labour to trafficking to the millions around the world who have lost their life savings, the issue of scams is one of the most pressing of our time. This book is the definitive story of how we got here, of who has profited and who has suffered, and goes beyond easy tropes and narratives. A clear, incisive, and must-read account'

Shibani Mahtani, co-author of *Among the Braves*

Ivan Franceschini is a lecturer at the Asia Institute, University of Melbourne. His expertise lies in the field of labour rights, with a specific focus on China and Southeast Asia. He co-founded the *Made in China Journal*, *The People's Map of Global China*, and *Global China Pulse*. His latest books include *Xinjiang Year Zero*, *Proletarian China*, and *Global China as Method*.

Ling Li is a project manager at Humanity Research Consultancy. She provides support to survivors of scam compounds in Southeast Asia, helping them to secure humanitarian aid and repatriation. She is currently pursuing a PhD at Ca' Foscari University of Venice.

Mark Bo is a civil society practitioner who has been based in East and Southeast Asia since 2006. He uses his background in corporate and financial mapping to investigate stakeholders involved in Asia's online gambling, fraud, and money-laundering industries.

Scam

Inside Southeast Asia's
Cybercrime Compounds

Ivan Franceschini, Ling Li, and Mark Bo

VERSO

London • New York

First published by Verso 2025

© Ivan Franceschini, Ling Li, and Mark Bo 2025

The author and publisher extend their gratitude to all those publications, detailed in the acknowledgements, in which earlier versions of these writings appeared.

1 3 5 7 9 10 8 6 4 2

Verso
UK: 6 Meard Street, London W1F 0EG
US: 207 32nd Street, New York, NY 10016
versobooks.com

Verso is the imprint of New Left Books

ISBN-13: 978-1-80429-690-5
ISBN-13: 978-1-80429-691-2 (UK EBK)
ISBN-13: 978-1-80429-692-9 (US EBK)

British Library Cataloguing in Publication Data
A catalogue record for this book is available from the British Library

Library of Congress Cataloging-in-Publication Data
A catalog record for this book is available from the Library of Congress

Typeset in Minion Pro by MJ&N Gavan, Truro, Cornwall
Printed and bound by CPI Group (UK) Ltd, Croydon CR0 4YY

Contents

Introduction   1

1. Rise of an Industry   33
2. Getting In   75
3. Inside the Scam Compounds   109
4. Players and Enablers   137
5. Getting Out   161

Conclusion   197

Acknowledgements   207
Index   209

Introduction

'I don't trust you. You are one of them, right? You all just want to sell me like some animal.' This was the first message a young Taiwanese woman named Alice (a pseudonym) sent to us when we reached out to her after she was rescued from a scam compound in Sihanoukville, Cambodia. Like the dozens of other survivors we met in the following months, her harrowing experience had left her unable to trust anyone.

In the ensuing two weeks, as we continued to exchange messages, Alice was always on edge. Penniless and paperless, she was staying in a safe house in Phnom Penh together with other survivors who mostly came from mainland China, waiting to find a way to return home to the small child she had left behind. It took some time, but eventually someone offered to pay for her journey back to Taiwan. Just a few days before her flight, she agreed to meet with one of us in a public place. It was then that she shared her whole story: 'I feel lucky because I was rescued very quickly, basically in a week. If I had been enslaved for a year or two, I might not be able to believe in humanity anymore. I know some of the victims have been brainwashed, or some have been tortured to the point that they are numb or have developed some mental illness. And at the same time, people outside, including my own family, think that I was trafficked because I am greedy and wanted to get rich overnight. So, I need to tell my story. I need to let them know the real situation.'

Knowing that she had been tortured and sexually abused in four different scam compounds, it was shocking to hear Alice describing herself as 'lucky'. She had been lured by a bogus job presented to her by a friend whom she trusted, a man in the Philippines who even paid for her visa and flight to Phnom Penh. When she arrived at her supposed new office in Sihanoukville, the supervisor informed her that she had been sold there to conduct online scams and that she would not be allowed to leave until she had earned enough money for the company. Threatening her with a stun gun, he said that if she did not comply, he would lock her up in a room and let several men rape her, which is exactly what happened soon after.

'At the beginning, they tried to force me to do pig-butchering work,' she said, referring to a type of online scam, called *shazhupan* (杀猪盘) in Chinese, in which scammers take on fictional profiles, initiate contact with hapless marks, and then slowly gain their trust before tricking them into fake investments.[1]

'I knew it was illegal, so I played dumb and said that I didn't know how to type. So, they assigned me to do cleaning and paperwork. Then they sold me again and again. I was repeatedly raped and almost forced to work in a brothel-like clubhouse in the last company.'

Alice eventually found a way to post a call for help on Instagram and was rescued before being sold a fifth time. Because of that cry for help, however, everyone in her social circles has come to know what happened to her, which has led to public shaming and is making her reintegration more difficult now that she is back home. As she told us: 'I want you to write about me. I am a victim of modern slavery, but no organisation is helping me. I also want to say it is not a matter of being greedy or stupid. It can really happen to anyone.'

A Booming Industry

Alice is just one of many affected by what the media dubbed a 'scam-demic', a surge in online fraud that gained worldwide attention following the onset of the COVID-19 pandemic in early 2020.[2] While online fraud

---

1 On pig-butchering scams, see Cassandra Cross, 'Romance Baiting, Cryptorom and "Pig Butchering": An Evolutionary Step in Romance Fraud', *Current Issues in Criminal Justice* 36(3), 2024, pp. 334–46; Fangzhou Wang and Xiaoli Zhou, 'Persuasive Schemes for Financial Exploitation in Online Romance Scam: An Anatomy on *Sha Zhu Pan* (杀猪盘) in China', *Victims and Offenders* 18(5), 2022, pp. 915–42.

2 Dominic Faulder, 'Asia's Scamdemic: How COVID-19 Supercharged Online Crime', *Nikkei Asia*, 16 November 2022.

operations can be found all over the world – one just has to think about the notorious Nigerian-prince advance-payment scams – this latest wave of online fraud has largely originated from one specific region: Southeast Asia.[3] It also presents some other new peculiar traits, most notably the emergence of new facilities – commonly known as scam compounds – where cyberfraud is practised on an industrial scale by a workforce that includes a significant number of people trafficked into forced criminality.

These scam compounds did not suddenly materialise out of thin air but should rather be seen as the latest development in a process that stretches as far back as Taiwan in the 1990s. It was at that time and in that place that entrepreneurial criminal groups began to experiment with the internet to conduct large-scale scams.[4] As Taiwanese law enforcement caught up, from the early 2000s these scammers turned their attention to mainland China, targeting it from locations in Taiwan while also establishing operations on the mainland itself.[5] Later on, in the early 2010s, as the authorities on both sides of the strait tightened up on online fraud and gambling, operations began to move into Southeast Asia, especially Cambodia, the Philippines, Myanmar, and Laos.[6] Even from their new bases, they continued to target the Chinese market.

According to our review of news reports of police raids from that time, those pioneering scam operations in Southeast Asia were often small scale

---

3   On Nigerian-prince scams, see Stephen Ellis, *This Present Darkness: A History of Nigerian Organized Crime*, Oxford University Press, Oxford, 2016, ch. 7. On the online scam industry in West Africa, see also the works of Suleman Lazarus, especially 'Social and Contextual Taxonomy of Cybercrime: Socioeconomic Theory of Nigerian Cyber-criminals', *International Journal of Law, Crime and Justice* no. 47, pp. 44–57. For a global overview of the online fraud industry, see 'INTERPOL Financial Fraud Assessment: A Global Threat Boosted by Technology', Interpol website, 11 March 2024.

4   For a thorough discussion of the origins of the industry in Taiwan, see Tseng Ya-fen 曾雅芬, 行骗天下: 臺灣跨境電信詐欺犯罪網絡之分析 (Global Networks of Fraud: Criminal Networks of Taiwan's Cross-Border Telecommunications Fraud), PhD dissertation, National Chengchi University, December 2016.

5   Jianxing Tan and Denise Jia, 'China's War on Rampant Telecom Scams', *Nikkei Asia*, 13 September 2022; Zhuang Hua 庄华, '论电信诈骗案件侦查突破口的选择' (Discussion on the Selection of Breakthroughs in Investigating Telecommunication Fraud Cases), 政法学刊 (Journal of Political Science and Law) 27(6), 2010, pp. 57–60.

6   Lennon Yao-Chung Chang, *Cybercrime in the Greater China Region: Regulatory Responses and Crime Prevention across the Taiwan Strait*, Edward Elgar Publishing, Cheltenham, 2014; Zhuang Hua 庄华 and Ma Zhonghong 马忠红, '东南亚地区中国公民跨境网络犯罪及治理研究' (Cross-Border Cybercrime of Chinese Citizens in Southeast Asia and Its Governance), 南洋问题研究 (Southeast Asian Affairs) no. 4, 2021, pp. 41–54.

and mostly located in apartments, villas, and hotel rooms. But soon things began to change. Although it is difficult to pinpoint an exact moment in time for this shift, available evidence indicates that from around 2016 onwards these operations started to assume industrial dimensions, coalescing into bigger scam compounds. Such a trend was acknowledged by China's Supreme People's Procuratorate, which in a 2023 report on telecom and online fraud noted that these operations had become increasingly 'monopolised' and less scattered, with large criminal groups often using 'technology parks' as a cover for their activities.[7]

These compounds in many cases are purpose-built for online operations, with offices, dormitories, and space for shops, entertainment, and other amenities for workers. In some cases, they are office buildings attached to or in the vicinity of public-facing casinos, or they may occupy the upper floors of a licensed casino. In others, they are repurposed condominiums and apartments. Many reports have focused on the presence of cyberfraud operations in special economic zones (SEZs), and a small number of such cases have been documented, for example in Cambodia and Laos.[8] They are not the norm, however, and this reporting often demonstrates confusion between self-described 'industrial' and 'technology' parks and SEZs.[9] There have also been reports of entire 'spinach cities' (菠城 *bocheng*) – a pun on the Chinese word for 'spinach' (菠菜 *bocai*), a homophone for 'gambling' (博彩 *bocai*) – purpose-built, especially in Myanmar's border areas, to host these types of operations.[10]

---

7   Supreme People's Procuratorate of the People's Republic of China, '检察机关打击治理电信网络诈骗及其关联犯罪工作情况 (2023年)' (State of the Prosecutors' Efforts to Combat Telecommunication and Online Fraud and Related Offences (2023)), Supreme People's Procuratorate website, 30 November 2023, spp.gov.cn.

8   On Cambodia, see 'MDS Henghe Thmorda Special Economic Zone', Cyber Scam Monitor, 6 November 2022; on Laos, see International Crisis Group, 'Transnational Crime and Geopolitical Contestation along the Mekong', ICG website, 18 August 2023.

9   An SEZ is a legal designation for a specific geographic area that is subject to economic regulations that differ from the rest of the country; usually they are created to promote export-oriented industries such as manufacturing. Given that the scam industry is illicit, any preferential rules on taxes, tariffs, and trade that may come with an SEZ are inconsequential. The principal draw for scam operators is the geographic location and permissiveness of the local environment.

10   See, for instance, Jason Tower and Priscilla Clapp, 'Myanmar's Casino Cities: The Role of China and Transnational Criminal Networks', United States Institute of Peace Special Report no. 471, 2020; Plato Cheng, 'Shwe Kokko Special Economic Zone/Yatai New City', People's Map of Global China, 18 August 2022.

As their business thrived, scam operations – most of which were still run by criminal groups from mainland China and Taiwan – increasingly resorted to deceptive and violent methods to recruit and retain their staff. Starting from around 2018, stories began appearing on Chinese-language social media of Chinese individuals getting tricked and often smuggled into Cambodia to work in scam compounds that they were not allowed to leave. There were also reports of Chinese nationals being kidnapped off the streets in places such as Sihanoukville, sold to scam operators by supposed friends and acquaintances, or reluctantly entering the industry due to unserviceable debts. Meanwhile, many individuals who had found their way into the sector knowing what kind of work they would be doing also found themselves trapped, their documents taken away and their liberty restricted.

When COVID-19 happened, it was a game-changer. The industry was already expanding rapidly, but as scam operators were achieving record profits capitalising on the misery and loneliness of people stuck in endless lockdowns, they needed a steady stream of new people to sustain their business. Still, travel restrictions made recruitment more challenging than ever. After the containment measures imposed by the Chinese authorities in early 2020 dried up the flow of new workers arriving through legal channels from mainland China, criminal groups running scam companies increasingly resorted to smuggling people out of the country. Whether they knew what they were getting into or not, these individuals often found themselves trapped in scam compounds, unable to return home because they lacked proper documents and, in many cases, had incurred substantial debts to their smugglers. At the same time, Chinese nationals already stranded abroad, often unemployed and facing financial hardships after losing their livelihood because of the pandemic, found themselves increasingly vulnerable. Many of them needed to make a living, no matter how, and entered the scam compounds.

During the pandemic, scam operations in Southeast Asia also expanded their reach beyond the Sinophone world. We were able to locate an early instance of a non-Chinese person trapped in a scam compound: in summer 2021, the local press in Cambodia reported that the husband of a Philippine national was claiming that his wife was being held against her will in a compound in Sihanoukville.[11] She had responded to a job ad

11   'Foreign Women Illegally Detained after Answering Facebook Job Ads', *Cambodia News English*, 26 July 2021.

posted on Facebook, and upon arrival her passport was immediately confiscated. Only after her story appeared in the English-language media was
she allowed to leave and return home.[12] Today, the workforce in Southeast
Asia's scam compounds is very diverse, with international organisations
active in the region claiming to have handled cases of at least forty nationalities trapped there.[13] With most cases going unreported, many more
nationalities are likely to have gone unrecorded.

Since the end of the pandemic, the industry continues to expand. The
scam-compound model – that is, cyberfraud on an industrial scale, often
performed by people being held in conditions akin to modern slavery
– was so successful that the existence of such facilities has now been
documented far and wide. In early 2023, the United Arab Emirates began
making headlines as an online scam and human trafficking hub.[14] In a
global warning issued in June 2023, Interpol said scam operations fuelled
by human trafficking had spread to West Africa.[15] The same month, media
outlets reported the discovery of the bodies of eight young workers who
had tried to quit their jobs at a cartel-run scam call centre in Mexico, only
to be brutally murdered and dismembered.[16] Later that year, over forty
Malaysians were rescued from a scam operation in Peru, and in 2024, a
police raid on a cyberscam operation in Zambia led to the eventual trial
and sentencing of over twenty Chinese nationals to up to eleven years
in jail.[17] This was followed by the arrest of over a hundred Chinese and
Malaysians for 'cybercrimes' in Nigeria, and dozens of Chinese nationals
in an Angolan call centre.[18]

Official data on the impacts of cyberscams are partial at best, in that

---

12   'Facebook Jobs Scam: Some Released, Others Still Held in Sihanoukville',
Cambodia News English, 26 July 2021.

13   United Nations Office on Drugs and Crime (UNODC), 'Casinos, Cyber Fraud,
and Trafficking in Persons for Forced Criminality in Southeast Asia', UNODC website,
September 2023, p. 10.

14   Andrew Haffner and Huang Yan, 'In Dubai, Chinese Industrial-Scale Scam Mills
Are Thriving', *Vice*, 5 May 2023.

15   'INTERPOL Issues Global Warning on Human Trafficking-Fueled Fraud', Interpol website, 7 June 2023.

16   Mark Stevenson, '8 Young Workers at Drug Cartel Call Center Killed, Bodies
Placed in Bags', Associated Press/AP News, 7 June 2023.

17   '43 Malaysians Freed from Phone Scam Syndicate in Peru Were Young People
Who Arrived a Week Earlier', Associated Press, 10 October 2023; Natasha Booty and
Wycliffe Muia, 'Long Jail Terms for Chinese Cybercrime Gang in Zambia', BBC News,
9 June 2024.

18   Solomon Odeniyi, 'Police to Charge 113 Foreign Nationals Arrested for Cyber-

they only consider reported cases in an industry where self-reporting is notoriously low as victims often feel too ashamed to share what happened to them. Also, scam patterns and the way law enforcement categorises them vary considerably from country to country, making it difficult to have a coherent and consistent dataset. Nevertheless, the available data are enough to give us a glimpse of the massive size of the industry today.

As we have seen, the Sinophone world is one of the main targets of these operations. In 2023 alone, the Chinese authorities claimed to have uncovered over 437,000 cases of telecommunication fraud and managed to stop scams with a total value of CN¥328.8 billion, roughly equivalent to US$45.29 billion.[19] In the same year, the Hong Kong authorities recorded 39,824 cases of fraud (a 3.8-fold increase from 2018), 70 per cent of which were internet-related, for a total loss of over HK$9 billion (US$1.15 billion).[20] In Taiwan, an all-time high of NT$8.878 billion (US$270 million) was reportedly lost to scams in 2023.[21] As for Singapore, the losses that year amounted to SG$651.8 million (US$492 million) in a record-high 46,563 reported cases – the third year in a row that Singaporean citizens had lost over SG$600 million to scams perpetrated by 'syndicated, well resourced, and technologically sophisticated' scammers based overseas.[22]

Southeast Asian countries have also been heavily targeted due to their geographical proximity to the scam operations. According to official data, in Thailand over THB63 billion (US$1.79 billion) were lost to cyberscams reported between March 2022 and May 2024.[23] In Vietnam, almost 17,500

crime', Punch, 4 November 2024; 'No Word on Dozens of Chinese Held in Angola for Running an Online Casino', The Macao News, 1 November 2024.

19   '2023年公安机关破获电信网络诈骗案件43.7万起' (The Public Security Organs Uncovered 437,000 Telecom Fraud Cases in 2023), 第一财经 (Diyi Caijing), 9 January 2024, m.yicai.com.

20   'Law and Order Situation in Hong Kong in 2023', Government of the Hong Kong Special Administrative Region website, 6 February 2024.

21   Hong Zongquan 洪宗荃, '台灣去年被詐騙金額創史上新高！「假投資」連3年第一 金管會提醒民眾要小心注意' (The Amount of Money Defrauded in Taiwan Hit a Record High Last Year! "Fake Investment" Ranks First for Three Consecutive Years, the Financial Supervisory Commission Reminds the Public to Be Careful), 新聞網 (FTNN), 12 February 2024.

22   Nadine Chua, 'Scam Victims in S'pore Lost $651.8m in 2023, with Record High of over 46,000 Cases Reported', Straits Times, 18 February 2024. For scammers being based mostly overseas, see David Sun and Jessie Lim, 'Scam Victims in S'pore Lost $633.3 Million in 2021', Straits Times, 16 February 2022.

23   Bloomberg News and Somruedi Banchongduang, 'Scam Losses Topped B60bn in Last Two Years', Bangkok Post, 13 June 2024.

fraud cases were reported in 2023 to a portal operated by the Ministry of Information and Communications, for a total loss of more than VNĐ300 billion (US\$12.24 million).[24] The Malaysian authorities recorded RM1.218 billion (US\$280 million) in losses to online scams in 2023.[25]

It has also been well documented how online frauds have targeted people far beyond the region.[26] In 2023, the FBI Crime Complaint Center received more than 69,000 complaints from the public regarding financial fraud involving the use of cryptocurrency, including investment, tech support, extortion, romance, government impersonation, and other types of scams. Estimated losses amounted to more than US\$5.6 billion, almost 50 per cent of the total losses associated with financial-fraud complaints.[27] While it is not possible to know for certain how many of these cases have links with Southeast Asia, given the timing and techniques employed we can safely assume that operations in Southeast Asia played an important role in this explosive growth. In one remarkable instance in which the Southeast Asia connection became explicit, the *Sydney Morning Herald* reported on an Australian woman duped into investing in fake cryptocurrency.[28] After realising she had been defrauded, she confronted the scammer, who confessed his identity as a twenty-year-old trapped in a scam operation being run from a compound in Cambodia. He told her that his bosses would punish him for poor performance and that he needed CN¥300,000 (US\$63,000) to be released.

---

24   'Vietnamese Users Report Losses of More Than \$12.24 Million Due to Online Fraud', *Viet Nam News*, 14 May 2024.

25   '34,497 Online Scam Cases Reported, Losses Estimated at RM1.2 Billion Last Year', *New Straits Times*, 18 March 2024.

26   See, for instance, 'The Pig Butchering Romance Scam', BBC World Service, 28 June 2023; *Forced to Scam: Cambodia's Cyber Slaves*, Al Jazeera, 14 July 2022; Cait Kelly, '"I Couldn't Escape": The People Trafficked into Call Centres and Forced to Scam Australians', *Guardian*, 2 April 2023; Wassayos Ngamkham and Chaiyot Puppatanapong, 'Police Raids Target Swindlers Preying on American Retirees', *Bangkok Post*, 21 March 2023; and Nicola Smith and Joe Wallen, 'Inside the Crypto "Prisons" Scamming Britons out of Their Life Savings', *Telegraph*, 24 January 2023.

27   FBI Internet Crime Complaint Center (IC3), 'Federal Bureau of Investigation Cryptocurrency Fraud Report 2023', FBI IC3 website.

28   Anna Patty, 'How a "Very Charming" Man Named Kevin Swindled a Sydney Woman out of \$220,000', *Sydney Morning Herald*, 16 December 2022.

Narratives of Victimhood

Stories such as the one that this man told his Australian target bring us back to how the current wave of online scams relies in part on the exploitation of an army of labourers, many of whom are forced to work under duress. Evidence has been mounting that today there are potentially hundreds of thousands of people toiling in hundreds of scam operations across Southeast Asia and beyond. While some enter willingly in the hope of making money, many others do not. Regardless of how people find their way into the compounds, often they are not allowed to leave without paying a substantial fee. Rescuers and anti-trafficking groups describe such payment as a 'ransom', and it sometimes amounts to tens of thousands of dollars. There is overwhelming evidence that torture, violence, and brutality are prevalent within many of these operations. Rescues are sporadic at best, hampered by the complicity or inaction of local officials, protection of local elites, and the mobile nature of the industry – which, to make things worse, is in some cases located in remote areas or even active conflict zones.

While largely the results of educated guesswork, estimates for the numbers of people involved are staggering. In a 2023 report, the United Nations Office of the High Commissioner for Human Rights stated that 'credible sources' indicated that at that time at least 120,000 people may have been held in situations where they were forced to carry out online scams in Myanmar, with another 100,000 in Cambodia.[29] Officials in both countries reacted angrily to this report, but in 2022 a senior official at the Cambodian Ministry of Interior admitted that the authorities estimated some 100,000 people in the country had been involved in 'illegal online gambling' – a euphemism often used by the Cambodian government to refer to online scam operations – before a short-lived crackdown was launched in September 2022.[30] Although he was referring to the overall workforce and not those who had been trafficked or forced to work, this gives an indication of the size of the industry.

---

29   United Nations Office of the High Commissioner for Human Rights (OHCHR), 'Online Scam Operations and Trafficking into Forced Criminality in Southeast Asia: Recommendations for a Human Rights Response', OHCHR Bangkok Office website, August 2023.

30   Huang Yan, 'Under Foreign Pressure, Cambodia Dismantles Some "Scam" Compounds', *Nikkei Asia*, 13 October 2022.

Still, not everyone agrees that these individuals should be regarded as victims. If we are to heed many officials from the region, these individuals should be considered criminals, or at least opportunists. As a Malaysian diplomat stated in February 2023, responding to public criticism of the Malaysian police mishandling the case of five nationals who had fallen prey to job scams in Cambodia: 'These five people are not victims because they do not fit the definition of "victim" ... [At least] two of them came here illegally after passing the border without the legal documents, and they do not have any proof [that they are] ... victims.'[31]

The Cambodian authorities have been particularly vocal in pushing the narrative that survivors of this industry should not be considered victims. Numerous officials have dismissed reports of forced labour, human trafficking, or slavery in the country's scam compounds, often describing incidents as nothing more than ordinary labour disputes. Indeed, these officials usually do not mention scams, instead referring to 'online gambling' or simply 'online work'. This perspective was fiercely promoted by Cambodian state actors throughout the pandemic and after. Back in December 2021, as the situation was increasingly being covered by international media, Kuoch Chamroeun, the former Preah Sihanouk provincial governor, explained that

> foreign workers have to spend thousands of dollars to process documents to get the job and they borrow some money from the company. When they borrow [a] company's money, they have to work for the company to pay back the money they owe ... After the provincial administration investigated these cases, we saw that there was no heavy abuse of their rights as alleged of people being detained to pay off debts because they are working to settle their debt with the company ... I have fixed at least three cases of this problem in one day and they all owe the company money.[32]

A few months later, in August 2022, he reiterated the same stance to a UN special rapporteur, stating that some people fabricated their stories simply because they wanted to change company.[33] Even on those rare

---

31   Taing Rinith, 'Attention Seekers: Untrue Statements on Human Trafficking Causing Harm', *Khmer Times*, 9 February 2023.

32   Son Minea, 'Governor Seeks Clarity on "Forced Labour" Claims', *Khmer Times*, 7 December 2021.

33   Sen Bao 森宝, '西港省长会见联合国人权专家: 20年前柬公民在国外遭贩卖,

occasions when senior Cambodian officials admit that there is a problem, they tend to minimise it. For instance, when a brief crackdown on the online scam industry launched in the fall of 2022, then prime minister Hun Sen acknowledged that thousands of foreigners had been lured to Cambodia, but then took care to specify that only hundreds were *real* victims.[34]

Unsurprisingly, lower-level officials toed the same line, with farcical results. When, in November 2021, a woman was rescued from a compound in Pursat, the provincial deputy police chief said that the problem was simply that 'she couldn't stay in the quarantine because it was too quiet'.[35] In January 2022, the police chief of Preah Sihanouk province laughed while commenting on the rescue of four Pakistanis from a compound: 'I would like to inform that there was no abduction, and they came to work here, but they found it difficult to eat because it was all Chinese food.'[36] In May 2022, when a man attempted to rescue a friend from a compound in Kampot, the police in Ruessei Srok Khang Lech commune commented: 'This is not detention, since they give him a salary … it is just they do not allow him to get out.'[37] In July 2022, the police chief of Preah Sihanouk commented on the rescue of ten individuals from a compound, saying that the complaint that brought about the rescue was defamatory because the captives 'were working, so this is not confinement'.[38] The police then focused their investigations on the complainant.

On the opposite front, the media and, belatedly, the international community, have explicitly called out forced labour, human trafficking, and modern slavery in the compounds. In July 2022, the US State Department's annual 'Trafficking in Persons' report downgraded Cambodia to

---

不希望"这种痛苦"在柬发生' (Preah Sihanouk Governor Met with UN Human Rights Experts: Cambodian Citizens Were Trafficked Abroad 20 Years Ago, and They Do Not Want 'This Kind of Pain' to Happen in Cambodia), 柬中时报 (Cambodia China Times), 20 August 2022.

34   Khuon Narim, 'Cambodia at Risk of Being Called "Worst Country" over Trafficking: PM', CamboJA News, 29 September 2022.

35   Mech Dara, 'Police Rescue Cambodian Woman from Try Pheap SEZ, Deny She Was Sold', Voice of Democracy, 18 November 2021.

36   Mech Dara, 'Four Pakistanis Rescued from Captivity, Forced Labor in Sihanoukville', Voice of Democracy, 13 January 2022.

37   Mech Dara and Andrew Haffner, 'A Friend's Journey Attempting Rescue from Alleged Slave Compound', Voice of Democracy, 24 May 2022.

38   Mech Dara, 'Police Help 10 Leave "Work" in Sihanoukville, but "Not Confinement"', Voice of Democracy, 26 July 2022.

Tier 3 – the lowest ranking – citing human trafficking in scam operations, the entertainment industry, and among migrant workers.[39] At the same time, international media widely framed the discussion as an issue of 'slavery'. One landmark moment in this regard was the release, in July 2022, of the documentary *Forced to Scam: Cambodia's Cyber Slaves*, produced by Al Jazeera.[40] After the video aired, international media coverage of scam operations grew exponentially, as did the idea that these compounds represented a new phenomenon called 'cyber slavery' – a term that previously had been sporadically used in other contexts, for instance to refer to North Korean state-sponsored hackers, but which in the past couple of years has come to be associated almost exclusively with the online scam industry.[41]

Since then, 'cyber slavery' has become a catch-all term to describe the situation of all people who were sold, kidnapped, or joined the online scam industry voluntarily but then found themselves trapped. The phrase has its merit in highlighting what is novel in this scene, that is, its virtual dimension: it emphasises the paradoxical nature of a situation that brings together the epitome of post-modernity, the internet, and something as brutal and primordial as slavery. Indeed, there is something new – and uncanny – in the phenomenon of individuals held in conditions of slavery while being almost perennially connected to the outside world through the internet, rather than being hidden from public view on fishing boats, in brick kilns, or in domestic abodes.

Still, the phrase may also present the issue as a wholly new form of slavery, obscuring continuities with modern slavery as we have understood it thus far. It also risks setting the so-called cyber slaves apart from other victims of human trafficking and forced labour in more traditional industries. For instance, particularly widespread among policymakers, civil society practitioners, and the public is the assumption that these individuals need to be computer-literate to do their job and, since they have to deal with international targets, better educated and skilled than typical victims of modern slavery. As a policy brief by the Bali Process Regional Support Office released in 2023 put it:

---

39 '2022 Trafficking in Persons Report: Cambodia', US Embassy in Cambodia website, 20 July 2022.
40 *Forced to Scam*, Al Jazeera.
41 Geoff White, *The Lazarus Heist*, Penguin Random House, London, 2022.

Given the skills needed to operate scams effectively, primarily computer literacy and language skills, the demographics scam centre recruiters target differs significantly from traditional trafficking victim profiles. Trafficking victims for scam centres are typically young, between the ages of 18 and 35, tech savvy, multilingual and educated … Many of those freed from scam centres have degrees, some at the graduate level. Proficiency in English and Chinese are particularly valuable to facilitate communication with both scam victims and the foreign crime bosses funding the scam operations, along with the knowledge of finance, investment, and cryptocurrencies, which is necessary for ensuring scams can be as accurate and convincing as possible.[42]

These assumptions have likely emerged due to various factors. First, due to the immense scope of the industry, its geographical spread, and the wide range of nationalities involved, we unavoidably have limited and fractured information on which to base our analysis. Second, survivors of the industry who have higher levels of education may be more likely to reach out to the media, and possibly more comfortable sharing their stories (potentially in English) with journalists than, for example, someone from a town in rural China with only a middle or high school education. Third, victim profiles differ depending on the country that they come from. For instance, many young unemployed Indian graduates with degrees in IT fields who emerged from university into an extremely unfavourable job market have ended up trapped in Southeast Asia's scam compounds.[43]

However, there is now substantial evidence that this depiction of the industry's workforce as highly educated is not entirely accurate, at least when it comes to Chinese survivors – who, as we have seen, constitute a large portion of the industry's workforce. A report released in 2023 by China's Supreme People's Procuratorate labels the Chinese nationals involved in the online scam industry as 'three lows' (三低 *sandi*), that is: young age, low income, and low education.[44] A survey that we conducted

42 See, for instance, 'New RSO Policy Brief Calls for Coordinated International Response to Huge and Growing Impact of Online Scam Centres', Bali Process website, 7 April 2023, baliprocess.net.

43 Anup Roy, 'Young Indians More Likely to Be Jobless if They're Educated', *Japan Times*, 29 March 2024; Agence France-Presse, 'Educated, Jobless and Angry: India's Young Graduates Drown in Despair Even as Economy Booms', *South China Morning Post*, 12 April 2023.

44 Supreme People's Procuratorate of the People's Republic of China, 'State of the

in 2023 among sixty-two survivors from mainland China confirms this pattern.[45] Our respondents were young overall – 15 per cent were minors, 55 per cent were below the age of twenty-five, and 86.7 per cent below thirty – and predominantly male (84.7 per cent). Their educational level was quite low, with 15 per cent having attended only elementary school and 45 per cent having a middle school diploma. Many of the Chinese survivors we interviewed for this book did not speak any language other than Mandarin Chinese or their native dialect, and this was often their first experience outside of China. In light of this, portraying cyber slaves as a separate category, generally better educated and skilled than the more traditional victims of human trafficking and forced labour, not only is potentially misleading but also increases the potential risk of law enforcement and government agencies questioning the motivations and accounts of survivors.

The idea of cyber slaves as a sort of privileged group among human trafficking survivors is also more likely to boost societal suspicion about them. Readers' comments on online media reports, especially on Chinese-language articles, are often unsympathetic, with many believing that those seeking rescue from scam compounds got what was coming to them. There is considerable reluctance among the public to regard the individuals who end up in the scam compounds as *real* victims. This hesitation is largely linked to widespread knowledge of the horrific psychological suffering and financial damage that scammers inflict on their targets. Moreover, even in cases where people have been deprived of their freedom, abused, and tortured, there is a lingering suspicion that these individuals *might* have known what they were signing on for, that they *could not* have been oblivious about the nature of the work when they accepted those tempting job offers. Once in trouble, they *might* have lied about how they were recruited and exaggerated the ill treatment in the hope of eliciting the sympathy of those whose help they were seeking, and, potentially, to avoid criminal charges.

Two dynamics well known in the field of criminological research are at play here. The first is what criminologists commonly call 'victim–offender

45   Ivan Franceschini, Ling Li, Yige Hu, and Mark Bo, 'A New Type of Victim? Profiling Survivors of Modern Slavery in the Online Scam Industry in Southeast Asia', *Trends in Organized Crime*, 6 November 2024.

overlap'. While victims and offenders are usually thought of as belonging to two separate categories, researchers have pointed out that the reality is not always clear-cut and the two groups should rather be seen as part of a spectrum. As early as the 1950s, scholars proposed the existence of three distinct categories: pure victims, pure offenders, and one-and-the-same individuals, who embody both victim and offender roles at the same time.[46] While this theorisation originally referred to people such as those involved in victim-precipitated homicides, the framework has proven applicable to other situations as well. For instance, the one-and-the-same approach has been employed to explain the role of individuals in pyramid schemes – an economic crime often employing cult-like tactics to recruit and manipulate participants with promises of financial gain for enrolling new members – and crypto scams.[47] The framework has also been applied to cases of intimate-partner violence, where prolonged exposure to abuse can eventually lead the victim to resort to violence, often as an act of self-defence or out of desperation.[48] Among those working to eradicate modern slavery, the victim–offender overlap has often been discussed in the context of commercial sex trafficking.[49] Recently, some researchers have also started applying the framework to victims of forced criminality in the online scam industry.[50]

The second dynamic is related to the so-called ideal victim. In the 1980s, Nils Christie pointed out that being a victim is not an objective position but rather has to do with the participant's definition of a certain

---

46   Martin F. Wolfgang, 'Victim Precipitated Criminal Homicide', *Journal of Criminal Law and Criminology* 48(1), 1957, pp. 1–11.

47   On pyramid schemes, see Branislav Hock and Mark Button, 'Non-ideal Victims or Offenders? The Curious Case of Pyramid Scheme Participants', *Victims and Offenders* 18(7), 2023, pp. 1311–34; on crypto, see Peter Howson, *Let Them Eat Crypto: The Blockchain Scam That's Ruining the World*, Pluto Press, London, 2023, p. 23.

48   John D. Hewitt, 'The Victim–Offender Relationship in Convicted Homicide Cases: 1960–1984', *Journal of Criminal Justice* 16(1), 1988, pp. 25–33.

49   See, for instance, Mary A. Finn, Lisa Muftić, and Erin Marsh, 'Exploring the Overlap between Victimization and Offending among Women in Sex Work', *Victims and Offenders* 10(1), 2015, pp. 74–94; Alexandra Baxter, 'Sex Trafficking's Tragic Paradox: When Victims Become Perpetrators', The Conversation, 22 May 2019, and 'When the Line between Victimization and Criminalization Blurs: The Victim–Offender Overlap Observed in Female Offenders in Cases of Trafficking in Persons for Sexual Exploitation in Australia', *Journal of Human Trafficking* 6(3), 2020, pp. 327–38.

50   Fangzhou Wang, 'Victim-Offender Overlap: The Identity Transformations Experienced by Trafficked Chinese Workers Escaping from Pig-Butchering Scam Syndicate', *Trends in Organized Crime*, 5 February 2024.

situation.[51] This led him to theorise the existence of 'ideal victims', which he defined as 'a person or a category of individuals who – when hit by crime – most readily are given the complete and legitimate status of being a victim'.[52] Scholars have since criticised how such views of victimhood have impaired efforts to provide support and justice to survivors based on their perceived moral shortcomings in comparison to these archetypes. This is particularly common in the field of sex trafficking and exploitation, where it is often upper-middle-class, attractive, educated individuals who receive the most focus and support.[53] This kind of construction of an ideal victim has also been highlighted in international criminal law, where victims are often characterised as vulnerable, dependent, and grotesque, resulting in a feminised, infantilised, and racialised stereotype of victimhood.[54] Another instance can be found in current public discourse about the war in Gaza, where intellectuals and activists have denounced biases in the way narratives of Palestinian victimhood are constructed.[55]

Survivors of the scam compounds hardly fit the image of the ideal victim. Not only is their blamelessness marred by the fact that they have committed crimes (albeit under alleged duress), but they are also mostly men in their prime, which is at odds with the stereotype of the weak and vulnerable victim. To make things worse, they are often believed to be well educated and endowed with valuable IT and language skills, all of which further contributes to undermining their claim to victimhood in the eyes of many. As a result, their ordeal does not end once they manage to exit the compounds, but it continues even after – first at the hand of the immigration authorities in the countries where they find themselves stranded, who often see them as nothing more than illegal migrants, and then in many cases after they return home, where they still face ostracism by their peers.

---

51   Nils Christie, 'The Ideal Victim', in Ezzat A. Fatah, ed., *From Crime Policy to Victim Policy: Reorienting the Justice System*, Macmillan, Handsmill and London, 1986, pp. 17–30.

52   Ibid., p. 18.

53   Robert Uy, 'Blinded by Red Lights: Why Trafficking Discourse Should Shift Away from Sex and the "Perfect Victim" Paradigm', *Berkeley Journal of Gender, Law and Justice* 26(1), 2011, pp. 204–19.

54   Christine Schwöbel-Patel, 'The "Ideal" Victim of International Criminal Law', *European Journal of International Law* 29(3), 2018, pp. 703–24.

55   Mohammed El-Kurd, 'The Right to Speak for Ourselves', *The Nation*, 27 November 2023.

Compound Capitalism

Criminologists have pointed out how any analysis of cybersecurity today should have a strong focus on offline, human, and contextual elements rather than simply looking at fast-changing technological threats and the challenges they pose.[56] The latest developments in the online scam industry have made this call more urgent than ever. If we look at current discussions in media and policy circles, Southeast Asia's cyberscam operations have largely – and rightly – been framed as a human rights crisis, with the tragedies of individuals trapped in the compounds taking the fore in public discussions. But it is also important to take a step back and look at the big picture to take stock of the industry as a whole.

Criminological research provides us with insight as to why certain geographical locations exert a powerful attraction for criminal actors. Scholars have listed a host of factors that act as a magnet for such groups, including mass demand, access to supply, lax law enforcement, high impunity or corruption, proximity to trafficking routes, porous borders, and the presence of brokers and facilitators.[57] The locations in Southeast Asia that have emerged as hubs for the online scam industry present several of these features. Federico Varese's research on the pull and push factors that lead mafia groups to branch out overseas has highlighted one additional factor: the sudden emergence of a new market.[58] While his analysis focuses specifically on mafia groups – which he defines as 'a group that supplies protection in the territory of origin' – this point also applies to the criminal groups that dominate the online scam industry.[59]

Scam compounds have mushroomed in the region due to the sudden emergence of a new market in which the interests between local elites and international crime groups could safely converge. On the one side, after years of wealth accumulation through land dispossession, logging, real

---

56   Jonathan Lusthaus and Federico Varese, 'Offline and Local: The Hidden Face of Cybercrime', *Policing* 15(1), 2021, pp. 4–14.

57   Carlo Morselli, Mathilde Turcotte, and Valentina Tenti, 'The Mobility of Criminal Groups', *Global Crime* 12(3), 2011, pp. 165–88, at p. 171. Tim Hall, Ben Sanders, Mamadou Bah, Owen King, and Edward Wigley, 'Economic Geographies of the Illegal: The Multiscalar Production of Cybercrime', *Trends in Organized Crime* 24(2), 2021: 282–307.

58   Federico Varese, *Mafias on the Move: How Organized Crime Conquers New Territories*, Princeton University Press, Princeton, NJ, 2011, and 'How Mafias Migrate: Transplantation, Functional Diversification, and Separation', *Crime and Justice* no. 49, 2020, pp. 289–337.

59   Varese, *Mafias on the Move*, p. 5.

estate speculation, and consolidating control of key industries, local elites remain on the lookout for ways to continue to maintain and expand their income streams.[60] On the other, criminal syndicates and shady business-people running online frauds have capital at their disposal, capacity to run complex scam operations, and networks through which to move illicit gains, but need safe havens from which to operate. The environment of impunity in which powerful elites operate in countries such as Cambodia and Myanmar presents a perfect destination for these groups to relocate and expand their activities, while creating new sources of revenue for those elites willing to act as protective umbrellas.

Still, none of this would have been possible without adding yet another element to the mix: the appearance of what some academics have called 'illicit infrastructure'.[61] Existing research has shown how the hacking community in recent years has undergone a substantial change, shifting from a model focused on the skilled artisanal labour of elite hackers to a top-down, concentric view in which less talented individuals use the sophisticated tools created by the former.[62] Concomitantly, the associated structures for buying and selling these tools have tended towards role specialisation and shifting to a service economy. This means that users – including scam operators – can now simply purchase these capacities as a service without having to possess or acquire technical skills themselves.[63] This illicit infrastructure, and the hidden work that sustains it, plays a fundamental role in supporting a broad array of illegal activities. In the online scam industry, it does so through the development of dedicated apps and websites, as well as the creation and curation of platforms and channels through which industry operators can launder the proceeds of their crimes, among many other services.

While all of this might suggest that the online scam industry has purely extractive relations with local society, this does not explain the industry's persistence once it takes roots in a certain location. This is because there

---

60 See, for instance, Neil Loughlin, *The Politics of Coercion: State and Regime Making in Cambodia*, Cornell University Press, Ithaca, NY, 2024.

61 Ben Collier, Richard Clayton, Alice Hutchings, and Daniel Thomas, 'Cybercrime Is (Often) Boring: Infrastructure and Alienation in a Deviant Subculture', *British Journal of Criminology* 61, 2021, pp. 1407–23.

62 Jonathan Lusthaus, *Industry of Anonymity: Inside the Business of Cybercrime*, Harvard University Press, Harvard, MA, 2018.

63 Collier et al, 'Cybercrime Is (Often) Boring'.

is one more aspect to consider: the role of local communities. Current discussions often overlook how it is not only local elites that profit from the existence of scam compounds; to a certain extent, surrounding communities benefit as well, be they local landowners, owners of small businesses catering to the compounds, or private citizens providing their services as cleaners, security guards, or construction, maintenance, and delivery workers. In impoverished areas, scam compounds often become a mainstay of the local economy, providing jobs and sources of income that are otherwise in limited supply. In places such as Myanmar, survivors have told us how one of their main concerns if they managed to escape was the danger of being sold back to the compound by the inhabitants of surrounding villages – they had seen this happen several times. This leads us to an uncomfortable truth: it is not only local elites that play a role in making the compounds viable, but also local businesses and individuals. The benefits they derive from the industry vary greatly, and many of the local people that play a role in the compound economy will do so due to lack of alternatives; yet as the compounds have grown, their integration into local communities is often considerable.

If these are the premises that made the emergence of scam compounds possible at this specific point in time in Southeast Asia, taking an even broader view, the evolution of the industry can also be seen as one of the latest manifestations of predatory capitalism, a model that we call *compound capitalism*. Compound capitalism combines some traditional elements of capitalist exploitation in novel ways. First, there is the issue of exceptionality.[64] As Quinn Slobodian has pointed out: 'Capitalism works by punching holes in the territory of the nation-state, creating zones of exception with different laws and often no democratic oversight.'[65] While traditionally this has occurred mostly in industrial zones and special economic zones (SEZs), scam compounds – with their high walls topped by barbed wire, heavily guarded entrances, and internal policing – represent the ultimate development of this perforation of state sovereignty: a situation that is paradoxically enabled by local and national state actors and complicated by the fact that the people locked inside remain constantly connected to the outside world through the internet.

---

64   Aihwa Ong, *Neoliberalism as Exception: Mutations in Citizenship and Sovereignty*, Duke University Press, Durham, NC, and London, 2006.

65   Quinn Slobodian, *Crack-Up Capitalism: Market Radicals and the Dream of a World without Democracy*, Allen Lane, London, 2023, p. 3.

Second, the labour regime in the scam operations is an extreme manifestation of a workplace-discipline model that is based on the provision and control of workers' accommodation. In modern industry, when employers choose to provide accommodation to their workforce, this may be because adequate facilities are lacking; it may be a cheaper option for employers, but it also has the effect of ensuring a reliable workforce by developing a more protracted and dependent relationship for their employees and their families.[66] While the wish to control workers and extract as much value as possible from their labour is not new, it has usually been masked with a paternalistic façade and the claim that workers are freely selling their labour. In some cases, though, the disciplinary nature of such an arrangement has been clear – as, for instance, in the compounds that until not so long ago were being built by mining companies in South Africa to house an all-male Black migrant workforce.

Created in the second half of the nineteenth century as a solution to the housing and control of Black workers, these compounds were 'bleak, functional barracks to which access [was] tightly controlled'.[67] The system did not allow rural workers recruited by local administrations to choose their destination or mode of transport; in fact, even to resign from a contract remained a criminal offence until 1974. While workers were not physically restricted to the space of the compound, managers would discourage visits to local townships, and apartheid laws prevented them from entering spaces reserved for white South Africans.[68] Discipline was usually harsh – Michael Burawoy referred to the compound manager as 'the supreme dictator' – with attempts to unionise violently crushed and control maintained by private security backed by the South African Police Force.[69] Although even in such a system workers managed to maintain a certain degree of agency, these compounds, and the migrant labour system they were based on, have been rightly defined

66   Chris Smith, 'Living at Work: Management Control and the Dormitory Labour System in China', *Asia Pacific Journal of Management* no. 20, 2003, pp. 333–58, at p. 333.

67   Jonathan Crush, 'Scripting the Compound: Power and Space in the South African Mining Industry', *Environment and Planning D: Society and Space* 12(3), 1994, pp. 301–24, at p. 302.

68   Andries Bezuidenhout and Sakhela Buhlungu, 'From Compounded to Fragmented Labour: Mineworkers and the Demise of Compounds in South Africa', *Antipode: A Radical Journal of Geography* 43(2), 2011, pp. 237–63, at p. 244.

69   Michael Burawoy, *The Politics of Production*, Verso, London and New York, 1985, p. 228.

as 'a cornerstone of the landscape of colonial and apartheid South and southern Africa'.[70]

A more recent instance was China's dormitory labour regime, which has operated since the 1980s and involved widespread provision of temporary company accommodation to workers in export-oriented factories in the south of the country.[71] In their seminal studies on the subject, Chris Smith and Pun Ngai cite the South African compound labour regime as one of the predecessors of this arrangement while also taking care to point out the differences, as mining compounds for Black workers in South Africa were more coercive, as well as 'racialized, colonial, male and factor restricted – accommodating workers close to where diamond and gold mines were located'.[72] However, in the Chinese case the exploitative nature of the system was also plain to see. Although the dormitory labour regime does not constrain workers' movements, by controlling the provision of accommodation for migrant workers who have no viable alternatives, employers maximise their utilisation of labour.[73] In this sense, China's dormitory regime is little more than 'a form of labour capture [that] allows access to cheap labour without a longer-term build-up of labour institutions that would lead to better working conditions and labour solidarities'.[74]

The labour regime that we are witnessing in the online scam industry today is much more coercive than any of these systems. Workers are often duped or drafted against their will, prevented from leaving, subjected to round-the-clock surveillance, and disciplined through the constant threat of arbitrary physical violence. As we have mentioned, many of those who enter willingly are also blocked from leaving, through either threats of violence or demands for exorbitant fees to break dubious contracts they

---

70   Charles Van Onselen, *Chibaro: African Mine Labour in Southern Rhodesia, 1900–1933*, Pluto Press, London, 1976; Crush, 'Scripting the Compound'; Bezuidenhout and Buhlungu, 'From Compounded to Fragmented Labour' (quote is from p. 238); Timothy Sizwe Phakathi, 'Worker Agency in Colonial, Apartheid and Post-Apartheid Gold Mining Workplace Regimes', *Review of African Political Economy* 39(132), 2012, pp. 279–94.

71   Chris Smith and Pun Ngai, 'The Dormitory Labour Regime in China as a Site for Control and Resistance', *International Journal of Human Resources Management* 17(8), 2006, pp. 1456–70; Pun Ngai and Chris Smith, 'Putting Transnational Labour Process in Its Place: The Dormitory Labour Regime in Post-socialist China', *Work, Employment and Society* 21(1), 2007, pp. 27–45.

72   Pun and Smith, 'The Dormitory Labour Regime in China', p. 1457.

73   Pun and Smith, 'Putting Transnational Labour Process in Its Place', p. 30.

74   Ibid., p. 29.

were forced to sign on arrival. It is the norm for operators to confiscate and hold workers' passports. And, unlike in South African mining compounds and Chinese dormitories, in today's scam compounds there is very little scope for solidarity, with workers often feeling uneasy around their peers, and fearing that they will be informed on if they express a desire to leave.[75]

There are also more subtle ways the workers in scam compounds are exploited. They are paid so-called salaries that are often much lower than promised and dependent on hitting performance targets. Interviewees told us how they had to pay a range of absurd fees for everything they used on site. To earn their keep, they are forced to work extremely long shifts, and even then their debts continue to accrue, adding to the ransom that their families may have to pay to get them out. At the same time, the compound economy is tightly controlled, and often the small businesses within the premises are run by friends and relatives of the managers, or people connected to them. These businesses thrive because they can take advantage of cheap or free labour and charge monopolistic prices that are substantially higher than in the outside world. Ultimately, workers in the scam compounds are exploited as both labourers and consumers.

Third, at a time when scholars debate surveillance capitalism, scam compounds represent yet another, extreme form of data extraction.[76] Unquestionably, the efforts of the global tech giants to extract data from a largely oblivious population are becoming increasingly sophisticated. From this point of view, there are certain uncomfortable similarities between legitimate tech companies and online scam operations. Even though the latter remain labour-intensive – unlike the largely automated efforts of commercial companies that engage in data extraction through algorithms – both business models are based on the ability to entice and retain their targets by making them addicted to services (such as a caring voice in a time of loneliness that is a hallmark of pig butchering and other romance scams) and then manipulating their behaviour. Scam operations can be as sophisticated as legitimate tech companies. There are reports of advanced apps being developed with the specific purpose of tricking hapless targets into handing over access to their accounts, and deep-fake technology is now also being used to trick victims into parting ways with their cash.[77]

75   'A Day in the Life of a Shwe Kokko Scammer', *Frontier Myanmar*, 1 June 2023.

76   Soshana Zuboff, *Surveillance Capitalism: The Fight for a Human Future at the New Frontier of Power*, Profile Books, London, 2019.

77   Sean Gallagher, 'Fool's Gold: Dissecting a Fake Gold Market Pig-Butchering

In a disturbing twist on the supposedly legitimate harvesting and trade in personal data that goes on around us every day, scammers are also known to recycle victim data, holding on to their details and approaching them later posing as companies that can help them recover assets. Victim lists are also sold to other scammers as potentially vulnerable targets.

Finally, just as capitalist exploitation is grounded in processes of dispossession and proletarianisation, the online scam industry preys on a workforce often rendered desperate by the lack of viable alternatives. This included people whose plight was exacerbated by the COVID-19 pandemic, but more broadly recruiters often target the young and people with limited economic prospects. There is no doubt that many individuals enter the scam compounds voluntarily, enticed by (often bogus) promises of high incomes and a good life. Yet, reducing the motivations of the industry's willing workforce to pure greed is an oversimplification. While the industry long predates the pandemic, COVID-19 acted as a catalyst, providing scam operators with a new pool of labourers desperate enough to be willing to turn a blind eye to conditions clearly too good to be true. As the industry, in turn, flourished by taking advantage of people's loneliness and desperation during the years of lockdown, we witnessed a predatory loop of desperation exploited at both ends, a dynamic akin to the ouroboros snake eating its own tail – which Nancy Fraser has aptly used as a metaphor for capitalism's cannibalistic tendencies.[78]

What about China?

There is one final question left to address: how does China fit into all of this? Since the outset, scam compounds have been strongly associated with China in current debates. Indeed, this connection is well founded if we consider that ethnic Chinese play a leading role in the sector, at least in Southeast Asia. Yet, there are several reasons why it is essential not to fixate upon this angle when discussing the industry. One is that if we look at online scam operations as a purely Chinese phenomenon, we risk overlooking the basic connections to local elites and society that allow

---

Scam', Sophos News, 13 February 2023, and 'Sour Grapes: Stomping on a Cambodia-Based "Pig Butchering" Scam', Sophos News, 28 February 2023; '"Deepfake" Scam in China Fans Worries over AI-Driven Fraud', Reuters, 22 May 2023.

78   Nancy Fraser, *Cannibal Capitalism: How Our System Is Devouring Democracy, Care, and the Planet – and What We Can Do about It*, Verso, London and New York, 2022.

these criminal groups to thrive. Another is that by reading the industry through a sweeping, racialising lens, we downplay the broader systemic factors that have engendered its transformation. Finally, the focus on Chinese-led criminal groups has obscured the important role of other participants in the industry, including those from other East and Southeast Asian countries.

Much of the discussion of the involvement of ethnic Chinese actors in the online scam industry has been framed in terms of Chinese mafias or triads. While triad groups do have a strong presence in the region, such generalisations about the backgrounds of the scam industry kingpins are often at odds with a general consensus among specialists on transnational crime that traditional Chinese organised crime and mafia groups are playing a declining role on the international stage.[79] Pioneering scholars Sheldon X. Zhang and Ko-lin Chin have explained this diminishing relevance through a 'structural deficiency perspective', emphasising how 'the very structure of triad societies, which has served these crime syndicates well for decades or even centuries, appears handicapped in a transnational environment', with their 'tendency towards permanency in pursuit of profits and control over vice businesses [rendering] these groups ineffective in expanding into uncharted territories where contingency, situational fluidity and legal constraints are the norm rather than the exception'.[80]

In their view, triads and other traditional ethnic Chinese organised crime and mafia groups have now been outflanked on the international stage by a 'new generation of non-traditional Chinese criminals' that has emerged starting from the early 1980s in the wake of China's economic reforms. Endowed with a strong entrepreneurial spirit, these 'freelance' criminals have been described as 'enterprising agents [who] have no identifiable organizations, no rigid structure, no clearly defined deviant norms and values'.[81] Departing from the fixed hierarchical structures of

---

79   Ko-lin Chin, Sheldon X. Zhang, and Robert Kelly, 'Transnational Chinese Organized Crime Activities', *Transnational Organized Crime* no. 4, 1998, pp. 127–54; Sheldon X. Zhang and Ko-lin Chin, 'Snakeheads, Mules, and Protective Umbrellas: A Review of Current Research on Chinese Organized Crime', *Crime, Law and Social Change* no. 50, 2008, pp. 177–95; Peng Wang, 'The Increasing Threat of Chinese Organised Crime: National, Regional and International Perspectives', *RUSI Journal* 158(4), 2013, pp. 6–18.

80   Sheldon X. Zhang and Ko-lin Chin, 'The Declining Significance of Triad Societies in Transnational Illegal Activities: A Structural Deficiency Perspective', *British Journal of Criminology* 43(3), 2003, pp. 469–88, at pp. 479–80.

81   Ibid., pp. 469 and 485.

traditional organised crime, they operate with structural fluidity and flexibility, qualities that enable them to '[expand] their territory and their range of activities to take advantage of conditions and markets in host countries'.[82] In fact, their transnational endeavours have been so successful that their involvement has been documented 'in all major types of criminal activity, from the trafficking of people, drugs, arms, organs, endangered animals and plants to gambling, prostitution, loan sharking, counterfeiting, money laundering, robbery, car and high-tech theft, extra-legal protection and extortion'.[83] This has been confirmed by scholars who have studied illegal and illicit industries as diverse as human trafficking and smuggling, the drug trade, sex trafficking, and illegal wildlife trading.[84]

Our own research on the cyberfraud industry bears this point out. It is extremely challenging to identify the actors that stand at the top of the scam compounds, with many obscured by proxies, yet it is clear that

---

82   Ibid, p. 469.

83   Wang, 'The Increasing Threat of Chinese Organised Crime', p. 12.

84   For human trafficking: Ko-lin Chin, *Smuggled Chinese: Clandestine Immigration to the United States*, Temple University Press, Philadelphia, PA, 1999; Sheldon X. Zhang and Ko-lin Chin, 'Enter the Dragon: Inside Chinese Human Smuggling Organizations', *Criminology* 40(4), 2002, pp. 737–68; Melvin R. J. Soudijn, *Chinese Human Smuggling in Transit*, Boom Juridische Uitgevers, The Hague, 2006; Sheldon X. Zhang, Ko-lin Chin, and Jody Miller, 'Women's Participation in Chinese Transnational Human Smuggling: A Gendered Market Perspective', *Criminology* 45(3), 2007, pp. 699–733; Sheldon X. Zhang, *Chinese Human Smuggling Organizations: Families, Social Networks, and Cultural Imperatives*, Stanford University Press, Palo Alto, CA, 2008; Yun Gao, ed., *Concealed Chains: Labour Exploitation and Chinese Migrants in Europe*, International Labour Office, Geneva, 2010; Daniel Silverstone, 'From Triads to Snakeheads: Organised Crime and Illegal Migration within Britain's Chinese Community', *Global Crime* 12(2), 2011, pp. 93–111; Joseph Whittle, 'Snakehead: The Extent to Which Chinese Organised Crime Groups Are Involved in Human Smuggling from China to the UK', *Trends in Organized Crime*, 2022. For the drug trade: Ko-lin Chin, *The Golden Triangle: Inside Southeast Asia's Drug Trade*, Cornell University Press, Ithaca, NY, 2009; Ko-lin Chin and Sheldon X. Zhang, *The Chinese Heroin Trade: Cross-Border Drug Trafficking in Southeast Asia and Beyond*, New York University Press, New York, 2015. For sex trafficking: Ko-lin Chin and James O. Finckenauer, *Selling Sex Overseas: Chinese Women and the Realities of Prostitution and Global Sex Trafficking*, New York University Press, 2012. For the wildlife trade: Daan P. van Uhm and Rebecca W. Y. Wong, 'Establishing Trust in the Illegal Wildlife Trade in China', *Asian Journal of Criminology* no. 14, 2019, pp. 23–40; Daan P. van Uhm and Rebecca W. Y. Wong, 'Chinese Organized Crime and the Illegal Wildlife Trade: Diversification and Outsourcing in the Golden Triangle', *Trends in Organized Crime* no. 24, 2021, pp. 486–505; Rebecca W. Y. Wong, *The Illegal Wildlife Trade in China: Understanding Distribution Networks*, Palgrave Macmillan, London, 2019, and 'Shadow Operations in Wildlife Trade under China's Belt and Road Initiative', *China Information* 35(2), 2020, pp. 201–18.

well-established criminal figures and triad groups are involved. However, rather than triads alone, the industry is dominated by a broad cohort of business-oriented, fluid groups that enter into partnerships both among themselves and with local elites to carry out their criminal activities in foreign countries. Even though many of these groups are led by ethnic Chinese individuals – in some cases fugitives wanted by the Chinese authorities who have acquired multiple foreign citizenships – they are flanked by a very diverse cohort. For instance, in Cambodia there is substantial evidence that ties scam compounds to Cambodian politicians and businesspeople, as well as investors from Myanmar, individuals linked to triad groups, and Macau gambling kingpins.[85] In Myanmar, the industry has close ties to ethnic armed organisations.[86] It is also established that ethnic Chinese crime groups work with their regional peers: indigenous recruiters and people traffickers in Vietnam, Indonesia, Malaysia, and Thailand play an important role in feeding labour into the compounds. Powerful businesspeople and elite actors from the region are also playing an increasingly significant role as financiers and owners of scam compounds, rather than simply partners or facilitators for Chinese groups.

The discourse that portrays the Chinese mafia or triads as the masterminds behind online scam operation in Southeast Asia misses this complexity and replaces it with a simplistic narrative that assumes the existence of highly hierarchical, centralised, secret organisations that control the industry in a top-down fashion. It is a discourse that has a long history and at times a distinct political bent. As criminologist Georgios Antonopoulos has explained, there is

a tendency on the part of the political realm, law enforcement agencies, many academics, and media not only to aggregate these 'organized crime' entities into one category but also to sclerotically identify specific

---

85 'Who's Who', Cyber Scam Monitor, cyberscammonitor.net; Neil Loughlin, 'Transnational Crime Meets Embedded Corruption in Cambodia', *Global China Pulse* 3(1), 2024.

86 Cheng, 'Shwe Kokko Special Economic Zone/Yatai New City'; Nanda, 'The Kokang Casino Dream', *Frontier Myanmar*, 23 July 2020; 'If They Catch Me, They'll Kill Me: Trafficked in Wa State', *Frontier Myanmar*, 9 December 2022; Kota Watanabe, 'Militia as a Coercive Broker: Border Guard Forces and Crime Cities in Myanmar's Karen Borderland', *Global China Pulse* 3(1), 2024; Xu Peng, 'The Political Economy of Ethnic Armed Organisations in the China–Myanmar Borderland: Opium, Gambling, and Online Scams', *Global China Pulse* 3(1), 2024.

'mafia characteristics' all these entities supposedly possess … and make assumptions about the supposed 'threat' they pose to China or the host societies when these entities are embedded in the Chinese migrant communities throughout the world.[87]

Joseph Whittle, another criminologist, has pointed out how the label 'organised crime' or 'criminal' has long been attached broadly and inconsistently to a range of actors of Chinese origin, with often racist undertones that fuel the perception of a fearsome 'Yellow' threat.[88] In his words: 'Focusing narratives and responses on organised crime enables a government to build solidarity through highlighting acts by the "other" (people outside of the mainstream), as being responsible for behaviour outside of social norms.'[89] In this sense, the current dominant discourses on ethnic Chinese transnational crime represent another instance of the 'otherisation' of China that tends to shift attention away from broader global trends and shortcomings that are inherent to Western societies, economies, and political systems as well.[90] More practically, by racialising the scam industry, we fuel discrimination and misunderstanding, including against Chinese individuals who are ensnared by it.

This does not mean that the involvement of ethnic Chinese criminal groups in the industry should be downplayed or ignored. Quite the opposite: if anything, this aspect deserves even closer attention – but a scrutiny that is grounded in solid research rather than sweeping assumptions. In this book, we frame the ethnic Chinese criminal syndicates behind the scam operations as an underexplored facet of what in recent years has come to be known as Global China.

Finding a definition more precise than *China outside of China* is a daunting task. In the words of sociologist Ching Kwan Lee, we are talking about a massive, multi-faceted phenomenon that

[takes] myriad forms, ranging from foreign direct investment, labor export, and multilateral financial institutions for building cross-regional

---

87 Georgios A. Antonopoulos, 'The Dragon's Shadow: An Introduction to the Special Issue on "Chinese Organized Crime"', *Trends in Organized Crime* no. 16, 2013, pp. 1–12, at p. 2.

88 Whittle, 'Snakehead'.

89 Ibid.

90 Ivan Franceschini and Nicholas Loubere, *Global China as Method*, Cambridge University Press, Cambridge, 2022.

infrastructure to the globalization of Chinese civil society organizations, creation of global media networks, and global joint ventures in higher education, to name just a few examples.[91]

According to Lee, there are at least three interpretations of Global China in circulation.[92] The first is the idea of Global China as *policy*, which refers to China's expansive official engagements beyond its geographical boundaries and national jurisdiction. The second is Global China as *power* and has a major focus on grassroots dynamics, asking questions about agency (who?), interest (why?), practice (how?), and consequences (so what?), attending especially to issues of resistance, bargaining, accommodation, appropriation, and adaptations by stakeholders in Chinese engagements overseas. Finally, the third approach takes Global China as a *method*, emphasising the *global* context, conditions, and impetuses of Chinese developments, and looking at links between China's domestic dimensions and broader trends. Rather than being mutually exclusive, these approaches should be seen as complementary, and when applied to the online scam industry, they all yield important insights.

Besides these three interpretations, it is also possible to distinguish between two *layers* in current analyses of Global China. The first, which we call *Global China from above*, largely coincides with what Lee frames as policy, and focuses on the state-led macro, top-down dynamics related to China's international engagements, including in the realms of geopolitics, geoeconomics, international trade, standard-setting, and participation in international organisations. The second is *bottom-up Global China*, which overlaps with the dynamics that Lee categorises as power, and includes all sorts of grassroots encounters between Chinese state and non-state actors and local communities in foreign contexts.[93] The online scam industry shows that there is also a third, less visible and largely overlooked layer, which we call *Global China's underbelly*. This layer includes the transnational operations of Chinese crime syndicates, their underground money flows, and their engagements with foreign counterparts, as well as China's efforts to pursue these actors.

---

91   Ching Kwan Lee, *The Specter of Global China: Politics, Labor, and Foreign Investment in Africa*, University of Chicago Press, Chicago, 2017, p. xiv.

92   Ching Kwan Lee, 'What Is Global China?', *Global China Pulse* 1(1), 2022, pp. 24–31; Ching Kwan Lee, 'Global China at 20: Why, How and So What?' *China Quarterly* no. 250, 2022, pp. 313–31.

93   Franceschini and Loubere, *Global China as Method*.

A thorough examination of this underbelly, including the online scam industry, challenges our understanding of Global China as monolithic, especially the views – dominant among proponents of the policy approach – of those who seek to find often tenuous connections between official and non-official actors with an eye to exposing Beijing's supposed nefarious plans for expanding its influence. There are certainly areas where state-linked actors intersect with companies and individuals with dubious backgrounds, and overseas Chinese criminal actors often profess support for the Chinese Party-State, or even unilaterally promote their projects as being state-endorsed. However, by researching the online scam industry, one realises what should already be obvious – that is, that the Chinese Party-State is far from being the omnipotent actor it is often purported to be, and that different Chinese actors can have very different, even conflicting, agendas.

The limitations of the global reach of the Chinese authorities are apparent if we consider that, for more than a decade, China's law enforcement has been tracking people and groups involved in the industry, both within China and abroad. It has conducted numerous arrests, but until recently relatively few key players have been apprehended and returned to China, even those operating in plain sight. This likely points to China's reluctance to expend political capital in demanding the arrest of individuals with connections to local political heavyweights, as well as the limitations of the Chinese state's ability to overcome local elite interests and the protection they provide to wanted individuals. It is certainly no coincidence, for example, that many of the Chinese individuals behind scam compounds in Southeast Asia have acquired Cambodian citizenship, which not only facilitates ownership of property, but also comes with a new name, visa-free travel in the ASEAN area, an extra level of obfuscation, and perhaps protection. It was not until 2023 that there was a significant shift. With negative sentiment growing both globally and within China, the Chinese authorities began to crack down much harder on the industry, exerting stronger pressure on other governments in the region. In Myanmar this led to a massive wave of deportations and the apprehension of high-profile Myanmar nationals who were previously seen as untouchable.

Methodology

While there is a wealth of excellent media reporting on this issue available, with this volume we hope to draw together this trove of information and offer a comprehensive overview of the online scam industry and its annexed humanitarian crisis. The book draws from extensive fieldwork conducted over several years in Southeast Asia, mostly in Cambodia. Two of the authors, Mark Bo and Ivan Franceschini, have been observing Chinese investment in Cambodia since the early 2010s: the former with a focus on both political dynamics and social and environmental impacts; the latter paying specific attention to issues around labour rights. The third author, Ling Li, has been intensively engaging with dozens of survivors of Southeast Asian scam compounds since 2022, interacting with local and international civil society organisations to bring them relief and supporting their requests for repatriation.

Besides combining our previous research and drawing on available media reports, scholarly literature, and material produced by civil society organisations, this book heavily relies on interviews with survivors of the scam compounds. The bulk of the information comes from in-depth interviews that Li conducted with ninety-six survivors in Cambodia, Myanmar, and Laos between 2022 and 2024. Of these survivors, seventy were from mainland China, eight from Taiwan, two from Hong Kong, five from Uganda, three from Malaysia, two from Sri Lanka, one from Bangladesh, one from the Philippines, one from Thailand, one from Vietnam, one from Cambodia, and one from Brazil. Seventy were men and twenty-six were women; twenty were in their teens (the four youngest were barely fourteen), fifty-two in their twenties, twenty-two in their thirties, and two in their early forties. These interviews were then complemented by – and cross-checked with – information coming from survivor testimonies collected by practitioners and journalists. We also spoke with non-governmental organisations, law enforcement, consular officers, members of rescue groups, and journalists who have been focusing on this issue in recent years. Needless to say, all survivors quoted in the book have been fully anonymised and the names should be considered pseudonyms.

We also drew on instant-messaging apps, online job-advertisement websites, and social media platforms that criminal groups utilise to recruit people into their operations. More specifically, we used Telegram to follow conversations among individuals involved in the scam industry and human trafficking. To do this, we joined numerous chat groups. Some were for jobseekers where scam companies advertised jobs; in others, members shared scam handbooks and techniques; some groups are used by disgruntled workers to try to expose their bosses, and others by brokers who post prices for selling and reselling people of different nationalities to online scam companies. We gathered numerous ads from Facebook promoting jobs in the industry and also used WeChat to examine the online activity of specific Chinese actors linked to the compounds, reviewing the material they posted on their feeds and then cross-checking it with other sources available on the web. Finally, we monitored Douyin and Jiandanwang, respectively the Chinese version of TikTok and a forum predominantly used by Chinese nationals in Cambodia, on the lookout for information about scam operations posted by anonymous whistle-blowers. While of uncertain provenance, these posts often included details about specific compounds, such as satellite images or information about the operation's inner workings shared by former workers. Although this type of information is often difficult to verify, these sources proved invaluable in pointing us in the right direction and allowing us to connect the dots of our research.

Additional sources included Chinese-language media based in Southeast Asia, which often report on issues related to the online scam industry, as well as the work of several bloggers, YouTubers, and influencers of various types who have used their platforms to share stories of people trapped in the compounds. These stories in some cases have moralistic undertones and there is often a tendency to be suspicious and critical of people who have survived the compounds, but nonetheless these voices are invaluable to those seeking to understand what is happening.

Finally, we reviewed the personal social media pages of businesspeople and elite actors linked to the scam compounds. Some of these individuals have no qualms about flaunting their attendance at public events linked to companies that we know to be linked to online scam operations, such as ground-breaking and opening ceremonies of hotels, casinos, and property developments, as well as private gatherings held by other notorious figures. The same goes for the websites and social media accounts of local state actors, where officials occasionally display interactions with companies known to be linked to criminal actors, including publishing photos of cash or in-kind donations received by state-aligned philanthropic associations. We also checked local business registries, where records of ownership, directors, addresses, and contact information can sometimes reveal unexpected links.

1

Rise of an Industry

'If you were Chinese, I would never have agreed to meet you,' a Chinese acquaintance told us when we sat down for coffee in Sihanoukville in early 2022. We had first met in the Cambodian city a couple of years earlier, before the pandemic, but much had changed since then. 'If you were Chinese, I would constantly be watching my back. Who knows, you might be coming with someone in a van and kidnap me right after we finish our coffee.' He then continued: 'We really cannot trust anybody here. On the one hand, the Cambodian police miss no opportunity to rip us [Chinese] off; on the other, we cannot trust any other Chinese, as there is always a chance that they might try to sell us off.' In these dire circumstances, his life was split between his workplace and his rented apartment, as he felt that stepping outside of these confines would put him in danger.

He had good reason to be concerned, as the reports – of scams, kidnappings, human trafficking, violence, and even murder – appearing daily in the Chinese-language press and social media in Cambodia made abundantly clear. Just a few weeks before our encounter, the corpse of a young Chinese woman was found handcuffed in a shallow grave in the city's outskirts, her body carrying the signs of extreme physical abuse.[1] The following month, only a few days before our meeting, the case of the 'blood slave' (血奴案 xuenu an) Li Yayuanlun broke. The Chinese man

---

1 'Police Investigate as "Tattooed" Woman's Body Found Handcuffed in Shallow Sihanoukville Grave', *Khmer Times*, 24 January 2022.

claimed to have been held prisoner in Sihanoukville by criminal gangs that had repeatedly drawn his blood to sell it – a story that made headlines all over the world, before being revealed as a partial fabrication (a story we return to in Chapter 5).[2] Behind stories such as these was the fact that by the time of our meeting, the city was teeming with compounds in which hundreds of scam companies run by transnational crime syndicates held masses of people in conditions akin to slavery.

The unusually high concentration of such operations, along with the rapidity with which the sector had transformed the city, put Sihanoukville at the very core of what the media were beginning to call a 'scamdemic'. But how did it come to this? How did a small city once famous as a destination for backpackers turn into a hub for human trafficking and online scams? To answer these questions, we need to take a step back and examine broader dynamics that underpin the rise of the online scam industry in East and Southeast Asia since the onset of the internet era in the 1990s.

Patriarch and Godfather

The origins of the online scam industry that dominates the news today lie in the Taiwan of the 1990s. It was then and there that pioneering scammers started experimenting with some of the sophisticated techniques of online fraud that we are still seeing today. Studies conducted by Taiwanese scholars highlight 1996 as an important watershed moment.[3] Before then, scammers were mostly small groups or even individuals who had to interact with their targets face to face to perpetrate their schemes. That year, however, as the Taiwanese authorities made it easier to acquire phone numbers and bank account passbooks, telecom scams started to emerge. These types of fraud were more high-tech, in that the perpetrators utilised various pretexts and high volumes of forged documents, personal account details, and phone numbers to induce targets to transfer

---

2   Alice Yan, '"Blood Slave" Kidnapped by Chinese Crime Gang in Cambodia Drained for Months and Threatened with Organ Harvesting', *South China Morning Post*, 17 February 2022.

3   For a thorough discussion of this literature and of the role of Taiwan in the rise of the online scam industry, see Tseng Ya-fen 曾雅芬, 行騙天下: 臺灣跨境電信詐欺犯罪網絡之分析 (Global Networks of Fraud: Criminal Networks of Taiwan's Cross-Border Telecommunications Fraud), PhD dissertation, National Chengchi University, December 2016.

money to accounts designated by the scammers. In one of the most notorious instances that occurred towards the end of the decade, local crime syndicates created a popular scratch-card lottery in which lottery buyers were led to believe they had won a prize and were then asked to pay taxes on their winnings before collecting.[4]

As law enforcement in Taiwan became increasingly strict, starting from the early 2000s the focus of the scammers turned to mainland China. At that time, the industry was dominated by Taiwanese gangs, who initially recruited people from Taiwan itself and China's Fujian province and only later expanded their pool to Guangdong and other inner provinces.[5] Online scams first made major headlines in China in 2004, with a case involving a well-known retired professor from a university in Beijing.[6] The man had received a text informing him that his mobile phone number had won the second prize in a lottery held to celebrate the tenth anniversary of Samsung's arrival in China, and that he would receive a Samsung television set and laptop as a prize. But there was a catch: he had to pay a 'service fee' of CN¥850, an insurance premium of CN¥2,000, plus the equivalent of 20 per cent of his personal income tax. After the professor took the bait, the fraudsters apologised for a supposed error in their computer system and informed him that he had won the first prize, not the second. Demands for more service fees, percentages of his tax, and insurance premiums ensued. In total, the man made eight payments amounting to CN¥147,000 (roughly US$17,700 at the average exchange rate that year) before realising it was all a scam. At that point, he sent a complaint to top leaders in the central government, setting in motion an investigation that eventually revealed that the scammer was an eighteen-year-old woman in Anxi, a county in Fujian province.[7]

Around the same time, another high-profile online fraud case was reported to the police, and the operator behind it also turned out to be

---

4   Jianxing Tan and Denise Jia, 'China's War on Rampant Telecom Scams', *Nikkei Asia*, 13 September 2022.

5   Zhuang Hua 庄华 and Ma Zhonghong 马忠红, '东南亚地区中国公民跨境网络犯罪及治理研究' (Cross-Border Cyber Crime of Chinese Citizens in Southeast Asia and Its Governance), 南洋问题研究 (Southeast Asian Affairs) no. 4, 2021, pp. 41–54, at p. 44.

6   '手机诈骗"大本营"揭秘 老教授8次被骗14.7万' (Mobile Phone Fraud 'Base Camp' Exposed: An Old Professor Was Defrauded of 147,000 in Eight Tranches), 北方网 (enorth.com.cn), 9 August 2004

7   '新闻会客厅: 破解短信诈骗迷局(组图' (Newsroom: Solving the Mystery of SMS Scams (Photos)), CCTV 《新闻会客厅》(CCTV Newsroom), 30 June 2004.

based in Anxi.[8] This was the beginning of the area's reputation as a so-called scam township (诈骗之乡 *zhapian zhi xiang*). Suddenly, Anxi was receiving huge attention not only from the Chinese media and public, but also from law enforcement bodies.[9] As one article published in the Chinese press at that time quipped: 'If Taiwan is the patriarch of the telecom fraud sector, then Anxi is its domestic godfather.'[10] Chinese journalists also emphasised other affinities between the two places, especially the existence of linguistic and ancestral connections, including the presence in Taiwan of 2.3 million people originating from Anxi, about 10 per cent of the island's population.[11] Significantly, Anxi's scam operations worked on a family-based model, supplemented by the hiring of external workers. These employees received either a fixed monthly salary of CN¥500 or a commission of 10–20 per cent of the money they generated. They were provided with food and accommodation, usually in a sealed-window suite, a set-up that eerily recalls today's scam compounds, even though we have no evidence that these workers were coerced to perpetrate the scams they engaged in. In addition, just like today's scam compounds, these operations were dynamic and could swiftly relocate to more remote areas in the event of a police investigation.

These developments led to increasingly strict law enforcement on the mainland. In 2003 and 2004 alone, Anxi was at the centre of more than 600 police investigations for online fraud launched by police in twenty-eight provinces and cities across the country.[12] On 1 June 2004, Fujian provincial authorities took the lead in launching a special campaign to crack down on fraud via mobile text messages and the internet. Later that year, the Ministry of Public Security expanded the campaign nationwide. Towards the end of the decade, in 2009, the signing of a Cross-Strait Joint Crime Fighting and Mutual Legal Assistance Agreement between mainland China and Taiwan singled out online scams for attention.[13]

---

8   Liu Haiying 刘海英, Guo Guihua 郭桂花, and Wang Dan 王丹, '厦门破获网络诈骗案 骗子骗去教授14万' (Internet Fraud Case Uncovered in Xiamen: Scammer Defrauded Professor of RMB 140,000), 东南早报 (Dongnan Zaobao), 17 July 2004.

9   See '中国诈骗基地深度揭秘番外篇（3）：诈骗教父安溪' (Extra Chapter with In-Depth Revelations about China's Fraud Base (3): Anxi, the Godfather of Fraud), 界面新闻 (Jiemian Xinwen), 13 June 2016.

10   Ibid.

11   Ibid.

12   Ibid.

13   For more details on these and other regulatory efforts in mainland China and

With scammers now having to find new bases for their operations, Southeast Asia – especially Cambodia, the Philippines, Myanmar, and Laos – emerged as their destination of choice.

Reviewing media and police reports of arrests and repatriations of Chinese nationals suspected of online fraud, mainland Chinese scholars Zhuang Hua and Ma Zhonghong were not able to locate any news of large-scale arrests in Southeast Asia before 2011, an indication that the industry had not yet taken root in the region.[14] The number of arrests spiked only in 2015, at the time of a renewed crackdown on online fraud in China. This hints at how regulatory changes and police crackdowns constitute a powerful push factor in determining the mobility of scam operators. On the pull side, parts of Southeast Asia were attractive destinations because of regulatory voids, lax law enforcement, and the existence of local elites and networks willing to act as protective umbrellas. Proximity to Taiwan and mainland China was also a plus, as fraudsters were easily able to travel back and forth, and secure a steady supply of Chinese-speaking workers. Even more important was the fact that those countries already had decent existing infrastructure, especially in terms of internet connectivity and telecommunications, in part thanks to their burgeoning online gambling sectors.

Zhuang and Ma highlight how after the pivot to Southeast Asia, Taiwanese gangs continued to play a prominent role in these operations, with people from mainland China in subordinate or ancillary roles.[15] Only later did mainlanders begin to play more prominent roles, eventually taking over existing businesses or starting their own, becoming the leading force in the industry. With successful operators returning to their hometowns and persuading relatives, friends, and neighbours to join them, some areas in mainland China came to be utterly transformed by the new-found prosperity of residents who had travelled to Southeast Asia to join the industry. Anxi was once again a notorious case in point. Visiting the place in 2023, a journalist from a Singaporean newspaper took care to note the presence of new multistorey houses alongside rows of older, dilapidated

---

Taiwan, see Lennon Yao-Chung Chang, *Cybercrime in the Greater China Region: Regulatory Responses and Crime Prevention across the Taiwan Strait*, Edward Elgar Publishing, Cheltenham, 2014.

14   Zhuang and Ma, 'Cross-Border Cyber Crime of Chinese Citizens in Southeast Asia and Its Governance'.

15   Ibid., p. 44.

brick houses, with BMWs, Mercedes-Benzes, Maseratis, and other luxury cars negotiating the rugged country roads.[16] She also spoke with local people who lamented the reputation this has brought to the town, once famous for producing some of China's best and most popular tea.

The Gambling–Scam Nexus

Since the move to Southeast Asia, online scams have continued to pro-liferate, with Chinese-speaking individuals remaining a major target even as the industry has rapidly expanded its reach all over the world. Although they were already raking in impressive profits, scam operators realised there was still much room for growth – they just had to find ways to secure larger workforces and supporting infrastructure to scale up their activities. While in the early days scam operations were often small-scale and mostly located in apartments, villas, and hotel rooms, in the late 2010s they began to coalesce into the scam compounds that are the focus of this volume. Zhuang and Ma highlight some key transfor-mations that occurred in this process.[17] These include the corporatisation (公司化 *gongsihua*) of the industry, which is now dominated by multi-layered operations where the masterminds at the top are invisible and the actual operations are conducted by subordinate workers; its so-called chainification (链条化 *liantiaohua*), as operators resort to external supply chains to procure personnel, personal information of potential targets, technology, and money-laundering services; and its merge (融合化 *ron-ghehua*) with the online gambling industry.

This last point hints at how online gambling plays an important role in explaining the rise of the online scam industry in Southeast Asia. As criminologist James Bank has pointed out, the online gambling and scam industries have been intimately intertwined from the very beginning of the internet era. Since its start in the mid-1990s, the online gambling sector has been marred by widespread illegal operations, cyberextortion, betting-related match-fixing, money laundering, and fraud and theft – all problems

---

16   Chen Jing, 'How Fujian's Tea Capital Became Known as a "Scam Town"', Think-China, 23 August 2023.

17   Zhuang and Ma, 'Cross-Border Cyber Crime of Chinese Citizens in Southeast Asia and Its Governance'.

that caused widespread alarm among law enforcement and policymakers.[18] In East and Southeast Asia, governments reacted in different ways. Some outright banned both the provision of and participation in online gambling; others decided to assign licensing monopolies to state-controlled bodies to regulate the industry and enjoy the revenues it generates.[19]

The Chinese authorities were among the former, and Chinese citizens have long been forbidden to gamble within the national borders, with the exceptions of the special administrative regions of Hong Kong and Macau. A judicial interpretation in 2005 made clear that the longstanding prohibition on gambling and opening casinos also applied to online gaming.[20] Chinese officials had particular reasons to be wary, as China's market has always been one of the biggest prizes for industry operators. Despite the prohibition, over CN¥1 trillion (roughly US$137 billion) a year was siphoned out of the country by offshore online gambling platforms in the late 2010s and early 2020s.[21] Chinese legislation on this issue has become increasingly harsh over the years: a 2021 amendment to the Criminal Law increased the statutory maximum penalty for the crime of opening a casino from three to five years, and introduced the crime of organising and participating in foreign (overseas) gambling.[22] The amended law also added that in cases where 'circumstances are serious' – including when Chinese citizens are organised to participate in overseas gambling – the penalty is further increased to ten years' imprisonment.[23]

Other governments, such as those of Cambodia and the Philippines, did not choose to follow China's path in banning online gambling. Instead, they chose to capitalise on it – and this is where things turned sour.

---

18   James Banks, *Online Gambling and Crime: Causes, Controls and Controversies*, Ashgate, Farnham and Burlington, VT, 2014.

19   Ibid., p. 34.

20   Junqing Zhang, 'Skin Gambling in Mainland China: Survival of Online Gambling Companies', *Cogent Social Sciences* 9(2), 2023.

21   Fan Dayu 樊大彧, '坚决打赢跨境赌博犯罪阻击战' (Resolutely Win the Battle against Cross-Border Gambling Crimes), 北京青年报 (Beijing Youth Daily), 25 April 2021.

22   Wu Pengyao 吴鹏瑶 and Xue Yongli 薛永利, '开设赌场犯罪高发，检察机关依法严惩！' (There Is a High Risk of Crime When Opening a Casino, and the Procuratorate Will Punish You Severely in Accordance with the Law!), WeChat channel of the Supreme People's Procuratorate, 29 November 2021.

23   See Article 303 of the Criminal Law of the People's Republic of China, available in an unofficial translation at chinalawtranslate.com.

Cambodia

As Teri Shaffer Yamada has shown, the gambling industry has a long history in Cambodia.[24] While in the colonial era the country had no casinos, things started to change in 1949, when the Cambodian government authorised the opening of the first state-run casino in Phnom Penh. In subsequent years, more casinos were established on Bokor Mountain, a favourite haunt of Khmer royalty and the wealthy elite, and a host of gambling dens opened in both Phnom Penh and Sihanoukville.[25] While the Cambodian civil war (1970–5), Khmer Rouge regime (1975–9), and subsequent Vietnamese occupation (1979–89) ostensibly put an end to these establishments, when Cambodia embarked on its neoliberal reforms in the 1990s, the country's new rulers relaxed anti-gambling restrictions, which led to the reappearance of such operations.

In 1994, the first mega-development deal signed by the Cambodian government that had emerged from the UN-led elections was for a resort and casino complex on an island off the coast of Sihanoukville. Although the details of the contract were never disclosed, it was reported at that time that the agreement included a seventy-year gambling licence and a twenty-year casino monopoly for the whole of Cambodia.[26] As that plan foundered due to internal squabbles among the Cambodian leadership and the opposition of local residents, the Malaysian company behind the development, Ariston Inc. – which assigned its subsidiary NagaWorld Ltd to operate the casino licence – relocated its operations to Phnom Penh. Initially, the casino was based on a barge moored on the Tonlé Sap River in the Cambodian capital. In 2003, it started operating from a new building in the very centre of the city, which later grew to become the two huge NagaWorld casino complexes that exist today. In the process, NagaWorld's monopolistic status changed, with the company being able to retain its original seventy-year casino licence and have its casino monopoly extended to 2035 (later extended to 2045), but only for Phnom Penh and all territory within a 200-kilometre radius.

According to the Law on Suppression of Gambling, passed in 1996, Cambodian citizens are not allowed to gamble anywhere on the national territory, and all types of gambling are forbidden except for those permitted

---

24   Teri Shaffer Yamada, 'Phnom Penh's NagaWorld Resort and Casino', *Pacific Affairs* 90(4), 2017, pp. 743–65.

25   Ibid., p. 753.

26   Ibid., p. 744.

by the government. But to accommodate visiting gamblers, the Cambodian authorities have granted licences to a growing number of casinos outside of Phnom Penh, especially in Sihanoukville and border areas such as Poipet and O'Smach on the Thai border and Bavet on the Vietnamese border.[27] In 2019, before the COVID-19 pandemic hit, 163 licensed casinos reportedly operated in Cambodia – ninety-one of them in Preah Sihanouk province – and state revenues peaked at US$85 million.[28] Although many closed during the pandemic, the number of licensed casinos has since climbed back to more than 180 in 2024.[29]

As the industry developed, numerous issues emerged around the proliferation of unlicensed venues and the challenges of collecting taxes even from supposedly legitimate establishments.[30] These problems were exacerbated both by the fact that Cambodia lacked comprehensive legislation for casino management and by the emergence of online gambling, which presented even greater complications when it came to regulation and taxation. In November 2020, the passing of a new, comprehensive Law on the Management of Integrated Resorts and Commercial Gambling represented the most significant legal development since the 1996 law.[31] As for online gambling, to the surprise of many, on 18 August 2019, the then prime minister Hun Sen announced that the Cambodian government would immediately stop issuing new online gambling licences and would not renew existing ones.

As Chinese nationals in the mainland were the top market for these online operations, it is widely believed that pressure from the Chinese government was behind the move. Yet the Cambodian authorities justified the decision with concerns related to public security. In the words of the directive: 'Some foreign criminals have taken refuge in the form of this gambling to cheat and extort money from victims, domestic and abroad, which affects the security, public order and social order.'[32] This provided

---

27   For the text of the law, see opendevelopmentcambodia.net.

28   Vann Vichar, 'No New Licenses for Online Gambling: Hun Sen', Voice of Democracy, 19 August 2023.

29   According to data published by the Commercial Gambling Management Commission of Cambodia.

30   Robin Spiess, 'Show Me the Money', *Southeast Asia Globe*, 4 June 2019.

31   'Cambodia – Law on the Management of Integrated Resorts and Commercial Gambling', IAGA.

32   Reuters, 'Cambodia to Ban Online Gambling, Cites Threat to Social Order', *Bangkok Post*, 16 August 2019.

an early indication that when the Cambodian government refers to online gambling, it is also talking about online scams and the criminality that seems to be inherent in both.

Hun Sen was not new to this kind of move and rhetoric regarding gambling. As early as December 1998, he ordered the immediate closure of more than a dozen unlicensed casinos in Phnom Penh, linking them to a high incidence of violent crime in the city.[33] A decade later, in 2009, he once again banned legally licensed venues hosting slot machines and electronic gaming machines, shutting down overnight sixty gambling clubs with valid licences, to 'protect public morals'.[34] However, unlike in these previous instances, the 2019 online gambling ban affected not only local industry players but also a large number of foreign investors. Many of these were the Chinese and Taiwanese who in the mid-2010s had flocked to Cambodia – especially to Sihanoukville – in the hope of taking advantage of a permissive regulatory regime at a time when the authorities in mainland China were cracking down hard on online gambling.

As it turned out, the ban proved transformative, rather than prohibitive. As we have seen, online gambling businesses have long been known to host scam operations on the side, and some scam companies present themselves as online gambling platforms but in fact run rigged games. This means that the infrastructure and workforce can be adapted to facilitate both gaming and scams, as can the platforms and networks that provide payment and money-laundering services. After the ban, raids on smaller operations began to increase, and many businesses based in villas and condos in well-populated areas started to clear out. As the smaller scattered operators began to disappear, the better-protected large-scale compounds came to the fore. While many operations in Cambodia shut down and a temporary outflux of Chinese nationals commenced, other online gambling and scam operators sought refuge within these compounds, which benefited from the protection of local partners and remained almost entirely ignored by law enforcement.

Just a short time after the ban came into force, the coronavirus pandemic broke out, further shaking up the industry. Before the ban, public-facing casinos had also started to host online gambling operations in offices above or adjacent to the in-person gaming and customer facilities. The

33   Shaffer Yamada, 'Phnom Penh's NagaWorld Resort and Casino', p. 763.
34   Ibid.

online areas, although hosted in the same complex as the casinos, were kept separate in secure annexed offices and dormitories for the staff, accessible only with key cards. When the pandemic took hold and decimated gambling tourism, many casinos and hotels switched their focus to renting out space to online companies or pivoted to running their own online operations, as did projects that had commenced construction prepandemic anticipating a continued upward trend in Chinese tourism. All this created more space for scam operators. While these locations do not always resemble the standard definition of a compound, workers in these casinos and hotels are often confined to their designated areas, or are unable to leave the walled grounds of the now secure establishments.

While some operators who wanted to hedge their bets or seek a more stable environment relocated to Laos or Myanmar, where a nascent online scam and gambling industry was then taking hold, online operations continued to thrive in Cambodia regardless of the ban, with media reports becoming increasingly frequent and detailed over the following years. Both local media and Chinese-language WeChat news accounts led the way and documented stories emerging from the compounds on an almost daily basis; international outlets picked these up and brought the issue to a global audience.[35] With the reputational harm reaching astronomical levels, and diplomatic pressure presumably building, the Cambodian government announced a major crackdown in September 2022. In the following three to four months there was a flurry of raids that took out a handful of operations, while other compounds went quiet, emptied out, and moved workers elsewhere.[36]

There followed a period of uncertainty as observers waited to see if the crackdown would be broadened or sustained, but by the end of the year law enforcement operations tailed off and shifted their focus to targeted rescues of workers who had been able to get a message to the newly established police helpline or their embassies. An announcement by the Preah Sihanouk provincial government in October 2022 instructed casinos and other establishments to cease 'closed-door operation', erect signs bearing the business name, and ensure their premises were accessible and their

35   On the role of beat journalists in exposing scam operations, see Danielle Keeton-Olsen, 'Scam Stories Hinge on On-the-Ground Journalism', *Global China Pulse* 3(1), 2024.

36   'Cambodia's Online "Crackdown" Six Months On (Part 1)', Cyber Scam Monitor, 25 June 2023; 'Cambodia's Online "Crackdown" Six Months On (Part 2)', Cyber Scam Monitor, 30 June 2023.

operations properly licensed.[37] It also ordered them not to hold workers' passports or other personal documents for extended periods of time. Many locations followed at least parts of these instructions, and previously heavily secured facilities opened their gates and erected signs. After the crackdown commenced, some journalists were even able to walk into once impenetrable compounds and observe deserted ground-floor businesses, noting the lack of activity in sites that had once housed thousands.[38]

Towards the end of the year, a large number of casino licences, including many referred to as temporary, were issued, in several cases to companies known to be involved in online operations. In mid-2023, a journalist from a local Chinese-language outlet visited known scam sites in Sihanoukville, including some that had been raided and some that had simply gone quiet, and reported that they were once again busy.[39] Gates were closed again – or at least entry and exit points were guarded by security – and numerous compounds erected signs bearing the names of casinos, even though they were clearly not public-facing businesses.

This shows that, while the short-lived crackdown shook up the industry and led to closures and relocations within Cambodia and to neighbouring countries, this was by no means the end for online gambling and scam operations in the kingdom. Instead, it represented another partial reconfiguration, with compounds in populated areas cleaning up their intimidating façades somewhat – erecting signs and presenting themselves as legitimate businesses – but otherwise coming back to life and getting back to work. Meanwhile, in areas further away from the public gaze, such as Koh Kong, Oddar Meanchey, Bavet, and Poipet, business apparently went on as usual. Reports of trafficking, confinement, and rescues began to gather attention, and a little more than six months after the crackdown, numerous well-documented scam operators made very public donations to the Cambodian Red Cross on the occasion of annual Red Cross and Crescent Day.[40]

37   Lay Samean, 'Preah Sihanouk Businesses Warned against Withholding Worker Passports, Closed-Door Operation', *Phnom Penh Post*, 10 October 2022.

38   Huang Yan 黄岩, '西港中国城凯博金水全部对外开放' (Sihanoukville China-town, Kaibo, and Jinshui All Open to the Public), *TNAOT*, 19 September 2022.

39   '去年918西港被关园区 现已陆续重新开工' (Parks in Sihanoukville, Shut Down during September Last Year, Have Gradually Reopened), 柬单网 (Jiandanwang), 23 June 2023.

40   Cyber Scam Monitor, 'Cambodia's Online "Crackdown" Six Months On (Part 2)'.

The Philippines

Regulation of the gambling industry in the Philippines has its roots in the martial law era. In 1977, the administration of Ferdinand Marcos established the Philippine Amusement and Gaming Corporation (PAGCOR), which was owned and controlled by the government, as the sole agency in charge of managing the casino and entertainment industry in the country. As Vicente Chua Reyes Jr has pointed out, this body was created for three main reasons: to prevent the proliferation of illegal casinos that had become rampant in the early 1970s; to complement the development of the tourism industry, which at that time had become one of the country's leading foreign-exchange earners; and to tap potential resources for the government to finance its development projects.[41] PAGCOR proved a significant success, with reports of its gaming operations generating about ₱73.11 billion (Philippine pesos, roughly US$1.24 billion) in 2023.[42]

To capitalise further on the gambling industry, upon taking office in 2016, President Rodrigo Duterte instituted the Philippine offshore gambling operators (POGO) scheme, a new policy that enabled online gambling firms targeting overseas customers to set up shop in major cities, such as Makati, Pasay, and Paranaque, thus expanding the space for these businesses to operate legally in the country.[43] Before then, such operations could only open in the areas managed by investment-promotion agencies, which were often located in export-processing zones or special economic zones away from the main urban centres. PAGCOR was put in charge of licensing all online gambling businesses nationwide. As in the case of Cambodian online gambling operations, the principal targets of POGOs were initially gamblers inside China, much to the ire of the Chinese government.

As he tried to bring the online gambling industry under state control, Duterte concurrently took action against some high-profile gambling operators. For instance, Macau gaming tycoon Jack Lam fled the Philippines in December 2016, after his casinos in the country were shut

---

41   Vicente Chua Reyes Jr, 'Networks of Dis(trust) and Gaming Development in the Philippines: PAGCOR and the Entertainment City', *Pacific Affairs* 90(4), 2017, pp. 725–42, at p. 734.

42   See 'Total Income from Gaming Operations of the Philippine Amusement and Gaming Corporation (PAGCOR) from Calendar Year 2018 to 2023', Statista, 18 July 2024.

43   Alvin Camba, 'Between Economic and Social Exclusions. Chinese Online Gambling Capital in the Philippines', *Made in China Journal* 5(2), 2020, pp. 209–17, at pp. 211–12.

down amid an investigation into illegal unlicensed online gambling and accusations that he had tried to pay bribes to secure the release of 1,300 arrested Chinese workers.[44] Later that month, Duterte openly threatened to ban online gambling in the country, only to have PAGCOR intervene to clarify that he was referring solely to unlicensed online gaming companies.[45] The following April, the Philippine government, in cooperation with its Chinese counterpart, cracked down on several illegal online gambling platforms, shutting four illegal websites run out of the Philippines, arresting ninety-nine people, and freezing more than a thousand bank accounts, while also threatening further raids.[46]

The Duterte administration was navigating opposing pressures. On the one hand, the online gambling industry was attracting huge amounts of capital from China, benefiting from improved bilateral relations that enticed not only investors but also large numbers of tourists – tourism which incidentally also created a pathway for illegal workers. On the other hand, there were pressures coming not only from the Chinese government, which was eager to see the industry in the Philippines banned, but also from the public. In 2016, online gambling firms, many of which were Chinese, were taking over entire condominium buildings or floors in Metro Manila, outbidding call centres that provide back-office services to Western multinational corporations, as well as Filipino buyers and renters.[47] This drove up real estate prices and even the cost of basic goods. At the same time, a massive influx of Chinese workers, many illegal, was perceived as stealing jobs from local people, causing considerable social tension.[48]

In 2019, facing renewed pressure from the Chinese authorities, Duterte openly declared that while he was not a fan of online gambling, he was not willing to ban this 'stupid activity' because of the impact this would have on the country's economy.[49] This concern might have been well founded

44   Niall Fraser, 'Gaming Tycoon Jack Lam Flees Philippines, Has Casinos Shut Down amid Sabotage and Bribery Allegations', *South China Morning Post*, 7 December 2016.

45   Reuters, 'Philippine President Duterte Says He Will Stop All Online Gambling', CNBC, 22 December 2016; Iriz Gonzales, 'Pagcor Clarifies Ban on Online Gambling', *Philippine Star*, 24 December 2016.

46   Neil Jerome Morales and Farah Master, 'As Philippines Joins China to Fight Illegal Gambling, More Scrutiny of Casinos Likely', Reuters, 8 May 2017.

47   Camba, 'Between Economic and Social Exclusions', p. 210.

48   'How Come There Are So Many Chinese Workers Here?', *Straits Times*, 7 February 2019.

49   'Duterte Rejects China's Call to Ban Philippine Online Gambling', Al Jazeera, 5 September 2019.

considering what happened to Sihanoukville after the online gambling ban, as we will discuss below. It is unclear whether these law enforcement actions caused anxiety among online operators, or if they simply wanted to diversify and expand their activities, but many companies that first set up in the Philippines later moved all or part of their operations to Cambodia, which was perceived as more welcoming due to its permissive legislation on gambling, lax legal supervision and enforcement, and friendly elite business partners. A similar reasoning applied to Myanmar later.

Under Duterte, POGOs were largely discussed in terms of the service they were set up to provide, that is, online gambling. However, after the new Ferdinand 'Bongbong' Marcos administration took office in 2022, PAGCOR came under increased pressure. From the moment POGOs started to be licensed in 2016, sporadic reports began to emerge that they were hosting scam operators and participating in serious transnational crimes, although not on the scale observed in Cambodia. In particular, thousands of Chinese travelled to the Philippines to work in POGOs, but by 2020, COVID-19 travel restrictions and fears of repercussions in China shrank the labour pool, leading to an increase in human trafficking and confinement of workers inside compounds. With the growing difficulty of staffing operations targeting Chinese gamblers, and with China blocking online gambling platforms and cracking down on financial flows, it is quite likely that a shift from gambling to scamming accelerated during this period. In 2022, it began to emerge that numerous POGOs shared a similar modus operandi, with increasingly numerous stories of trafficked workers, bonded labour, scams, and brutality coming to light.

In late 2022, with opposition to POGOs growing among the public and lawmakers, senators rejected a roadmap presented by PAGCOR that would allow online gambling operators to continue to do business in the country under proposed tighter regulation.[50] The debate quickly became increasingly polarised, with critics linking these operations to scams, unpaid taxes, money laundering, prostitution, modern slavery, and the kidnapping and murder of (mostly) Chinese nationals, while proponents touted POGOs' importance for revenue generation and job creation.[51] As some local administrations began to impose deadlines for existing online gambling establishments to terminate operations in the territory under

50   'Pagcor Must End Its Love Affair with POGOs', *Manila Times*, 25 November 2022.

51   See, for instance, Erik Gibbs, 'PAGCOR Dismantling Calls Grow in the Philippines amid New Accusations', casino.org, 24 January 2023.

their purview, in March 2023 Senator Sherwin Gatchalian, chair of the Philippines' Ways and Means Committee, presented a report to a Senate plenary session on the impacts of the industry and recommended a permanent ban on offshore gaming operations.[52] He referred to POGOs as a breeding ground for financial crimes, with the Anti–Money Laundering Council deeming POGOs and their service providers 'highly vulnerable to money laundering'. With many operators avoiding their tax obligations, the senator's report found POGOs' benefits to the country 'overrated, moderate and erratic', with the costs outweighing the benefits.

Concrete evidence of some POGOs' role in human trafficking and online scams really came to dominate headlines in 2023. In May, a massive police raid on a business park in Pampanga, north of Manila, resulted in the rescue of over 1,100 people from more than ten countries who had allegedly been forced to operate crypto scams. It was later revealed that the scam operators subleased this space from a licensed POGO.[53] In late June, another huge raid took place in Las Piñas City at the complex of Xinchuang Network Technology. AP News reported that the raid, which saw police backed by commandos, picked up more than 2,700 workers from eighteen different countries.[54] On 1 August another raid took place, this time targeting Rivendell Global Gaming in Pasay City.[55] On that occasion, police found around 460 Filipino workers and over 180 foreigners, seizing hundreds of phones, computers, and SIM cards, as well as papers with scripts for romance scams and devices used for mass text blasting.[56]

In light of these occurrences, the continuation of the POGO industry put the Philippines even further at odds with China, which on multiple occasions directly called on the government to shut it down.[57] According to the *Manila Times*, in November 2022 the Chinese authorities were getting

52   See, for instance, Mariel Celine Serquina, 'Pasig Ordinance to Prohibit Renewal, Granting of New Online Gambling Permits', CNN Philippines, 27 December 2022; Beatrice Pinlac, '"Game Over": Gatchalian Wants Permanent Ban on POGOs', inquirer.net, 22 March 2023.

53   Senate of the Philippines, 'Hontiveros: POGOs Used as Legal Cover for Scam Hubs', press release, 30 May 2023.

54   '2,700 People Tricked into Working for Cybercrime Syndicates Rescued in Philippines', Associated Press/AP News, 27 June 2023.

55   Emmanuel Tupas and Marc Jayson Cayabyab, '650 Workers Held in Pasay POGO Raid', *Philippine Star*, 3 August 2023.

56   Joviland Rita, 'Alleged Cybercrime Hub Raided in Pasay; Around 650 Held Including Foreigners', GMA News Online, 2 August 2023.

57   Muhammad Cohen, 'Philippine POGOs Stick with Chinese Betting, Tempting

closer to placing the Philippines on a blacklist as a tourist destination due to the government not taking action to close POGOs.[58] Indeed, in his presentation to the Senate in March 2023, Senator Sherwin Gatchalian described the POGO industry as 'inherently unstable due to the out-sized foreign regulatory and political risks involved', with most customers betting through POGOs being Chinese nationals, which is 'problematic' due to gambling being outlawed in China.[59] Eventually, in July 2024, the Marcos administration caved in and put an end to the controversial scheme. The country's Bureau of Immigration immediately followed suit by ordering all registered foreign workers employed by POGOs, estimated at around 20,000 (including many Chinese), to leave the country within two months.[60] While the move earned vocal praise from the Chinese Embassy in Manila, its long-term effects remain to be seen.[61] Even prior to the announcement of the ban, hundreds of online gambling and scam hubs simply operated without licences, so implementation of the ban on licensed operations will not be a panacea.

Local Power Brokers and Areas of Exception

While the existence of a permissive environment for the gambling indus-try can work as a significant pull factor, this is not the only factor that draws scam operators to certain locations. The existence of local power brokers willing to act as facilitators and protective umbrellas in exchange for a hefty share of the profits is also essential. This applies to both Cam-bodia and the Philippines, but it emerges with even more clarity when we examine the rise of Myanmar and Laos as scam hubs. Laos also brings to light one additional dynamic: that some areas of exception set up for development purposes, such as special economic zones (SEZs), can morph into crime hubs.

Beijing's Wrath', iGB, 13 February 2023; Cliff Venzon, 'Manila Vice: Xi and Duterte Grapple with Online Casino Crime', *Nikkei Asia*, 24 December 2019.

58   Rigoberto D. Tiglao, 'China Likely to Blacklist PH as a Tourist Destination Because of POGOs', *Manila Times*, 23 November 2022.

59   Pinlac, '"Game Over"'.

60   'All POGO Workers to Leave', Philippines Bureau of Immigration press release, 24 July 2024.

61   Jim Gomez, 'China Issues Rare Praise to Philippine President for His Ban on Chinese Online Gambling Operators', Associated Press/AP News, 25 July 2024.

Myanmar

The 1986 Law on Gambling completely prohibited gambling of any sort in Myanmar, although illegal casinos were operating with the permission of the then military junta. During the partial democratic transition between 2011 and 2021, reforms were introduced to regulate gambling. This included a 2013 Myanmar Investment Commission notification that allowed casinos to operate for foreigners in hotels in 'restricted areas' with the permission of the military-controlled Ministry of Home Affairs.[62] In June 2019, a new law permitted gambling venues for foreigners countrywide (as in Cambodia, gambling continued to be prohibited for local citizens), although a licensing regime was never established. Regardless of the regulatory framework in place, casino industries developed, particularly in border areas controlled by militia groups and self-administered territories. These regions are not all easily accessible, operation costs are higher than elsewhere in mainland Southeast Asia, and the risk of conflict is high. In this environment, the online industry was likely attracted by the opportunity to establish itself in places that are in many regards lawless, effectively ruled by warlords, who have for years operated myriad criminal operations, many of which are transnational in nature.

The growth of the online scam industry began to attract closer scrutiny around 2020, initially focusing on the township of Myawaddy in Kayin State, which borders Thailand.[63] The state is home to the Karen National Union (KNU) and its armed wing, the Karen National Liberation Army (KNLA), which has fought a decades-long battle against the central government for the autonomy of Karen areas. In the 1990s, a group split from the KNLA and established the Democratic Karen Buddhist Army, which signed a ceasefire with the military junta and joined it in its battle against the KNU. In 2010, this group formally came under the command of the military and became the Kayin Border Guard Force (Kayin BGF), which now controls a large part of the area in which Myanmar's southern scam industry thrives. Here, scam compounds expanded exponentially, including the notorious Shwe Kokko Yatai New City, as well as dozens of other locations reported to be populated by workers from across the region and beyond, many of whom are held against their volition.[64]

---

62 'The Republic of the Union of Myanmar, Myanmar Investment Commission, Notification No. 1/2013', Asia Pacific Energy Portal, 31 January 2013.

63 Formerly known as Karen State, and still referred to as such by many.

64 Alastair McCready and Allegra Mendelson, 'Inside the Chinese-Run Crime Hubs

Northern Myanmar initially received less attention in the global media, but there, just as in Kayin State, scam compounds were also rapidly proliferating. Again, this took place in areas under the control of ethnic armed organisations, mainly in Wa State, a self-governing area within Shan State, and the Kokang Self-Administered Zone, which was governed from 2010 to early 2024 by a border guard force under the command of the central government and the current ruling military junta. With scam sites in the north much less accessible to the wider world than Myawaddy – which is so close to Thailand that it can be viewed from the banks of the Moei River on the Thai side of the border – and predominantly staffed by Chinese workers rather than the international workforce that can be found in Myawaddy, these operations were slower to catch global attention; but reports in Chinese mainstream and social media have for years recounted tales of lawlessness and brutality in the north, with heavily secured sites guarded by soldiers provided by local armed groups.

This changed dramatically in September 2023, when a series of major raids orchestrated by Chinese and local police hit online fraud sites in Wa State.[65] These raids continued into the following month, and on a single day in October, 2,349 people suspected of being involved in online scams in Wa State were handed over to Chinese police on the Yunnan border, bringing the total number of deportations to over 4,600.[66] Piecemeal law enforcement actions had taken place in various parts of Myanmar in the months prior to this, but reports only covered the repatriation of a few dozen people, and many observers continued to dismiss these as drops in the ocean, failing to take down the real power players behind the scenes. However, in October there was a shift in this sense too, with China issuing wanted notices and offering rewards for tips leading to the apprehension of Chen Yanban (also known as Bao Yanban) and Xiao Yankuai (also known as He Chuntian), alleging they were ringleaders of fraud gangs targeting Chinese citizens. Unlike with previous wanted notices issued for Chinese nationals suspected of perpetrating overseas fraud, these men were public figures: Chen was Wa State minister of construction, and Xiao the mayor

---

of Myanmar That Are Conning the World: "We Can Kill You Here", *South China Morning Post*, 22 July 2023.

65   Yang Zekun, 'Police in China, Myanmar Bust 11 Scam Dens', *People's Daily*, 6 September 2023.

66   'Myanmar Hands China Over 2,300 Telecom Scam Suspects', Xinhua, 16 October 2023.

of Wa State's Monglin county.[67] Soon after, according to a document from the Wa State Central Committee, the two were dismissed; Chen Yanban had his United Wa State Party politburo position revoked and was expelled from both party and military.[68]

This dramatic shift was not limited to Wa State. In the Kokang Self-Administered Zone, which sits along the border with China's Yunnan province, rumours began to circulate in October that executives of the huge conglomerate Fully Light Group (福利来集团 *fulilai jituan*), which had long had interests in casinos and later expanded into online operations, had been arrested while on a business trip to China.[69] The rumours turned out to be true, making this a significant development as the company is chaired by one of the founders of the Kokang Border Guard Force, a subdivision of the Myanmar military comprising former insurgents that sits under the Myanmar military and was installed after the latter took control of the area in 2009. Public attention shifted on 27 October, when Operation 1027 was launched by the Three Brotherhood Alliance, a coalition composed of three groups: the Arakan Army; Myanmar National Democratic Alliance Army; and Ta'ang National Liberation Army. The Alliance rapidly hit military and border trade posts across Shan State, and, with the Kokang Border Guard Force on the back foot, this offensive moved in on the Kokang Self-Administered Zone and encircled its bases of power, including its capital, the major scam hub of Laukkai. In early January 2024, the Alliance announced it had taken control of the town.[70]

Amid the fighting, thousands of scam workers in Laukkai and other areas managed to flee their compounds, while others were locked inside or moved by their bosses. Whether motivated by principle or in an attempt to garner the favour of China, or a mixture of the two, the Brotherhood Alliance had declared at the outset that wiping out fraud parks was a

---

67 Criminal Investigation Bureau of the Ministry of Public Security, '公安机关公开通缉陈岩板（鲍岩板）、肖岩块（何春田）2名电信网络诈骗犯罪集团头目' (Public Security Organs Release Wanted Notices for Chen Yanban (Bao Yanban) and Xiao Yankui (He Chuntian), Two Leaders of a Criminal Telecommunications Network Fraud Group), CCTV, 12 October 2023.

68 Agence France-Presse, 'Myanmar Rebels Fire Top Officials Wanted by China for Online Scams', *Barron's*, 18 October 2023.

69 'ကိုးကန့်လုပ်ငန်းရှင် ၁၁ ဦးကို တရုတ်ရဲဖမ်းဆီး' (Chinese Police Arrest 11 Kokang Entrepreneurs), BBC News Burmese, 3 October 2023.

70 'Myanmar Rebels Claim Control of Key Town Near Chinese Border', Reuters, 6 January 2024.

central objective of the operation. In November, reports emerged that in late October a large number of Chinese nationals had been killed escaping one infamous Laukkai compound known as Crouching Tiger Villa (卧虎山庄 *wohu shanzhuang*).[71] Reports vary as to the severity of the incident, but it seems likely it did occur, with several unconfirmed accounts stating that among the dozens killed were four undercover Chinese police officers. This was followed by another batch of arrest warrants issued by the Chinese police for members of the Ming family, whose patriarch, Ming Xuechang, allegedly owned the Crouching Tiger Villa compound.[72] Those arrested included his son, who held a senior military position in Kokang. Just four days later, China's Ministry of Public Security reported that these individuals had been 'brought to justice', with the son, daughter, and son-in-law of Ming Xuechang handed over to Chinese police. Ming Xuechang allegedly shot and killed himself during a raid on his home.[73]

Although this was a huge development, and the Ming family was a powerful one, they are not among the so-called Four Families that have long been known to control the administration, police, military, and organised crime that Kokang had become famous for. Their moment came soon enough though, and in December a batch of ten wanted notices was issued by China for members of the Bai, Wei, and Liu clans.[74] Among them was the previously untouchable Bai Suocheng, former chairman of the Kokang

71   Jonathan Head, 'The Chinese Mafia's Downfall in a Lawless Casino Town', BBC News, 23 November 2023.

72   Criminal Investigation Bureau of the Ministry of Public Security, '公安机关公开通缉明学昌、明国平、明菊兰、明珍珍4名缅北果敢自治区电信网络诈骗犯罪集团重要头目' (Public Security Organs Release Wanted Notices for Four Important Leaders of Criminal Telecommunications Network Fraud Group in the Kokang Self-Administered Zone in Northern Myanmar, Ming Xuechang, Ming Guoping, Ming Julan, and Ming Zhenzhen), CCTV, 12 November 2023.

73   Criminal Investigation Bureau of the Ministry of Public Security, '缅北果敢电诈集团重要头目明国平、明菊兰、明珍珍被成功缉拿归案' (Key Leaders of Kokang Online Fraud Group in Northern Myanmar Ming Guoping, Ming Julan, and Ming Zhenzhen Successfully Arrested and Brought to Justice), 澎湃 (The Paper), 16 November 2023; Criminal Investigation Bureau of the Ministry of Public Security, '缅北果敢电信网络诈骗犯罪集团首犯明学昌畏罪自杀' (Ming Xuechang, Lead Criminal of the Kokang Telecom Internet Fraud Crime Group in Northern Myanmar, Committed Suicide in Fear of Punishment for His Crimes), *China News*, 17 November 2023.

74   Criminal Investigation Bureau of the Ministry of Public Security, '公安机关公开通缉白所成、魏怀仁、刘正祥等10名缅北果敢自治区电信网络诈骗犯罪集团重要头目' (Public Security Organs Release Wanted Notices for Bai Suocheng, Wei Huairen, Liu Zhengxiang, and 10 Other Key Leaders of Telecom Network Fraud Criminal Groups in the Kokang Self-Administered Zone in Northern Myanmar), Xinhua, 10 December 2023.

region. Other targets included the heads of powerful criminal business enterprises and Kokang military units, including the executive director and general manager of the Fully Light Group, of which Bai Suocheng was also the chairman. On 30 January 2024, in an event extensively publicised by Chinese state media, six of the ten wanted family members were arrested, handed over to Chinese police, and put on chartered flights to China. This included the heads of three of the four Kokang crime families.[75]

The sudden shift of events in northern Myanmar dealt a massive blow to the online gambling and scam industry, with compounds raided, workers and bosses fleeing, and heavy fighting forcing even the hardiest of operators to shut down. By the end of November 2023, China reported that a staggering 31,000 people had been handed over to Chinese police.[76] By the end of the year, according to China's Ministry of Public Security, this had risen to 41,000.[77] In August 2024, the ministry reported that this had exceeded 50,000.[78] Although Chinese nationals made up the majority of workers in these areas, media reports spoke of Thais, Filipinos, Malaysians, Vietnamese, South Koreans, Singaporeans, Hongkongers, and others being evacuated from the area in their hundreds.

During these massive upheavals, all eyes shifted to the southern cluster of scam operators. The situation in Myawaddy remained quiet. No similar law enforcement action took place in the township, suggesting that China's priorities and influence, at least for the time being, were focused on areas closer to its borders. There was one event in March 2024 during which the Myanmar junta and Chinese and Thai governments cooperated to facilitate the repatriation of over 800 Chinese nationals from compounds

---

75 '10 Major Criminal Suspects Transferred Back to China from Myanmar', Xinhua, 31 January 2024.

76 Criminal Investigation Bureau of the Ministry of Public Security, '打击缅北涉我电诈犯罪取得显著战果 累计3.1万名电信网络诈骗犯罪嫌疑人移交我方' (Remarkable Results Have Been Achieved in Combating Telecom Fraud Crimes Involving China in Northern Myanmar. A Total of 31,000 Telecom and Online Fraud Suspects Have Been Handed Over to Us), Consulate-General of the People's Republic of China in Luang Prabang, 21 November 2023.

77 Yang Zekun, 'Ministry Releases Details of Successful Crackdown on Telecom and Online Fraud', *China Daily*, 5 January 2024.

78 Criminal Investigation Bureau of the Ministry of Public Security, '公安部: 近年来累计抓获缅北涉诈嫌疑人5万余名' (Ministry of Public Security: In Recent Years, More Than 50,000 Fraud Suspects Have Been Arrested in Northern Myanmar), CCTV, 27 August 2024.

in Myawaddy.[79] This received limited attention in the Chinese press, and only later did it become clear that the release was the result of a negotiation with the Kayin BGF and compound owners, who perhaps wanted to release some pressure and reduce the risk of major action taking place, as it had in northern Myanmar.

Even though at the time the Chinese-born mastermind of the Yatai New City scam haven in Shwe Kokko, She Zhijiang, resided in a jail cell in Thailand fighting his deportation to China, the scam industry continued to thrive in the Myanmar–Thai border area. Pressure did continue to build though, and with nationals from across the world trapped in Myawaddy, various embassies and foreign ministries released a steady stream of warnings and statements about the risks of going to the area and detailing efforts to rescue their citizens. In May 2024, the Kayin BGF announced that all foreigners involved in online fraud operations in the area had to leave by October or face punishment.[80] Although this deadline passed, many major compounds continued to operate in and around Myawaddy, although some did begin to relocate further south.[81]

The crackdown in the north of the country sent shockwaves through the industry, but even though thousands of people were arrested and evacuated from Wa State and the Kokang region, this represented a reshuffling rather than a purge. Although the industry may not rebuild in those areas in the immediate future, groups quickly moved to other parts of Myanmar, crossed the border to Laos, or relocated to Cambodia.

Laos

Located where Laos, Thailand, and Myanmar converge, the Golden Triangle region has long been infamous for its links to transnational crime, including the trafficking of narcotics and wildlife.[82] Since the mid-2000s, the Lao government has sought to develop this area, with the explicit goal of eliminating its negative reputation.[83] Deals were signed but it

79   'Thailand Facilitates Transfer of 900 Scam Victims from Myanmar to China', Reuters, 3 March 2024.

80   Saw Lwin, 'Myanmar Junta-Linked Armed Group Orders Foreign Scammers Out of Myawaddy', *Irrawaddy*, 7 May 2024.

81   Naw Betty Han, 'South for the Winter: Myanmar's Cyber Scam Industry Migrates', *Frontier Myanmar*, 29 August 2024.

82   International Crisis Group, 'Transnational Crime and Geopolitical Contestation along the Mekong', ICG website, 18 August 2023.

83   National Committee for Special and Specific Economic Zone Secretariat Office,

was not until around 2014 that significant development commenced, and the previously rural riparian area began to transform into a major border casino zone, dubbed the Golden Triangle Special Economic Zone (GTSEZ). The mastermind behind this transformation is Zhao Wei, a seasoned gambling kingpin born in China's northeastern Heilongjiang province, who made his name in the casinos of Macau before moving to northern Myanmar, then Laos.

Reports in the Chinese media on nationals being arrested and deported for involvement in online gambling and scams in Laos can be found at least as far back as 2011.[84] Since then, arrests have occurred across several provinces, but as the GTSEZ expanded, the online industries coalesced around it. As global attention fell on the regional scam industry, more information began to emerge from the zone, with illegal online gambling and cyberscams now added to the long list of crimes associated with it.[85] Located on the frontier, in close proximity to Myanmar, Thailand, and China, and flanked by the Mekong River, the GTSEZ presented a perfect location for scam operators.

As has occurred elsewhere in the region, after several years of scammers operating with apparent impunity from the area, with workforces bolstered by trafficked labour from across the world, pressure on Laos led to an uptick in law enforcement action in late 2023. This picked up pace the following year, and in August 2024, over 700 people from fifteen countries were detained.[86] In the following days, the Lao government announced that strict inspections would soon be conducted across the zone. At the same time as pressure was growing on the GTSEZ, an increasing number of reports emerged from Cambodia and Thailand of Chinese nationals being caught illegally crossing the border from Laos, again indicating a shift in workforce brought about by law enforcement action.

Despite its notoriety, the GTSEZ has been able to host a range of major criminal actors and continues to expand, with an international airport

'Development Strategy for Special and Specific Economic Zone (SEZ) in the Lao PDR, 2011–2020', 2012.

84   Wen Haixuan 文海宣, '冒充司法工作人员 跨国电信诈骗团伙32人获刑' (32 Members of a Transnational Telecommunications Fraud Gang Impersonating Judicial Personnel Were Sentenced), 中国法院网 (China Court Net), 19 September 2013.

85   International Crisis Group, 'Stepping into South East Asia's Most Conspicuous Criminal Enclave', ICG website, 17 January 2024.

86   Namfon Chanthavong, 'Golden Triangle Seizes Telecom Fraud Network in Major Crackdown', *Laotian Times*, 20 August 2024.

completing construction in 2024. Reports frequently describe the zone as existing outside of the law, with the SEZ management responsible for order and security. Numerous media articles have quoted local officials lamenting their inability to enter the zone without support at the national level, which until recently has generally not been forthcoming.[87] While Zhao Wei is undoubtedly a powerful regional actor, with strong connections to armed groups in Myanmar, he would not have been able to operate what effectively became a transnational crime zone without establishing strong connections with elite actors in Laos. Yet, the expansion of this zone so close to China has clearly caused increasing frustration, with Chinese police tracing online gambling and scams targeting its citizens to operations inside it. In 2024, a feature on Chinese state broadcaster CCTV included an interview with a Chinese police officer who called the GTSEZ a 'cancerous area' plagued by crime.[88] The police actions launched in mid-2024, surely in large part a result of growing anger from Laos's northern neighbour, show that elite power is not unlimited; but it remains to be seen if the crackdown will be sustained or if it is just another temporary show, after which the industry will go back to business as usual.

Sihanoukville: Rise and Fall of a Frontier City

So far, we have taken a bird's-eye view to track the development of the online scam industry in East and Southeast Asia. It is equally important not to lose sight of the dramatic impact that online scam operations can have at the grassroots. The fate of Sihanoukville was entangled in the transnational ebbs and flows of the online gambling and scam industries. What happened there was not entirely unique – roughly at the same time as the city grew into a global online scam hub, we witnessed the nascent establishment of 'spinach cities' in Myanmar, the growth of scam compounds in Cambodia's border areas and capital city, and the transition of already affirmed gambling venues (such as those located in Laos's GTSEZ)

---

87   Alastair McCready, 'Will Laos' Economic Zones Boost Growth or Bring In Criminals?', *Nikkei Asia*, 10 October 2023.

88   Criminal Investigation Bureau of the Ministry of Public Security, '全民反诈在行动–斩链行动' (National Anti-Fraud Action: Operation Chain Cutting), Sohu, 24 June 2024.

into the online fraud business.[89] What renders the case of Sihanoukville particularly poignant is the high concentration and visibility of online gambling and scam operations on its territory, which have completely and rapidly changed the urban landscape and economy, transforming the city into a symbol of the industry.

The Romanticised Before (1950s–2017)

Founded in the mid-1950s around a then new deep-water port funded by France and named after the late Cambodian king and long-term ruler Norodom Sihanouk (1922–2012), the Sihanoukville of old is often remembered as an enchanted place. Youk Chhang, director of the Documentation Centre of Cambodia, a nongovernmental organisation (NGO) that played a fundamental role in documenting the atrocities of the Khmer Rouge, has described how, when he was growing up in Cambodia in the 1960s, he used to hear about the city in popular music.[90] Although he had never visited the place, his youthful fascination was also fuelled by the fact that Jacqueline Kennedy had travelled there in 1967 to inaugurate a boulevard named after her late husband, John F. Kennedy. When he first went to Sihanoukville in the early 1990s, he was not disappointed:

> This first visit to Sihanoukville had been wonderful, I would even say magical … on that day of September 1992, all we could see was a small town with a huge, huge, long beach. The ocean deep blue, the sky blue. It was like heaven. Going up that mountain and seeing this beautiful landscape, you felt on top of the world. And nobody was there.[91]

We had a chance to visit the place ourselves several times in the late 2000s and early 2010s, and have some very distinct memories of a somnolent town of low-rise buildings, with seaside resorts beside white-sand beaches where one could lie in a hammock and simply relax. The temptation to nostalgia is strong. Yet even at that time it was widely known that, behind the beautiful scenery, the city was a flawed paradise. Not only were

---

89   Jason Tower and Priscilla Clapp, 'Myanmar's Casino Cities: The Role of China and Transnational Criminal Networks', United States Institute of Peace Special Report no. 471, 2020; International Crisis Group, 'Transnational Crime and Geopolitical Contestation along the Mekong'.

90   Youk Chhang, 'Cambodia's History, Viewed through Sihanoukville', *The Diplomat*, 16 November 2021.

91   Ibid.

certain areas a haven for sex tourists, including several notorious paedo-
philes, but it was also a favourite haunt of a handful of Russian oligarchs
and gangsters, who for years dominated the city with their extravagant
behaviour and penchant for violence.

In the early 2010s, Sihanoukville was the long-term home of a growing
community of about 200 former Soviet citizens and attracted as many as
5,000 to 6,000 Russian-speaking tourists every year.[92] They had their own
Russian-language newspaper, a monthly Russian community meeting, at
least six Russian restaurants, street signs in Russian, and a Russian-owned
beachside disco. There were also plans to build the first Russian Orthodox
church in the city, which eventually came to fruition a few years later.[93]
Money – often of uncertain provenance – was pouring in. At the same
time, the situation was quickly shifting as new Chinese investors began
to eye the lucrative opportunities in the city.

In fact, China's presence in Sihanoukville goes way back. Under the
Khmer Rouge regime (1975–9), the city was the site of one of the main
Chinese aid projects in what was then known as Democratic Kampuchea:
the reactivation and expansion of an oil refinery that had been built by a
French company in the 1960s and had been abandoned due to continuous
attacks from Cambodian and Vietnamese communist insurgents and US
bombing in May 1975. According to Henry Locard:

> The entire peninsula of Kampong Som [now Sihanoukville], the coun-
> try's high sea harbour, was something of a haven of near normality in a
> sea of misery in this particularly wretched Southeast region. This had
> to be so for the visiting Chinese sailors or other foreign visitors. The
> Chinese built a long pier and warehouses, while the oil refinery, burnt by
> the Khmer Rouge in the early days of the civil war, was being repaired
> by Chinese experts, and was planned to reopen in 1980.[94]

In *Brothers in Arms*, Andrew Mertha documents in painstaking detail the
bureaucratic and personal challenges that Chinese workers faced as they
attempted to rebuild the refinery, their long-ago voices resonating with the

92   Olesia Plokhii, 'Sihanoukville Becomes Unlikely Slavic Haven', *Cambodia Daily*,
15 November 2011.
93   'Construction of the Church of Greatmartyr and Healer Panteleimon Begins in
Sihanoukville (Cambodia)', Orthodox Christianity, 10 September 2014.
94   Cited in Andrew Mertha, *Brothers in Arms: Chinese Aid to the Khmer Rouge
1975–1979*, Cornell University Press, New York, 2014, p. 100.

complaints of some of their successors of today as they bemoan the lack of skills of Cambodian co-workers and the impossibility of understanding who is in charge of what.[95] The refinery would never be completed, the project reaching a premature end due to the onslaught of internal purges in the Khmer Rouge bureaucracy and then the Vietnamese invasion. As Vietnamese forces entered Kampong Som, the place 'became noteworthy' as a 'site of the disorganized and panic-ridden retreat of the Chinese'.[96] Convinced by Khmer Rouge propaganda into believing that all was well on the Vietnam front, Chinese technicians and workers took a while to realise the impending danger. It was then too late for them to escape, and as many as 200 became de facto prisoners of war.[97]

Fast-forward two decades. In the newly pacified Cambodia of the 1990s, Sihanoukville gained renewed importance as the country's only deep-water port, which made it an important hub for international trade. In the new millennium, Chinese businesses began to gain a new foothold in the city and the surrounding Preah Sihanouk province. An important event in this sense was the establishment of the Sihanoukville Special Economic Zone (SSEZ) – a development that would later be branded a landmark project of the Belt and Road Initiative (BRI) in Cambodia.[98] A priority of both the Chinese and the Cambodian governments since its approval in 2006, the project showcased the alignment of their agendas in that period, with Cambodia prioritising the zone's development to attract foreign capital and build its export capacities, and China eager to push its well-established manufacturers to head overseas and seek lower-cost production bases and explore access to foreign markets.[99]

---

95   Ibid., ch. 5; Ivan Franceschini, 'As Far Apart as Earth and Sky: A Survey of Chinese and Cambodian Construction Workers in Sihanoukville', *Critical Asian Studies* 52(4), 2020, pp. 512–29.

96   Mertha, *Brothers in Arms*, p. 117.

97   Ibid.

98   The SSEZ has attracted much scrutiny from both civil society and academia. See, for instance, Deborah Bräutigam and Xiaoyang Tang, 'Economic Statecraft in China's New Overseas Special Economic Zones: Soft Power, Business or Resource Security?', *International Affairs* 88(4), 2012, pp. 799–816; Inclusive Development International, 'Sihanoukville Special Economic Zone', People's Map of Global China, updated on 31 March 2021; Neil Loughlin and Mark Grimsditch, 'How Local Political Economy Dynamics Are Shaping the Belt and Road Initiative', *Third World Quarterly* 42(10), 2020, pp. 2334–52; Mark Bo and Neil Loughlin, 'Overlapping Agendas on the Belt and Road: The Case of the Sihanoukville Special Economic Zone', *Global China Pulse* 1(1), 2022, pp. 84–97.

99   Ibid.

Boom …

The transformation of Sihanoukville began abruptly in the mid-2010s, accelerating around 2017, as online gambling operators set up shop in the city. They soon spread rapidly across Cambodia, but Sihanoukville was the perfect location: relatively good access to the capital, Phnom Penh, a functioning airport, and plenty of land – much of it already grabbed by local elites – available for purchase or rent; an already thriving in-person gambling industry; and very lax law enforcement. Possibly, it was made even more desirable by the impending construction of China-funded infrastructure, especially a new expressway that would connect the city to Phnom Penh, dramatically cutting travel time between the two cities.

Given these considerations, industry operators began to descend *en masse* upon the city, investing not only in their online activities, but also in a host of new casinos, hotels, and entertainment venues, most of which were targeting the rapidly growing Chinese market. This generated a bubble that at its peak in 2019 produced an annual revenue conservatively estimated between US$3.5 billion and US$5 billion a year, 90 per cent of which came from online gambling.[100] The Chinese population in the city grew exponentially, as did the percentage of businesses owned by Chinese nationals, which in mid-2019 was a staggering 90 per cent of the total in the city.[101]

Cambodian landowners were able to profit from this windfall by renting or selling their land and properties to deep-pocketed Chinese investors at hugely inflated rates – at prices as much as fifteen times pre-2017 levels, according to one report.[102] At the same time, however, local people and businesses unable to afford the rising rents and costs were pushed further to the margins or forced to leave altogether.[103] Concurrently, a ramping up of evictions of small seaside businesses, ostensibly aimed at beautifying the beaches for the benefit of the expected inflows of Chinese tourists, further hit the local community.[104] The erasure of these types of resorts

---

100   Shaun Turton, 'In Cambodia's Boomtown, a Gamble on Chinese Money Goes Sour', *Nikkei Asia*, 10 January 2020.

101   Hin Pisei, 'Chinese Own More Than 90% of Sihanoukville Businesses, Says Report', *Phnom Penh Post*, 2 July 2019.

102   See, for instance, Hannah Ellis-Petersen, '"No Cambodia Left": How Chinese Money Is Changing Sihanoukville', *Guardian*, 31 July 2018.

103   Hin Pisei, 'Chinese Influx Pushing Locals, Westerners Out of Preah Sihanouk', *Phnom Penh Post*, 18 September 2018.

104   See, for instance, Robin Spiess, 'Evictions Sweep Away Sihanoukville Beach

led to a reduction in low-budget travellers and, combined with the transformation of the city into a massive construction site, put off any tourists not looking for high-end hotels and gambling. All the while, there were widespread concerns about the quality and safety of the new buildings that were mushrooming at record speed all over the city. These worries came to a head on 22 June 2019, when a building under construction in the centre of Sihanoukville came crashing down, killing twenty-eight workers and family members who were living on the site. Four Chinese nationals were eventually charged with causing involuntary bodily harm and causing damage with aggravating circumstances.[105]

To make things worse, public security also became a serious concern in the city at around the same time. In January 2018, authorities in China launched a three-year campaign known as 'sweeping away the black and eliminating the evil' (扫黑除恶 *saohei chu'e*), to root out 'underworld forces'.[106] Destinations such as Sihanoukville likely presented an enticing prospect to gangsters trying to avoid the crackdown. Reports of kidnappings, human trafficking, and forced labour to fuel the burgeoning online gambling and scam industry in Sihanoukville started appearing with increasing frequency in Chinese-language media. In July 2018, as the presence of illicit online operations was becoming better known, the Chinese Embassy in Cambodia released a warning about the 'high-paying traps of online gambling recruitment' – one of the earliest instances of such

---

Businesses', *Phnom Penh Post*, 8 January 2018; Danielle Keeton-Olsen and Moeurn Voleak, 'After Sihanoukville Beach Stalls Removed, Future Development Unclear', Voice of Democracy, 17 February 2020.

105   Khan Leakhena, 'Four Chinese Nationals Charged with Manslaughter over Building Collapse', Voice of Democracy, 25 June 2019.

106   See Sheena Chestnut Greitens, 'The Saohei Campaign, Protection Umbrellas, and China's Changing Political-Legal Apparatus', China Leadership Monitor, 1 September 2020. The Chinese government was not playing around. In early 2021, the Chinese authorities triumphantly announced that over the previous three years they had busted more than 3,600 mafia-like groups, 1.3 times as many as the total of the previous ten years (see 'China Makes Remarkable Results in Gang Crime Crackdown', Xinhua, 28 March 2021). They also reported that another 89,742 cases involving gang-crime-related corruption and 'protective umbrellas' that shelter gangs had been handled nationwide in the same period, and that Chinese courts had concluded 32,943 gang-related cases, involving more than 220,000 suspects. Illegal income worth CN¥137 billion (US$21 billion) was confiscated and 2,668 cases in which public officials had given protection to criminal gangs were closed (see Shan Yuxiao and Matthew Walsh, 'China Gang Crackdown Led to Tens of Thousands of Cases', Caixin Global, 9 March 2021).

advisories that we were able to locate.[107] The embassy encouraged Chinese nationals planning to come to Cambodia, especially young people, to be vigilant about offers of well-paid jobs as typists or network technicians, or in network customer service and network promotion, regardless of whether these were promoted in online advertisements or through introductions by friends or relatives.

Alarm about public security in Sihanoukville peaked in May 2019, when a security-camera video showing the body of an assassinated Chinese man being thrown out of a car in broad daylight made the rounds on social media.[108] A couple of days later, Cambodia's national police released a report that revealed that Chinese nationals were the top perpetrators and victims of crime among foreigners in the kingdom during the first quarter of the year.[109] Of 341 arrests, 241 were Chinese nationals.

Amid growing public fear, another video went viral later in the month. It showed a Chinese man wearing a white T-shirt, defiantly declaring: 'If Sihanoukville will be safe or chaotic in the next three years is under my control'; another nineteen shirtless Chinese men menacingly crowded behind him.[110] The men, some heavily tattooed, were in a dormitory room like those found in scam compounds. The clip triggered strong feelings in the Cambodian population and further fuelled concerns about gangsters from China taking over the city. Rebuttals by the Chinese Embassy in Phnom Penh – that this was just a prank by ordinary workers from Chongqing who had arrived in Cambodia only a few months earlier – were met with scepticism.[111] As similar stories piled up, it became increasingly untenable for the Cambodian authorities to ignore what was happening on the coast. The ban on online gambling soon followed.

---

107   Chinese Embassy in Cambodia, '再次提醒在柬中国公民循正规途径来柬工作' (Chinese Citizens in Cambodia Are Once Again Reminded to Follow Formal Channels to Work in Cambodia), Chinese Embassy in Cambodia website, 19 July 2018.

108   The video is available on the YouTube channel of 柬中时报 (Cambodia China Times), YouTube.

109   Taing Vida, 'Chinese Top Foreign Crime List', *Khmer Times*, 8 May 2019.

110   Andrew Nachemson and Kong Meta, 'Chinese Gang Threatens Chaos in Cambodian Province as Rift Deepens between Locals and New Arrivals', *South China Morning Post*, 14 May 2019; Zhuang Pinghui, 'Chinese "Gangster" Video That Caused Cambodia's Police Chief to Intervene "Was a Prank"', *South China Morning Post*, 16 May 2019.

111   Khan Leakhena, 'Authorities Continue to Investigate "Just for Fun" Gangster Video', Voice of Democracy, 20 May 2019; Iem Bunhy, 'Chinese "Prank" Video Is No Joke for Cambodia', *Phnom Penh Post*, 11 June 2019.

… *and Bust*

The day in 2019 when then prime minister Hun Sen announced the online gambling ban, 18 August, was a watershed moment for Sihanoukville. No one was more aware of this than the Chinese diaspora in Cambodia, who began to refer to the event simply as '818' – a supposedly auspicious number transformed into a symbol of doom. If up to that point the city's economy was soaring, afterwards the edifice showed hints of cracking. Signs began to emerge that many operations had closed and rushed to relocate, dragging with them not only their workforce but also that of ancillary industries. According to some sources, an estimated 10,000 Chinese citizens fled Sihanoukville in the space of a few days after the ban was announced.[112] Reports followed of masses of Chinese leaving the city and Cambodia and, in January 2020, Cambodia's Immigration Department revealed that about 447,000 Chinese nationals had left the kingdom.[113] While this is a huge number, there was no breakdown to indicate how many of these departures were residents and how many were short-term visitors. During the same period there were 323,000 inbound Chinese travellers, meaning the net influx of Chinese was down by more than 100,000 people. While it is not possible to isolate any other potential factors that could have caused this drop, it can be assumed that 818 had an impact.

Several casinos shut in a matter of weeks, with many more laying off staff, leaving at least 7,000 Cambodians unemployed by the end of the year.[114] The real estate bubble burst and construction halted on many projects, often leaving workers unpaid and in limbo. Commercial rents dropped by about 30 per cent and hotel room rates decreased by up to 50 per cent.[115] According to a survey by the Chinese-founded Federation of Business Associations of Preah Sihanouk Province cited in *Nikkei Asia*, between August 2019 and early January 2020, almost 800 restaurants had gone bankrupt and daily orders had plummeted by more than 80 per cent.[116] As many restaurants generated the bulk of their income from

---

112 '10,000 Chinese Citizens Flee Sihanoukville in Days after Cambodian Online Gaming Directive: Report', Inside Asian Gaming, 5 September 2019.

113 Ben Sokhean, 'Immigration Dept Says 400,000 Chinese Have Left Because of Online Gambling Ban', *Khmer Times*, 1 January 2020.

114 Prak Chan Thul, 'Thousands Lose Jobs, Casinos Shut as Cambodia Bans Online Gambling', Reuters, 31 December 2019.

115 Turton, 'In Cambodia's Boomtown, a Gamble on Chinese Money Goes Sour'.

116 Ibid.

serving online gambling or scam workers, restaurants' daily earnings had fallen from an average of US$1,500 to US$200, while monthly earnings from food delivery dropped from US$3,000 to US$800. Livelihoods were destroyed, leading business owners to flee the city without paying their rent and bills to avoid further losses. In some extreme situations, suicides were reported.[117]

The story of a middle-aged woman from eastern China whom we met in Sihanoukville towards the end of 2019 gives us a glimpse into the plight of small-business owners at that time. She had arrived in the city in August 2019 to open a modest guesthouse in Otres Village, on the outskirts of Sihanoukville's new urban sprawl. On arrival, she rented a piece of land and a small building for more than US$4,000 a month, paying a three-month deposit and a one-month advance. She then spent a substantial amount of money to renovate the property. But, as it turned out, this was the worst possible time to invest in the city. At first, she could rent rooms for US$50 a night, but after the online gambling ban, she suddenly found herself unable to attract guests and had to slash the rate to US$10–15. As if that were not enough, at the end of September, three Chinese guests attacked her. They forced her to transfer CN¥12,000 (roughly US$1,700) to their WeChat account, give them US$600 in cash, and hand over her recently bought phone. A security camera in the lobby captured their images, but when the woman went to the local police to report what had happened, they showed no interest. From that moment, she lived in terror. She wanted to go back to China, but she stood to lose too much money so was reluctant to give up everything and decided to stay.

As official disclosure of actions to implement the 2019 ban is extremely limited, it is difficult to say how much this shift was due to enforcement and how much was due to the fear and uncertainty that the ban created among operators. In any case, any alarm generated was soon overtaken when, only a few months later, the onset of the COVID-19 pandemic dealt Sihanoukville an even bigger blow. Although Cambodia emerged from 2020 with relatively low numbers of confirmed infections, the impact on

---

117   For mentions of suicides among Chinese business owners, see '西港一中国投资者自杀身亡' (A Chinese Business Owner Commits Suicide in Sihanoukville), *TNAOT*, 26 March 2020; Huang Yan 黄岩, '官方数据：西港有1155栋烂尾楼' (Official Data: Sihanoukville Has 1,155 Unfinished Buildings), *TNAOT*, 4 July 2022; '中国商人投资柬埔寨遭遇烂尾楼：投资几千万月前靠卖豆腐为生' (Chinese Businessmen Invest in Cambodia and Cannot Finish Their Building: They Invested Tens of Millions and Now Make a Living by Selling Tofu), 凤凰周刊 (Phoenix Weekly), 6 August 2022.

global travel meant that regular tourism dropped to almost zero, and after China imposed strict travel restrictions, gamblers and online gambling and scam workers could no longer travel to and from the country. The pandemic took hold in Cambodia in early 2021, resulting in temporary lockdowns, which further pounded the economy. In May 2022, the Preah Sihanouk provincial government reported that only 31,258 foreigners of sixty nationalities were still legally residing there, including 23,375 Chinese citizens.[118] This does not capture those who had entered the country illegally or those with no registered presence in the province, but still indicates a sharp decline.

Many Chinese developers decided to write off their losses and flee. Having lost faith in the future of the city and worried about the contractual obligations that bound them to pay exaggerated rents even in the face of an economy that was collapsing, they chose to evade their legal obligations and return to China. In so doing, they left behind hundreds of buildings at different stages of completion. On one hand, this spelled the ruin of local landowners, many of whom had sought to capitalise on the gambling-fuelled boom. As one of them complained to a journalist from Voice of Democracy (VoD) in July 2022: 'I borrowed money to buy land worth more than $200,000 because I thought it was a great opportunity ... We could earn $7,500 [per month] – why wouldn't we dare to pay $2,000 per month [in loan repayments]? The banks were happy to lend money between $200,000 and $300,000.'[119] On the other hand, this caused mayhem among the Chinese and Cambodian workers employed on these sites, many of whom were not notified that their bosses had fled and continued to work for weeks or even months without being paid.

We were in Sihanoukville between December 2019 and January 2020, right before the pandemic hit, and encountered several of these workers. While by that time many Cambodian workers had already returned to their homes in the provinces, having received the back salaries they were owed – which were much lower than those of their Chinese colleagues – or having given up on being paid at all, many of their Chinese counterparts were still stuck in the city. Many were living in conditions of destitution in the half-finished construction sites, unable to go home, either because

118   Voun Dara, 'Preah Sihanouk Issues Report on Foreigner Presence', *Phnom Penh Post*, 29 May 2022.

119   Mech Dara, '1,000 Unfinished Constructions Show Aftermath of a "Boom"', Voice of Democracy, 13 July 2022.

they did not have the money or because they were still clinging to the hope of retrieving the (often significant) amounts they were owed. As we have recounted at length elsewhere, this was a heartbreaking experience.[120]

When we returned to the city in early 2022, these workers were gone. As we visited the construction sites where we had conducted our survey, only faint traces of the former occupants lingered: the frames of the beds where they slept, a table, a wash basin, a soy sauce bottle, and broken glasses. Almost all the smaller private constructions remained abandoned; only the largest sites, many of which were being handled by Chinese state-owned companies, had been completed or were nearing completion. This was reflected in official data. According to an official from Cambodia's Ministry of Economy and Finance, as of early July 2022, Sihanoukville had 1,155 projects that remained incomplete, accounting for 70–80 per cent of all the buildings in the city.[121] Although some buildings have restarted construction, this situation was still dragging on at the time of writing in late 2024, despite various attempts by the Cambodian government and Chinese business associations to find viable solutions.[122]

---

120   For these accounts, see Franceschini, 'As Far Apart as Earth and Sky'.

121   Huang, 'Official Data'.

122   With the city reduced to such a devastated landscape, on 7 July 2022, representatives of Chinese investors and local Cambodian landlords met under the auspices of Cambodia's Ministry of Finance and the Preah Sihanouk provincial government to discuss possible solutions (see Huang, 'Official Data'; Shaun Turton and Huang Yan, 'Stuck in Sihanoukville: Projects Grind to Halt in Cambodia Resort Town', *Nikkei Asia*, 5 August 2022). On that occasion, Chinese investors bemoaned how security issues, including recurrent kidnappings, had impacted the confidence of existing and potential investors and raised six suggestions, the most important of which was that local landlords take a share in the projects. They also called for rent relief, preferential taxation on construction, and an official land valuation system to keep prices under control. These requests, however, seemed to go nowhere. When, in late August 2022, we met some Chinese businessmen in Sihanoukville who had incurred significant losses due to the bust of the local economy, they shared their frustration and explained to us how their latest approach was to try to petition the Cambodian prime minister to declare the COVID-19 pandemic an 'act of God' so that they could benefit from some reduction in the leases they had to pay. A few months later, in October 2022, the Cambodian government then set up an inter-institutional commission tasked with resolving the issue of unfinished buildings in Preah Sihanouk province (May Kunmakara, 'Unfinished Preah Sihanouk Building Team Formed', *Phnom Penh Post*, 2 November 2022), and in early April 2023 an official incentive package was announced, even though at the time of writing it remains to be seen whether the measures will have any actual impact (Lu Jiming 陆积明, '柬埔寨政府提供激励配套 帮助西港烂尾楼复工' (Cambodian Government Provides Incentive Packages to Help Unfinished Buildings in Sihanoukville Resume Work), 柬中时报 (Cambodia China Times), 5 April 2023).

The Turn to Scams

Although the online gambling ban had clear immediate impacts, this moment paradoxically marked a point when awareness of the scale of the online industries and their associated crimes really came to the fore. Scam operations had existed for years in the city, often discreetly hosted within the same sites that were home to ostensibly more legitimate gambling activities. As news emerged of the hardships occurring in Sihanoukville, it became clear that business was still booming in many of the larger hotel- and casino-based online scam operations, and in the major compounds that proliferated across the city. Many companies providing real online gambling services (rather than rigged games or scams) probably left, and recently arrived scam operators and smaller players with less established connections probably got cold feet. At the same time, however, the compounds became increasingly closed off, and failing casinos converted premises to provide more space for online operations. In both cases, security increased and the movement of workers in and out became tightly restricted.

Reports emerged of scam operations, detention, and human trafficking linked to dozens of compounds in Preah Sihanouk province alone, which were still operating after the ban came into place. Several of these compounds housed thousands of workers. In the middle of a systemic collapse, the online scam industry perversely became a major economic pillar of Sihanoukville, again feeding businesses such as restaurants and shops that had few other customers and providing employment opportunities to locals as security guards, delivery workers, suppliers, and other ancillary roles. At the same time, as it became increasingly difficult for workers to travel to Cambodia due to pandemic travel restrictions and reductions in flights, these operations resorted to violent means and trickery to find and retain their staff, and increasingly turned to smuggling to bring them to Cambodia.

For the duration of the pandemic, grisly stories of people trapped in compounds in Sihanoukville and forced to perpetrate scams under the constant threat of violence continued to trickle out of the city. Although some parts of Sihanoukville had long had a bad reputation, a Pandora's box had been opened. A review of crime reports by VoD in early 2022 found cases of abandoned bodies, homicides, assaults, firearms, extortion, and detention throughout the city.[123] In January 2022, two bodies were

---

123   Mech Dara and Danielle Keeton-Olsen, 'Crimes in Shadows: Sihanoukville's Grisly Reports, Pressure on Journalists', Voice of Democracy, 11 March 2022.

found in shallow graves on land adjacent to a scam compound in Otres Village – one of them the young handcuffed woman we mentioned at the beginning of this chapter.[124] In March, a security guard was found hanged in one of the buildings of this compound. When asked by VoD about this case, local police had limited information. An officer told the reporter that the area was hard to police: 'These places don't allow us to go in.'[125] When asked how many suicides and deaths had occurred at such compounds, he said: 'I forget it because there are so many, and I don't know which is which. Some cases we know, while others we don't know about.'

As such stories became widespread in Chinese and international media, in February 2022 the so-called blood-slave case embodied the decline of Sihanoukville's reputation. Even though it was later discovered that Li Yayuanlun had lied about having his blood repeatedly extracted by his captors, the story had already gone viral, cementing the city's reputation among the Chinese public as a hellish place.

For months the Cambodian authorities continued to deny that the waves of accounts coming from survivors of scam compounds were true, insisting that these were just labour disputes or that the stories were fabricated. As the governments of nearby countries became increasingly vocal in demanding clarity about the fate of their citizens trapped in Cambodia, however, the issue began to garner attention from every quarter. This was especially true of China, but the wider world also began to take note, and the United States downgraded Cambodia to the lowest-possible ranking in its 2022 'Trafficking in Persons' annual report, which included multiple references to trafficking associated with the scam industry.[126] Under the weight of this pressure, the Cambodian government eventually had to change tack.

As noted earlier, a nationwide crackdown on 'illegal gambling' began in September 2022, focusing heavily on Sihanoukville. This led to raids of various gambling locations, including small local gambling rooms and a handful of major compounds that were known to be running illegal online gambling and/or scam operations. Soon after, official statements shifted drastically, and Cambodian officials began to admit that human

---

124   Mech Dara, 'Spate of Violent Crimes against Foreigners Nabs More Than 20 Suspects', Voice of Democracy, 2 February 2022.

125   Mech Dara, 'Body Found Hanging in Sihanoukville's Alleged Slave-Compound Area', Voice of Democracy, 18 March 2022.

126   '2022 Trafficking in Persons Report: Cambodia', US State Department website.

trafficking and detention were happening, and that as many as 100,000 people may have been involved in 'illegal gambling' (officials still appeared reluctant to acknowledge that many operations were in fact conducting online fraud).[127] In Sihanoukville, ten compounds are known to have been raided, although only five were shut – and two of them re-opened months later. Others were tipped off that raids were coming and conducted orderly evacuations of their staff – something that we witnessed first-hand, as we were in the city at that time – or were simply told to stop operating.[128] An exodus of gambling and scam workers from Sihanoukville occurred, with reports that some people had moved to compounds in other parts of the country or elsewhere in Southeast Asia, especially Myanmar and Laos.

After the flurry of activity that followed the 2022 crackdown, the Cambodian government adjusted its public position. While Cambodian officials are now less likely to deny outright the existence of the industry, these operations are presented as something that has been largely dealt with, but which law enforcement continues to take seriously. There is no doubt that Sihanoukville now occupies a less prominent place in Southeast Asia's online scam ecosystem than it has in the past. Over the past couple of years, more peripheral locations in Cambodia have established themselves as online scam hubs, most famously the border towns of Bavet and Sampov Poun, on the border with Vietnam, and Poipet, on the border with Thailand, plus a host of other largely remote places across the country.

Yet the scam industry has clearly not left the city altogether. While some compounds remained empty after the 2022 crackdown, others have since quietly resumed operations or simply changed tenants. During several trips there in 2024, we saw several of the better-known compounds closed off once again (despite orders from the city for all businesses to open their gates) and guarded by security, with clear signs of life visible from outside, such as laundry on balconies, and signs advertising space for rent. In the words of a survivor who passed through a few notorious scam compounds in the city months after they had supposedly been cleared in the crackdown:

127   Mech Dara, 'Officials Speak Out on Compounds: As Many as 100,000 Foreign Nationals Came to Cambodia', Voice of Democracy, 30 September 2022.

128   Sen Bao 森宝 and Jia Hao 嘉豪, '西港省长: 10个园区被查封, 所雇用的3000余名外国人中有930人非法入境' (Governor of Sihanoukville: 10 Compounds Were Sealed and 930 of the More Than 3,000 Foreigners Employed Entered the Country Illegally), 柬中时报 (Cambodia China Times), 12 October 2022.

Right after [the September crackdowns] happened the compounds did make some changes, but as more time has passed and it seems people have forgotten, the companies are slowly returning to their previous ways of operating … They might be afraid to buy and sell people now, but companies are slowly starting to detain and restrict people's freedom again.[129]

Push and Pull

The dynamics highlighted in this chapter show the extreme mobility, adaptability, and opportunism of the shady capital that fuels the online scam industry. They also point to some of the powerful push and pull factors that determine the mobility of these operations. On the push side, regulatory and law enforcement crackdowns factor heavily in scam operators' decision to relocate from one place to another. It was growing pressure from authorities in Taiwan and mainland China that first encouraged the scam operations led by ethnic Chinese groups to relocate to Southeast Asia in the early 2010s, and the same dynamic has been at play repeatedly since then. We saw it in extreme situations such as the conflict in northern Myanmar or more targeted crackdowns under the Duterte administration in the Philippines.

Still, for a crackdown to be effective, it needs to be sustained by longer-term measures enforced by strong institutions. If local authorities rely only on a campaign model to launch occasional ad hoc offensives, online scam operations simply make a comeback soon after the heat has died down and public attention has shifted elsewhere. This, for instance, is what we have seen in Cambodia since the short-lived crackdown of late 2022. These are sometimes the same returning groups, or entirely new ones. After all, the infrastructure is still there and, most often, so are the protective umbrellas that supported their businesses in the first place.

In the Introduction, we mentioned how criminologists have identified the sudden emergence of a new market as a necessary condition for transnational criminal groups to transplant to a certain area. That is certainly the case for the online scam industry, as the sector counts on a virtually unlimited global market where there is not, nor can there ever be, a single

---

129   Cindy Liu and Jack Brook, 'Kidnapped, Beaten and Ransomed in Post-crackdown Sihanoukville', Voice of Democracy, 1 May 2023.

dominant player. We also mentioned how a new illicit infrastructure, comprising software designers, tech support, and money-laundering marketplaces, provides services to industry operators regardless of their physical locations. Under such levelling circumstances, it is the existence of local elites able and willing to shield these actors from unwanted scrutiny in exchange for hefty profits that makes a difference. Ethnic armed organisations have been playing this role in Myanmar's border areas; in Cambodia and the Philippines, business elites and corrupt elements in the political class, law enforcement, and the military have played a crucial role. As crackdowns mostly focus on lower-level players and frontline scammers, these individuals rarely end up behind bars. Even when that happens – or on those rare occasions when there is a radical overhaul of the political apparatus, as in northern Myanmar in late 2023 – they may be replaced by other actors willing to play the same role.

There are, of course, other conditions necessary for a location to become attractive to scam operators. One is the existence of adequate physical infrastructure, as we have seen in the case of Sihanoukville's relinquished casinos, hotels, and compounds. Another condition is porous borders, which allow scam operations to procure their workforce by air, land, or sea through either legal or illegal means. In Myanmar, Kayin State is accessible from Thailand, as is northern Myanmar from China; this not only facilitated a steady supply of workers but also allowed many local compounds to take advantage of the telecommunications infrastructure of their neighbouring countries.

At the time of writing, in late 2024, things are in flux. The Marcos government in the Philippines has now banned POGOs, the Cambodian authorities have announced further crackdowns on the industry, Laos has imposed a deadline for online operators to leave the Golden Triangle SEZ, and turmoil in Myanmar continues; meanwhile, the situation on the ground is fluid. Although it is impossible to predict where the industry will be heading next, there are plenty of places in the world that fit the conditions outlined above. As far as we know, scam compounds are well established in the United Arab Emirates, and there is evidence of the industry expanding as far afield as Serbia, Turkey, Georgia, Mexico, Peru, Sri Lanka, India, and West and Central Africa. It can be expected that Southeast Asia will remain an important base, but groups may increasingly seek to hedge risks by exploring new territories.

Global law enforcement is slowly catching up, but it is chasing a moving target. In early December 2023, Interpol announced the results of its first operation specifically targeting the phenomenon of human-trafficking-fuelled fraud, resulting in the arrest of over 280 people and rescue of almost 150 people across twenty-seven countries.[130] Later the same month it shared details of another global operation that targeted cyber-enabled scams, with 3,500 arrested and the seizure of over US$300 million in assets across thirty-four countries.[131] Also in December 2023, the first international sanctions explicitly targeting actors for their involvement in human trafficking linked to the scam industry were announced by the United Kingdom. They targeted individuals connected to the GTSEZ in Laos, as well as those involved in scam operations in Myanmar, including Chinese businessmen and Kayin Border Guard Force officials, and companies linked to scam compounds in Cambodia.[132] Sanctions from the United States followed in 2024, with the Department of the Treasury specifically targeting a ruling party senator in Cambodia for his alleged links to the industry.[133] Freezing or seizures of crypto wallets linked to cyberfraud are becoming increasingly common, even though these are just drops in the ocean of profits the industry is making.[134] Unfortunately, given the astronomical riches on offer from the industry, its ability to traverse jurisdictions, its linkages to local and transnational crime networks, as well as the persistence of the baggage of human misery it relies on, these efforts may hinder the industry but will not eradicate it. The online scam industry is unlikely to go away any time soon.

---

130   'INTERPOL Operation Reveals Further Insights into "Globalization" of Cyber Scam Centres', Interpol website, 8 December 2023.

131   'USD 300 Million Seized and 3,500 Suspects Arrested in International Financial Crime Operation', Interpol website, 19 December 2023.

132   HM Treasury, Office of Financial Sanctions Implementation, 'Financial Sanctions Notice: Global Human Rights', UK government website, 8 December 2023.

133   US Department of the Treasury, 'Treasury Sanctions Cambodian Tycoon and Businesses Linked to Human Trafficking and Forced Labor in Furtherance of Cyber and Virtual Currency Scams', US Department of the Treasury website, 12 September 2023.

134   See, for instance, 'Following Investigations by Tether, OKX, and the US Department of Justice, Tether Voluntarily Freezes 225M in Stolen USDT Linked to International Crime Syndicate', Tether website, 20 November 2023; Tom Wilson and Poppy McPherson, 'U.S. Seizes Crypto Linked to Southeast Asian Investment Scam', Reuters, 13 December 2023.

2
Getting In

Before ending up in a scam compound in Myanmar, Zhang had a stable job at the Lushan Botanical Garden in Jiangxi province, China.[1] During the COVID-19 pandemic, he lost his position and found himself in severe financial stress due to family illness and debt. With a PhD from the Chinese Academy of Sciences, he chose to pursue new opportunities overseas, where salaries were higher, and eventually got recruited by a company in Singapore.[2] Everything appeared promising, until repeated visa delays prompted his agent to suggest that he work temporarily at the company's office in Thailand. Aware of the reports about people getting tricked into the scam industry in Southeast Asia, Zhang was initially hesitant, but after thoroughly checking the company's documents and confident in the legitimacy of the onboarding process, he chose to trust the agent. However, soon after he arrived in Thailand, his phone, ID card, and passport were confiscated, and he was taken to a scam compound in Myawaddy Township, just over the border in Myanmar's Kayin State. There, he was forced to perpetrate pig-butchering scams, posing

---

1   Zhang Xu 张旭, '中科院博士揭露缅甸园区电诈细节: 诈骗模式广为人知, 业绩一直在下滑' (A Doctor from the Chinese Academy of Sciences Reveals the Details of Electronic Fraud in Myanmar's Industrial Park: The Fraud Model Is Widely Known and Performance Has Been Declining), 界面新闻 (Jiemian News), 15 September 2023.

2   Li Yuning 李雨凝, '中科院博士, 卷入缅甸诈骗风暴后' (Doctor of the Chinese Academy of Sciences, after Being Involved in the Myanmar Fraud Storm), 搜狐 (Sohu), 27 September 2023.

as women to convince targets in Europe and North America to invest in cryptocurrencies.[3]

Once inside, Zhang heard stories of people who had successfully managed to escape and began contemplating doing the same. Yet he soon realised that regaining his freedom would be exceedingly difficult. Not only did the walls stand four to five metres high, with high-voltage electricity cables on top and armed sentries monitoring the perimeter, but there were also checkpoints every few hundred metres outside, with more armed guards surveilling the compound's surrounding areas. Any attempt to flee was met with a threat of lethal force from the guards stationed inside or outside. Being unfamiliar with Myanmar and lacking financial resources to bribe people to guarantee his safety, Zhang ultimately abandoned the notion of escaping.[4] Instead, he contacted media in China, which, intrigued by the fact that he had a PhD, quickly picked up the story. The persistent media coverage put significant pressure on the group holding him, which agreed to reduce the ransom they were demanding from CN¥120,000 to CN¥59,000. Eventually, Zhang's family paid the ransom and he managed to get out.[5]

Since Zhang had a PhD from an elite institution, his story made headlines in China, triggering indignation among the Chinese public. Still, not all people who survive Southeast Asia's scam compounds receive the same level of attention and sympathy. In late 2023, at roughly the time when Zhang's ordeal was going viral on Chinese social media, Yun and Pei, two youths from China's Sichuan province, were scrolling Kuaishou, a popular Chinese live-video platform, when they noticed what looked like a promising opportunity. Aged seventeen and twenty, they had been scraping a living on construction sites around their hometown, and here was a job that promised to pay nearly double their daily wage, plus food and lodging. After receiving a first positive response, they embarked on a journey to a coastal city in Guangxi province for an interview in

3   Zhao Min 赵敏, '中科院博士讲述被骗缅甸历程，曾因"泄密"被关私人监狱' (A Doctor from the Chinese Academy of Sciences Tells How He Was Deceived from Myanmar and Was Imprisoned in a Private Prison for 'Leaking Secrets'), 新京报 (Beijing News), 12 September 2023.

4   Zhang, 'A Doctor from the Chinese Academy of Sciences Reveals the Details of Electronic Fraud in Myanmar's Industrial Park'.

5   '被骗缅甸中科院博士：曾被打近百棍，诈骗园区更关注反诈新闻' (A Doctor from the Chinese Academy of Sciences Was Tricked into Myanmar: Beaten Nearly a Hundred Times, the Scam Compound Pays More Attention to Anti-Fraud News), 红星新闻 (Red Star News), 16 September 2023.

person. There, their enthusiasm quickly turned to fear, as their prospective employer threatened them with violence if they did not board a boat. Soon, they were in Vietnam, where they spent a couple of days under guard in a hotel before being transported by car to Bavet, a Cambodian border town.

In Bavet, they discovered the job they had been recruited to do. Yun and Pei were taken to a compound hosting both online gambling and cyberfraud operations. They were told they would have to engage in online scams. Unwilling, they tried to escape but were caught by security guards and beaten badly. After being locked up in a dormitory for several days, they finally agreed to learn the scam techniques. In a stroke of luck, they were soon moved to another compound and managed to contact relatives back in China through WeChat. Their families promptly reported their situation to the authorities in China and the Chinese Embassy in Cambodia. Finally, in January 2024, they were rescued by Cambodian police.

A continent away, another invisible story was unfolding. George, a young Ugandan man in his early thirties, had taken advantage of the rare opportunity to spend four years in India working towards an IT-related degree.[6] After graduating, he returned to Kampala, where he worked as a freelancer, fixing systems, configuring routers, installing cables, and the like. Then COVID-19 hit, and everything slowed down. With his livelihood at stake, in November 2020 he decided to move to Dubai. Once there, he found that life was hard: 'I was just doing anything ... freelancing still, I can say. Like doing minor jobs, small jobs, odd jobs, simple jobs ... you get paid cash, do a job and get paid instantly. Because I had a visa that I had to renew every three months, and also had accommodation to pay for. So that means I had to keep moving, like, as I look for a job, I had to keep working also ... to sustain myself there.'

For this reason, when in August 2022 a friend mentioned a well-paid IT job opportunity in Laos, he jumped at it. 'Some company was looking for guys to manage their data and it was just a simple six-months contract,' he recounts. His friend introduced him to a woman from the company, who offered him a basic monthly salary of US$1,500, plus allowances and commissions. Accommodation would be provided, and expenses covered. She introduced the company, and everything seemed to check out. Once George agreed, the woman took care of his visa and bought his flight and

---

6 George recounted his story in detail in a series of multimedia articles and podcasts that we published with The Conversation in February 2025. See 'Scam Factories: the inside story of Southeast Asia's brutal fraud compounds', The Conversation, 24 February 2025.

insurance. Soon, he was on his way to the Golden Triangle, on Laos's border with Myanmar and Thailand.

There, he was asked to sign a contract that was completely different from the one discussed in Dubai, and which put him in substantial debt to the company. His passport and phone were taken away and he was introduced to his new job: using pre-written scripts to contact people from all over the world and scam them into putting money into fake investments. For two months he dragged his feet, insisting that he was simply an IT guy and that he should be asked to do the work he was good at, until one day he was sold to a second scam company in Myanmar. The people who traded him did not even tell him how much they gained from the transaction: 'They don't tell you [how much they sell you for]. They just tell you: "We own you. We bought you." … It's weird. It takes you back to the, the ages of the slave trade in Africa … it was hard to believe when someone tells you: "I own you."' He was supposed to be gone for only six months – but it would take him a whole year to find his way back to Kampala.

Just like Zhang, Yun, Pei, and George, every year thousands of people are tricked, trafficked, and sold to scam operators throughout Southeast Asia and beyond. As we have seen in the Introduction, the United Nations Office of the High Commissioner for Human Rights estimated that in 2023 at least 120,000 people were being held in situations where they were forced to carry out online scams across Myanmar, with another 100,000 in Cambodia.[7] Such numbers remain vigorously contested by local state officials and are very hard to confirm. On the one hand, many areas where scam compounds are located are inaccessible, with the sites closed to the public and heavily secured, so it is very difficult to gather reliable data. On the other, the backgrounds and motivations of those working inside vary. While many have been duped and trafficked, others enter the industry in full knowledge that they are going to engage in illegal work and approach their tasks as a job just like any other. Others again know (or think they know) what they are getting into, but when they see the actual conditions and attempt to leave they find they are trapped, their documents withheld and their debt to the company mounting as absurd fees imposed by the managers accrue.

---

7   United Nations Office of the High Commissioner for Human Rights (OHCHR), 'Online Scam Operations and Trafficking into Forced Criminality in Southeast Asia: Recommendations for a Human Rights Response', OHCHR Bangkok Office website, August 2023.

Establishing how people end up in the scam compounds is always tricky. Knowing that it could undermine people's motivation to help them, and that they may face criminal charges in both their home country and the location of the scam operation, some survivors are disincentivised to admit they have entered the industry willingly. Further complicating things, there are cases where abuses have been exaggerated in order to elicit public sympathy, creating inconsistencies in survivors' stories that, when exposed, ultimately undermine efforts to support them. This occurred in the case of Sihanoukville's so-called blood slave mentioned in the previous chapter, where a semi-fictitious story recounted by a survivor backfired spectacularly, providing the Cambodian authorities with new ammunition to deny the existence of scam compounds in the country and even arrest key individuals involved in rescue operations.

It is exactly this ambiguity and the resulting distrust towards the testimonies of survivors that in mid-2022 led a civil society organisation to declare that it would stop rescuing individuals who had entered the compounds after a certain date. According to this reasoning, due to the significant media coverage that the online scam industry was receiving at that point, it was impossible for people who ended up in the compounds after that date not to know what they were getting into. More widely, there have been morally charged debates about what to make of those who, willingly or under duress (or any degree in between), make scam operations possible. Should those who knew (or should have known) the work was likely to be illegal and still entered the industry, only to find themselves trapped, be considered victims at all? Oftentimes, these discussions have served as little more than a distraction from the structural reasons that make so many people vulnerable to the lure of the industry, including the widespread immiseration brought about by the COVID-19 pandemic.

In this chapter we attempt to complicate the picture of how people end up trapped in Southeast Asia's scam compounds by describing several ways in which this can happen. In so doing, we hope to show how many survivors find themselves in their predicament due to a combination of desperation, bad luck, and naïvety. More specifically, we focus on seven aspects: deceptive job ads; the role of professional brokers on the scam operators' payroll; recruitment by friends or relatives; the lure of social media influencers; trafficking by organised crime groups; kidnappings; and sales between compounds.

Job Ads

Job adverts are a very common recruitment method used by scam operators. Circulated through various job-recruitment websites and social media, these announcements often do not specify the type of work but in many cases carry similar hallmarks. In a typical example, one message posted in 2020 in Chinese on a public Facebook group for jobseekers in Cambodia reads: 'Are you looking for work? I have a job for a man or woman between 18 and 30, 6,000 yuan with possible salary raise depending on your performance. Accommodation provided. Basic requirements: knowing how to type and communicate in Chinese. Location: O'smach. Please DM me if interested.'[8] Instant-messaging apps including Telegram, Line, WeChat, and QQ are also common recruitment grounds. Telegram is particularly popular among recruiters for scam companies, with a single ad sometimes including dozens of vacancies, promising high salaries, commissions, year-end bonuses, and promotion opportunities. Based on our observation, on a single day, more than one hundred job ads can be posted by different actors in a single Telegram group chat.

According to the Hong Kong–based NGO Branches of Hope, several red flags make these dubious job offers stand out.[9] First, the job is generally described in vague terms, with calls for 'app developers', 'engineers', 'HR managers', 'crypto investors', or 'translators', but without any detailed description of the tasks involved. Second, the prospective employer promises to cover food, accommodation, and travel expenses. Third, there are language requirements (often Chinese and English, but also other languages depending on the market being targeted), and a mismatch between the salaries offered and the level of skills required, which usually do not go beyond basic computer literacy, with no previous experience needed. Fourth, the ads target younger individuals, aged between eighteen and thirty-five, of various nationalities. Fifth, the positions are often in places known for their association with online gambling and scamming – although this is also sometimes circumvented by pretending that the position is in a 'safe' place in the region, such as Thailand. Finally, there may be compensation fees for early termination

---

8   The post appeared in the 柬埔寨人才市场 (Cambodia Talent Marketplace) Facebook group on 3 June 2020. It is long gone (although we have a screenshot), but the group can be viewed at facebook.com/groups/2671365012894245.

9   Seminar presentation on 9 December 2022, quoted with permission.

of the employment or, conversely, a notable emphasis on the fact that no such fees will be levied.

Although they often carry these tell-tale signs, many of these ads appear on legitimate websites alongside regular positions, leading many job-seekers to trust them. When deceptive recruitment is in play, the whole process is often engineered to reassure the target that the job is genuine. At least three of our interviewees told us that they were already aware of the existence of scam operations when they fell for phoney job offers. These informants came from different places – Malaysia, mainland China, and Taiwan – but their stories are remarkably similar. They all lost their jobs during the pandemic and started looking for work on legitimate main-stream platforms. On the surface, the recruitment process was standard and professional, with background checks and one or two rounds of video interviews, followed by formal offer letters. Feeling confident that their level of education and work experience would make them unlikely targets for scam operators, they boarded the flights to Thailand and Cambodia that the recruiters had bought for them, only to find themselves trapped in scam compounds in Sihanoukville and Myanmar.

Some ads involve sectors that have nothing to do with IT, such as con-struction, food, and tourism. For instance, Yun and Pei, the two Chinese youths we encountered at the beginning of this chapter, were lured through an advertisement for construction work within China. Others target specific skilled professionals, such as engineers, chefs, dancers, make-up artists, and photographers. In some cases, recruiters proactively reach out to people who have posted their profiles online. Sometimes they offer to cover travel expenses for freelancers to meet the management, which is not unusual in some industries. For instance, in early 2023 a digital media outlet in mainland China received distress messages from over fifty individuals trapped in a scam compound in Myanmar.[10] These people identified themselves as engineers and shared a common narrative: they had all come across an enticing job offer for a 'Thai/Singapore project' in a WeChat job-hunting group that offered: 'Work five days and get two days off, eight hours a day, and a monthly salary of CN¥19,000 after taxes.'

---

10   For this story, see '男工程师赴泰国遭遇噩梦：20万元被转卖至万人诈骗营！同伴痛悔：当时深信不疑' (A Male Engineer Went to Thailand and Encountered a Night-mare: 200,000 Yuan and He Was Resold to a Scam Compound with Thousands of People! Companion Regrets: He Believed It Deeply at the Time), 上观 (Shanghai Observer), 24 March 2023.

The ruse was well crafted, and did not arouse the suspicions of the applicants. The offered amount was in line with what a Chinese engineer working overseas could expect, and some of them had been introduced to the opportunity by friends. Moreover, the recruiter provided photos of the dormitories, canteen facilities, and the machinery that would be used in the supposed factory. Encouraged by the seemingly legitimate opportunity, over a hundred people applied, and seventy-eight were offered the job. Organised into five groups, they boarded flights from China to Thailand under the belief that the factory, which supposedly dealt with fishmeal production, was located in Mae Sot, near the Thai border with Myanmar. Only after being smuggled into Myanmar did they realise that they had been deceived and sold into one of the most notorious scam compounds in the region.

A common strategy particularly widespread in mainland China and Taiwan is to hire people ostensibly for *daigou* (代购) work – that is, the practice of dispatching professional shoppers abroad to buy commodities on behalf of individuals in their home country. As disposable incomes and desire for foreign and luxury products grew among the Chinese population, *daigou* became a major industry, with buyers sending or bringing products into the country that are otherwise difficult to find or subject to high taxes. The practice is also prevalent in Taiwan, as there is demand for products, especially from Southeast Asia, that are not widely available there. In one example, in mid-December 2022 the Taiwanese police raided two buildings, one in New Taipei and the other in Taoyuan, that were suspected of hosting online scam activities.[11] They discovered fifty-eight people who had been lured by the scam group, imprisoned, and forced to engage in criminal activities.[12] Three corpses – two male and one female – were also found inside, bearing the marks of the physical violence they received while still alive. The Taiwanese police later found out that this group not only held people in Taiwan, but also sold people to scam compounds in Myanmar under the pretence of sending them there for *daigou*.

---

11   Zhang Fangrong 張芳榮, '專訪! 緬甸興華園區死裡逃生　她親揭淡水詐團藏鏡人' (Interview! She Narrowly Escaped Death in Myanmar's Xinghua Park and Now Personally Exposes the Hidden Proxy of the Danshui Scam Group), 鏡週刊 (Mirror Media), 14 December 2022.

12   Ibid.; '台灣女直播主涉「柬埔寨詐騙」! 逃出受害女控「害死3人」' (Taiwanese Female Live Broadcaster Involved in 'Cambodia Fraud'! Victim Who Escaped Accuses Her: 'She Killed Three People'), 三立新聞網 (SETN), 26 December 2022.

A female live broadcaster who displayed a very luxurious lifestyle on social media was identified by the Taiwanese media as a key player in this operation.[13] According to their investigation, the woman did not work alone but oversaw a network of other live broadcasters who helped her to peddle luxury goods on the internet. She also had three 'district representatives' working for her, with several collaborators below them using various ploys to trick people into scam compounds.[14] One of her alleged victims, a young woman surnamed Lin, recounted her ordeal to journalists. In early July 2022, the influencer had published a Facebook post saying that she was looking for people to help with her *daigou* business by buying Buddhist amulets in Thailand. Sensing a good opportunity to travel overseas and earn some easy money, Lin contacted her and together they made arrangements for the trip. When she arrived in Bangkok, Lin was picked up by a friend of the influencer and transported to a scam compound in Myanmar.[15] There she discovered that what awaited her was not a three-day shopping spree, but rather four gruesome months of forced sex work and online scamming. In late November, she finally managed to contact her family in Taiwan. Only after her relatives paid almost US$10,000 to the scam company was she finally released and able to return to Taiwan.

As public awareness about the industry has grown, some online scam operations have started to come up with creative ways to repackage their hiring practices. One common strategy has been to acknowledge the existence of problems in the online industries, while claiming to be different. Two companies located within a compound in Bavet, Cambodia, provide us with good examples.[16] In the first case, the website of one 'online gaming' company had several pages warning jobseekers about the risks of being tricked by fake roles in Southeast Asia and falling victim to human

13   '釀3死詐團案新進度?! "台灣總代表"曝光' (New Progress in the Case of the Three Deaths Perpetrated by the Scam Group?! 'Taiwan General Representative' Exposes), 華視新聞 (CTS News), 14 December 2022.

14   Zhang, 'Interview!'

15   Wu Zheyi 吳哲宜, '被直播主騙去緬甸淪「豬仔」！她逃生成關鍵證人　淚訴被餵毒品逼賣淫: 男會被剁手指' (I Was Deceived by the Live Broadcaster and Went to Myanmar to Become a 'Piglet'! She Escaped and Became a Key Witness. She Cried and Complained about Being Fed Drugs and Forced into Prostitution: Men Would Have Their Fingers Chopped Off), 風傳媒 (Storm Media), 15 December 2022.

16   'Bavet Moc Bai Casino Profile', Cyber Scam Monitor, 31 January 2023, retrieved from web.archive.org/web/20230704093105/https://cyberscammonitor.net/profile/bavet-moc-bai-casino.

trafficking, encouraging people to seek work through reputable employers, such as itself.[17] In the second case, the company – which was mentioned on several online message boards as a scam operator – presented itself as a responsible player in a sea of unscrupulous actors, warning jobseekers to look out for recruitment scams.[18]

This second case makes a particularly riveting read. On one of its websites, the company published the story of a woman who claimed to have travelled to Cambodia for work only to realise that she had been hired by a 'black company' that would not let her leave the building, did not pay as promised, and demanded a fee when she asked to quit.[19] Upon hearing about the good working conditions at the 'virtuous' company – the one publishing this story – she approached them for an interview. This led to her being offered the job and her new employer even 'compensating' the previous one. Still, had she checked the website of her new employer, this (probably fictitious) woman might have been slightly suspicious. An FAQ page stated that if employees quit, they would have to pay official expenses and possible 'compensation costs from other companies', unless they stayed for at least six months.[20] In the same page, responding to the question 'If I can't perform, will I be sold to another company?', the company said it prohibited human trafficking, and unhappy staff needed only write a resignation letter to be allowed to leave.[21] On another webpage, the company denied being engaged in online scams, and in yet another it stated that it allowed employees to move freely, never sold employees, and did not take away their passports.[22] As the old Latin saying goes: 'Excusatio non petita, accusatio manifesta' (unsolicited excuse, manifested accusation).

---

17   The page has now been deleted, but an archived version can be viewed at web.archive.org/web/20221220073258/https://www.defi8k.com/2022/01/canh-bao-viec-lam-tai-sihanouk-campuchia.html.

18   As above, the page has been deleted, but can be viewed at web.archive.org/web/20221219165052/https://taipei101group.com/viec-lam-tai-campuchia-2022.

19   'Cạm Bẫy Mắc Kẹt Ở Công Ty Đen Và Quá Trình Đến Với Taipei101' (Taipei-101 Company and the Process to Taipei101), Taipei101 company webpage, 28 October 2021, web.archive.org/web/20220925021449/https://taipei101tuyendung.com/cam-bay-mac-ket-o-cong-ty-den-va-qua-trinh-den-voi-taipei101.

20   'Những Câu Hỏi Thường Gặp Xoay Quanh Taipei101 Tuyển Dụng' (Frequently Asked Questions about Taipei101 Recruitment), Taipei101 company webpage, web.archive.org/web/20220924153853/https:/taipei101tuyendung.com/nhung-cau-hoi-thuong-gap.

21   Ibid.

22   'Sự Thật Việc Công Ty Taipei 101 Lừa Đảo Người Sang Campuchia' (The Truth about Taipei 101 Company Scamming People to Cambodia), company website, 13 July 2021, web.archive.org/web/20220924170544/https:/taipei101tuyendung.com/

Professional Brokers

Another channel through which people end up in the scam compounds is through professional brokers, whose costs are borne by the scam company and accrue to the debt that these individuals and their families may later be required to pay to secure their release. These brokers – some of which are legally registered agencies – are contracted by scam companies specifically to lure people in.[23] Many of them work remotely and flexibly in countries where scam operators seek workers to staff their activities, a condition that presents some advantages but also makes them more likely to get caught by the police in the country where they work.[24] In December 2023, for example, a Vietnamese woman who had worked as an interpreter for online companies in Cambodia was sentenced to sixteen years in jail by a Vietnamese court for trafficking nine people to Cambodia after promising them customer service work.[25] She had received US$2,900 in brokerage fees at a rate of US$300–500 per person. At least one of those she duped was described by Vietnamese media as 'a friend', who then shared the opportunity with four of her relatives. After seven of these people escaped, they reported the broker to the police in Vietnam, which led to her arrest. The court heard that she had been travelling to and from Cambodia since 2019, during which time it can be assumed she had trafficked more people.

In some cases, brokers themselves are trapped inside the scam compounds and engage in these activities to make money or simply to survive (sometimes both), further blurring the line between victim and perpetrator. A Rest of World report from 2022 recounts the story of a Vietnamese woman who was trafficked to Cambodia, where she was resold several times, an experience she described as 'hell'.[26] Eventually, she managed to

cong-ty-taipei-101-lua-dao; 'Tập Đoàn Taipei101 Có Uy Tín Không?' (Is Taipei101 Group Reputable?), company website, undated, vieclamcampuchia.vn/tap-doan-taipei101.

23   Chen Sisi 陈思思 and Wang Shi 王时, '在家"躺着"就赚钱？ 哈市警方捣毁一个"吸粉引流"电信网络诈骗团伙' (Make Money While 'Lying' at Home? Harbin Police Smashed an 'Attract Fans and Drain Them' Telecom and Internet Fraud Gang), 搜狐 (Sohu), 14 May 2020.

24   '藏身境外的"荐股"骗子遥控境内"引流"团伙，44名涉案人里甚至还有学生' (The 'Stock Recommendation' Scammers Hiding Abroad Remotely Controlled the Domestic 'Drainage' Gang, and Even Students Were among the 44 Involved), 新浪网 (sina.com.cn), 18 February 2022.

25   Vinh Tho and Doan Cuong, 'Vietnamese Interpreter Gets 16 Years for Cambodia Job Scam', Tuoi Tre News, 5 December 2023.

26   Danielle Keeton-Olsen and Lam Nguyen, 'How Cambodia's Scam Mills Reel in New "Cyber Slave" Workers', Rest of World, 10 November 2022.

climb the ranks to become a recruiter herself – an uncomfortable transition that points to the dehumanising capacity of the industry, even though this specific person apparently 'made peace with her role in hiring people into a business that deceived and traumatized her'. Another Vietnamese man trafficked to a compound in Cambodia tricked three of his friends into joining a scam operation after being offered US$100 for every person he recruited: 'In order to have money and not be starved and be beaten, I tricked three of my friends into coming here … But I did not receive any money.' He returned to Vietnam after his family paid a ransom, but was arrested for his role in trafficking others.[27] In another case reported in Malaysian media, a woman who had been trafficked to Myanmar was told she could not leave unless she found someone to replace her.[28] Similarly, three of our interviewees in Myanmar were given the choice of paying a ransom or recruiting at least five people in order to be released.

Professional brokers may spend months building personal connections with their targets. These people can pose as a fellow townsman (老乡 *laoxiang*), an attentive match on a dating app, or even a team partner in online video games. After building up trust, they bide their time before bringing up an unmissable job opportunity abroad. For instance, one of our interviewees from China teamed up with a stranger named Feifei on the online video game *Dota*. As they got to know each other, he learned that his new teammate was also from his hometown. After several weeks of playing and chatting together through the game, they became close friends and Feifei even bought some in-game virtual equipment for him. When they added each other on WeChat, our interviewee saw that Feifei often shared photos of fancy dinners and luxury cars, so he surmised that the man was from a rich family. Little did he know that this 'pretending-to-be-rich package' is a trick commonly used by recruiters, who share photos of luxury bags, sports cars, and fancy lifestyles on social media to attract the attention of their targets.[29] Convinced by months of interactions and consistent displays of wealth, when Feifei presented him with a job opportunity in Cambodia, our informant accepted without hesitation – only to find himself trapped in a scam compound.

27   Danh Toai and Pham Linh, 'Human Trafficking Victim Tricks to Sell Close Friend to Cambodia', *VNExpress*, 18 February 2023.

28   Fernando Fong, 'From Hope to Horror: Sickly Woman Falls for Job Scam, Ends Up in Myanmar', *Rakyat Post*, 27 August 2023.

29   Tanran Fengyun 坦然风云, '在朋友圈暴富，一个淘宝就够了' (Get Rich in the Circle of Friends, a Taobao Is Enough), 网易 (NetEase), 9 October 2019, 163.com.

A similar strategy was employed on Xiao Zheng, a Chinese man who got trapped in a scam company in Phnom Penh in 2021:

> I know the person who sold me through online gaming, he plays very well, so we teamed up together. One day, he asked me if I was from Anhui province because my accent sounded familiar. Then he said he was from Lu'an city, and at that time I thought, wow, he's a fellow towns-man. What a coincidence! I never expected to be deceived by him. Later, while playing games, he casually mentioned that he worked in Cambo-dia, saying his job was so easy that he had become lazy and unmotivated. I was jealous because I had just graduated and was working so hard for a little over 3,000 yuan [roughly US$420] in China. Hearing what he said, I was curious, and he briefly described his work situation. He said he worked in procurement for a company, a job with no technical skills and very little to do. Then he started encouraging me to also work in Cambodia. At first, I was hesitant, but he constantly shared photos of his fancy life and salary slips. Then I decided to go to join him in his company.

In cases where deception is used to ensnare people, the relationships that develop are sometimes so intimate that they leave deep emotional scars. When one of our interviewees was telling us his story of being tricked by someone from his hometown, the pain and disappointment on his face were obvious: 'I really saw him as a true friend. Really. Because he once helped me a lot during my hardest time. Especially as he is also a person from my hometown, you know that kind of bond, right? I definitely trusted him more than others. So, when he asked me whether I wanted to go to work as a chef in Cambodia, I agreed and just went.' Alice, the young Taiwanese woman whose story we recounted at the very beginning of the book, was also betrayed by a colleague she had met at her workplace in the Philippines:

> To be honest, at that time I was being severely bullied by all my col-leagues in the Philippines, except him. That was a new workplace for me, and I did not have any friends there. He was the only person who would greet me, ask how I was, and care about my feelings. So, when he said that he knew of a new work opportunity in Phnom Penh and suggested that I change work environment, I trusted him.

To convince their targets to take the bait, recruiters offer company-sponsored flights and promise to handle visas, work permits, and associated fees. Most of our interviewees arrived in their destination country legally, and some indicated that the scam companies are well connected with the immigration authorities. In the Philippines, the authorities have been investigating connections between the traffickers and immigration and airport personnel, with reports implicating officers and staff in facilitating Filipinos leaving the country with dubious work papers, as well as allowing foreigners destined for online work to enter the Philippines without adequate paperwork.[30]

Freelance Recruiters

In the same Rest of World article mentioned above, one Vietnamese man told the reporters: 'The reason people still go to scam companies is because they are scammed by friends and family.'[31] While identifying this as the easiest way to recruit people, he took pride in the fact that he had never done that. These so-called friends and family are what we call freelance recruiters – opportunists who are not always part of the industry but often know people who are and exploit these connections to make some easy money by taking advantage of vulnerable acquaintances, friends, or even relatives. We had close experience of this when, in 2022, a relative of one of the authors was approached by her music tutor, a Chinese woman living in Cambodia, who asked if she was interested in translation work at a company operating in a notorious scam compound on the coast. When she expressed surprise at the offer and said she knew the reputation of that location, the tutor said not to believe everything the media reports, and that women are free to come and go from the compound.

Stories of people tricked into the compounds by family members are not uncommon, especially in China. In early 2023, the Chinese media widely reported the story of Hao, a forty-year-old man whose gaming

---

30   'Immigration Chief Calls for Coordinated BI, Airport Authority Probe into Human Trafficking Scheme', Rappler, 30 November 2022; William B. Depasupil and Bernadette E. Tamayo, 'DoJ Orders Probe on Recruitment Scam', *Manila Times*, 1 December 2022.

31   Keeton-Olsen and Nguyen, 'How Cambodia's Scam Mills Reel in New "Cyber Slave" Workers'.

company went bust during the COVID pandemic.[32] Heavily indebted and at a loss about how to make a living, he heeded the advice of one of his uncles, who told him about an unmissable opportunity in a 'call centre' in Myanmar. Once he got there, he realised that it was a scam compound and that he was not allowed to leave. The uncle was also working for the compound, earning a fee ranging from CN¥10,000 to CN¥20,000 for every individual he recruited. Hao spent two months inside before managing to escape. Once he got out, he became famous as an anti-scam TikToker. In another case that occurred in April 2023, an underage girl was intercepted at Kunming airport en route to Cambodia, where she believed a well-paid job was waiting for her.[33] She had been talked into it by a distant relative she had not seen in a long time and expected to be paid US$1,500 per month, with food and accommodation covered, although she had no clue where she would work nor what she would do. The police called her parents, and she was eventually persuaded to return home.

Many of these brokers exploit the bonds of trust and solidarity derived from sharing the same place of origin – ties that have always been a powerful driving force for Chinese international migration. In Phnom Penh, we encountered a nineteen-year-old man we will call Xiaozan. He had arrived in the Cambodian capital in 2019 to work on the construction site of a new shopping mall, but only a few months later found himself unemployed due to the COVID-19 outbreak. This is how he recounted his ordeal:

> I come from a poor family, and my father, also a construction worker, taught me the skills. [In 2019] I travelled to Phnom Penh with some friends because there were many projects here. However, I lost my job due to the COVID-19 pandemic and couldn't afford the US$4,000 flight ticket back home. During that time, I also met my [Cambodian] wife, so I wanted to do everything to stay. With no other skills besides construction work, I accepted a job offer from a fellow townsman I knew

---

32   '起底缅北诈骗① | 惊魂59天! 园区高墙电网、保安荷枪实弹、一个人能卖25万到30万 … 想挣大钱却沦为"猪仔"' (The Scams in Northern Myanmar ① | 59 Days of Shock! The Compound Has High Walls and Electric Wires, Security Guards Are Armed with Live Ammunition, and One Person Can Sell for 250,000 to 300,000 … He Planned to Make a Lot of Money, but Became a 'Piglet'), 半岛网 (Bandaowang), 7 September 2023.

33   '月薪1500美金? 云南一未成年女孩称要去柬埔寨务工, 结果 …' (A Monthly Salary of US$1,500? An Underage Girl from Yunnan Said She Was Going to Cambodia to Work, but …), 网易 (NetEase), 19 April 2023, 163.com.

since I arrived in Cambodia to work as a maintenance worker in Sihan-oukville. It seemed reasonable because I knew there were many casinos and online businesses in Sihanoukville that needed workers, and the salary they offered was comparable to my previous job. However, the moment I settled in, they confiscated my passport. I was powerless. I had no money, no connections, do not speak the local language to ask for help, and now don't even have any identity [documents].

In Sihanoukville he was severely beaten, and eventually sold to five different compounds. As he was not provided any medical care, only painkillers, this resulted in a permanent injury to his leg (when we met him in Phnom Penh in July 2022, he was still limping). Still, he felt he was lucky, because he was young and able to learn quickly in the initial weeks when he was trained on how to operate the scams. Others had it much worse: he knew of several workers who barely knew how to type and were badly tortured.

The fact that personal relations play a fundamental role in the recruit-ment patterns of the online scam industry, at least when it comes to ethnic Chinese victims, is borne out by the previously mentioned survey we conducted in 2023 among a sample of sixty-two Chinese survivors.[34] Our survey revealed that as many as 79.4 per cent of our respondents had found their jobs through personal acquaintances, against only 8.8 per cent who had been recruited through social media (they specifically mentioned Douyin, Xiaohongshu, and WeChat), 8.8 per cent who had gone through employment agencies, and barely 2.9 per cent who had fallen for ads on job-advertisement platforms. Asked about their relationship with the people who introduced them to the industry, 46.9 per cent stated that they were friends, 21.9 per cent acquaintances or fellow townspeople, 9.4 per cent relatives, and 6.2 per cent business relations. Only 6.2 per cent of the respondents indicated that they were tricked by strangers, and 3.1 per cent by someone they met on the internet.

The existence of opportunist brokers among one's social circles can lead to a general breakdown of societal trust, especially in proximity to the scam compounds. As one of our interviewees in Sihanoukville told us: 'The person you are eating dinner with now can be the one who sells

---

34   Ivan Franceschini, Ling Li, Yige Hu, and Mark Bo, 'A New Type of Victim? Pro-filing Survivors of Modern Slavery in the Online Scam Industry in Southeast Asia', *Trends in Organized Crime*, 6 November 2024.

you tomorrow.' In such contexts, any basic social interaction becomes fraught with risk. During one of our visits to the city in early 2022, a Chinese food-delivery worker we had never met before had no qualms to share with us the story of how he had sold someone to a scam company:

> This guy owed me money. After I urged him three times to pay me back and he refused to do so, I decided to call a manager I know from one of the compounds. I asked him to come around the restaurant I work for, and the compound car waited there and took him. He didn't struggle when he saw the compound people, he knew it was me, and it is quite normal in Sihanoukville when you don't have money to pay back.

Asked about the reasons that had prompted him to act that way, he said: 'I had no choice but to do so. The police here are not doing anything, and I need the money for my family. I didn't take anything more than what he owed to me from the compound. What I did was just transfer the debt to the compound, and he will work for them to pay back. It is fair.' He was speaking in a calm tone, as if this was nothing out of the ordinary.

Social Media Influencers

In May 2024, a social media influencer was arrested in India in a human trafficking case.[35] According to Indian police, he had sent thirty-three people abroad – twelve to Laos, twelve to Armenia, four to Bangkok, three to Canada, and two to Singapore – on the pretext of helping them secure jobs, but once they arrived at their destination, they were forced to commit cyberfraud. While the man was allegedly directly involved in trafficking these people, social media influencers sometimes play a more subtle role. It is not uncommon for people to end up in scam compounds after heeding the call of some influencer who extolls Southeast Asia as a place where anyone willing to work hard can fulfil their dreams of prosperity. These influencers often bring up how easy it is to find attractive local women – whom they describe as 'beautiful, obedient, and eager to find Chinese boyfriends.'[36]

---

35   Express News Service, 'Social Media Influencer Bobby Kataria Sent 33 People Abroad on Job Promise: Gurgaon Police', *Indian Express*, 1 June 2024.

36   See, for instance, this video published by an influencer on Douyin on 9 May 2021: douyin.com/video/6960267391943101733.

Some influencers also bring up enticing job opportunities with major local companies which, unbeknown to viewers, are directly involved in or linked to the scam industry. This approach is adopted by several Chinese-speaking Myanmar or Cambodian influencers. They introduce their audience to their hometowns by showing them luscious landscapes and discussing local politics and culture, but their videos invariably end up with investment or employment opportunities. An influencer from Kokang, Myanmar, is a good example of this approach.[37] In her videos, she frequently named three companies as pillars of the local economy, claiming that they work in real estate and tourism and create many employment opportunities for Chinese youths willing to travel there. Although it is unclear whether the woman was aware, all the companies are known to be also involved in scam-related activities.

In some cases, links between the influencers and the scam companies have been proven beyond any reasonable doubt. We found at least two such cases, both of which involved Myanmar nationals who claimed to be descendants of the Chinese Expeditionary Force, a military unit dispatched to Burma and India by Chiang Kai-shek to aid Allied efforts against the Imperial Japanese Army during the Second World War.[38] The two men posted patriotic content to advertise their affection for China and the Chinese people. One of them, a young man named Li Saigao, shared several videos of himself wearing a military uniform and singing red songs. His handsome looks and patriotic speeches received widespread engagement from his audience in China, with his Douyin account quickly skyrocketing in 2021 to nearly 2 million followers. In February 2022, however, local police in Shijiazhuang, in China's Hebei province, posted an announcement accusing him of involvement in the online scam industry.[39] Concurrently, police in Zhangjiajie, Hunan province, accused

---

37   Huichanjuan 灰产圈, '缅北最深的套路是美女, 每天在互联网上诱骗中国人偷渡前往参与电诈和网赌' (The Most Common Trick in Northern Myanmar Is Beautiful Women, Who Use the Internet Every Day to Trick Chinese People into Illegally Crossing the Border to Participate in Electronic Fraud and Online Gambling), 搜狐 (Sohu), 2 March 2022.

38   Jinrong Baguanü 金融八卦女, '围猎中国人的"危险网红": 冒充远征军后裔, 骗赌要钱还要命' ('Dangerous Internet Celebrities' Hunting Chinese People: Pretending to Be Descendants of the Expeditionary Army, Scamming for Money and Life), 财经头条 (Sina Financial Toutiao), 24 February 2022.

39   '警方实锤百万网红李赛高: 小心电信诈骗' (The Police Hit Million-Follower Internet Celebrity Li Saigao: Beware of Telecom Fraud), 福州新闻网 (Fuzhou News), 23 February 2022.

him of working for Henry Group, a company notorious for engaging in human trafficking, online scamming, and money laundering in North Myanmar; they issued a warning against accepting any job offers in the country.[40] Around the same time, some of his followers pointed out that in the background of one of his videos they heard the sound of people getting beaten up, and a female voice shouting: 'I am sorry, I don't dare to do it anymore.'[41] Although he denied any wrongdoing, as more evidence of Li Saigao's involvement in the online scam industry was shared on the internet, his accounts were blocked by Douyin and other platforms.

Organised Crime Syndicates

As we have already discussed, the online scam industry is dominated by non-traditional ethnic Chinese criminal groups endowed with a strong entrepreneurial spirit. Yet traditional organised crime groups, including triad or triad-linked groups from Hong Kong and Taiwan, are also known to play a role. Former 14K triad leader Wan Kuok-koi (also known as Broken Tooth) is known to associate with several key industry actors, and he is also one of the investors behind the Dongmei Park scam site in Myanmar, which has been linked to human trafficking and forced criminality.[42] There are no doubt instances where traditional organised crime actors are linked directly to the compounds, but evidence suggests one area they are heavily involved in is recruitment and trafficking. In Taiwan, local media have extensively reported on cases of individuals kidnapped or tricked by local mafia groups such as the United Bamboo Gang (竹聯幫 *zhulianbang*), the Thento Union (天道盟 *tiandaomeng*), the Four Seas Gang (四海幫 *sihaibang*), the San Guang Gang (三光幫 *sanguangbang*), and the Feng Fei Sha Gang (風飛沙幫 *fengfeishabang*).[43]

40   Ibid. Henry Group is led by the Wei family, whose patriarch was arrested in Myanmar in January 2024 and handed over to Chinese police, as discussed in Chapter 1.

41   Susu Yule 素素娱乐, '网红李赛高的身份证明来了! 属于缅北军政人员, 年龄才 22岁' (Internet Celebrity Li Saigao's Proof of Identity Is Here! He Belongs to the Political Personnel of the Northern Myanmar Army and Is Only 22 Years Old), 网易 (NetEase), 25 February 2022, 163.com.

42   'The Karen Border Guard Force/Karen National Army Criminal Business Network Exposed', Justice for Myanmar website, 22 May 2024; Isabelle Qian, '7 Months inside an Online Scam Labor Camp', *New York Times*, 17 December 2023.

43   For instance, in April 2023, a Taiwanese court sentenced a reported member of

Over the years, these Taiwanese groups have formalised much of their activity by registering companies, with representatives assuming company titles and handing out business cards.[44] According to one report from TVBS News, some have registered new companies and then used these start-ups to place job advertisements on legitimate websites in order to lure recruits.[45] These shell companies present themselves as operations where much of the work can be done online, such as studios producing games or music. Initially, they onboard the new staff and operate normally so as not to arouse suspicion among their recruits. Then, once trust is established, the managers arrange a 'team-bonding trip' to Southeast Asia for the staff. It is often only when they get off the plane and are met by vans that bring them to the scam compounds that they realise something is off.

Traditional organised crime groups have the advantage that they can count on their own protective umbrellas in the locations where they are based. In May 2023, a Taiwanese police chief was dismissed and detained for allegedly colluding with criminals engaged in human trafficking to Cambodia.[46] He faced corruption charges for allegedly receiving money in Tether cryptocurrency tokens worth NT$1 million (US$32,609), as well as charges of forgery, illegal access to and use of personal information, and leaking confidential files. Investigators said he accessed restricted police files to obtain personal information of kidnapped people, which he then passed to Tu Cheng-che, an alleged gang leader, who used it to apply for passports and access bank accounts. Tu reportedly engaged in extortion,

the Bamboo Union to eighteen years for trafficking eighty-eight people into fraud rings in Cambodia, while eight of his accomplices received terms of between eleven and sixteen and a half years. According to the prosecutors, the gang had received US$18,000 per person. See Lin Chang-shun and Matthew Mazzetta, 'Crime Ringleader Gets 18 Years for Trafficking 88 Victims to Cambodia', Focus Taiwan, 13 April 2023. On the involvement of Taiwanese gangs in the online scam industry in Southeast Asia, see also Jason Pan, 'Three Gangs to Blame for Most Trafficking: Police', *Taipei Times*, 10 November 2022; Zhang Fangrong 張芳榮, '【黑幫掮客賣豬仔2】台灣「豬仔」柬埔寨搶手 黑幫掮客仲介1人賺60萬' (Gangster Brokers Selling Two Piglets: Taiwan's 'Piglets' Are Popular in Cambodia, Gangster Brokers Earn 600,000 Yuan per Person), 鏡週刊 (Mirror Media), 23 July 2022.

44   Kong Delian 孔德廉, '台灣黑幫、柬國詐騙集團: 跨國博弈餘燼下新生的人口販運鏈' (Taiwanese Gangs, Cambodian Fraud Syndicates: A New Human Trafficking Chain in the Ashes of Transnational Games), *The Reporter*, 9 August 2022.

45   '公司突豪爽旅遊! 員工「整車載走」一開門全傻了: 怎柬埔寨?' (The Company's Sudden Adventurous Trip! The Employees Were All Dumbfounded When They Opened the Door: Why Cambodia?), TVBS, 16 August 2022.

46   On this case, see Jason Pan, 'Police Chief Detained in Corruption, Bribery Probe', *Taipei Times*, 5 May 2023.

online scams, and human trafficking. His associates posted job ads on social media, then seized and tied up the people who came for interview, forcing them to give their bank details for use in money laundering. Some were forced to work for online scammers in Cambodia. Tu and his associates went into hiding in 2022 following police raids, but were tracked down and arrested in March and April 2023.

Traditional organised crime groups also supply scam operations with associates who already have experience in money laundering, phone scamming, lottery fraud, and other grey industries (灰产 *huichan*). Not only are these skilled professionals, but they also willingly engage in criminal activity, which makes them highly sought after. Given the huge profits involved, some syndicates not directly involved in online scams have attempted to capitalise on the industry by dispatching their members to more specialised gangs, and organised crime groups from different countries frequently cooperate transnationally to share their workforce.[47] Gang leadership send junior members (小弟 *xiaodi*, or little brothers) to support allied gangs in their online scam work abroad; in return the recipient gang sends back a share of the profits, usually in the form of cryptocurrency.

Yet not all of those dispatched by these syndicates go voluntarily. Further confirming the moral ambiguity of the industry, many follow the same trajectory as civilians, getting tricked and being sold from one compound to the next. One of our interviewees, a former member of a Hong Kong triad, was originally dispatched to Sihanoukville by his boss with the stated aim of laundering money. Once there, however, he was asked to do online fraud instead. Being inexperienced in this line of work, he was slow on the uptake. Facing exhausting work hours, endless criticism, and physical beatings from the managers, at the first opportunity he contacted his boss to request a transfer. He ended up at another scam operator in Myawaddy in Myanmar, where he says he was treated much better.

---

47   Guo Ying 郭穎, '臟款逾2億! 竹聯幫勾結「柬」詐團　詐騙洗錢' (The Stolen Money Exceeded 200 million! The Bamboo Union Gang Colluded with Cambodian Fraud Groups to Commit Scams and Launder Money), TVBS, 6 December 2022; Yao Yuehong 姚岳宏, '《自由日日shoot》黑幫營造海外淘金熱 騙國人到柬埔寨西港 恐2千人' (Mafia Faked Money Opportunities Abroad and Lured Approximately 2,000 Taiwanese to Sihanoukville, Cambodia), 自由時報 (Liberty Times Net), 27 July 2022; Chen Lifei 陳立非 and Li Yao 李耀, '不到四天就有一起案件, 台湾枪击案为何创下新高?' (There Was One New Case in Less Than Four Days: Why Did the Shootings in Taiwan Hit a New High?), 环球时报 (Global Times), 19 November 2022.

In the summer of 2022, as mainstream coverage of scams in Cambodia and Myanmar increased in the Hong Kong media, some operators in Myawaddy decided to offload their Hong Kong staff. With his parents' help, the young man got his ransom paid and was one of the first to leave his company. During our interview with him, he revealed to us how triad members are tricked by their bosses into joining scam companies:

> To be honest, a lot of triads in Hong Kong would sell their members for online scam work. Sometimes they would make up some excuse, pretending to send members for training programmes abroad; other times, they would just openly tell their members that they are sending them to Cambodia for online scamming. But usually, if triad leaders know that the working environment they are going to send people to is very bad, like in those compounds where people are not allowed to sleep at all, then they just make up these nice excuses.

He also mentioned two other people whom he had met when he was in Sihanoukville: 'They are from a gang in Taiwan, and they were tricked by their leader to come to Cambodia. They knew they were going to do something bad, but they just did not expect the conditions under which they were going to work could be so terrible.'

Aside from the internal dissatisfaction from disgruntled members as news of these betrayals spread, gangs also often face each other in conflicts for power, money, and staff – a dynamic that is referred to as 'black eat black' (黑吃黑 *hei chi hei*) in Chinese-language media.[48] In one particularly gruesome case, a Taiwanese gang that directly managed a scam company in Cambodia sent one of its workers, a man who himself had previously been tricked into the industry, to pick up five new Taiwanese recruits, handle their passports and visas upon arrival, and bring them to the compound.[49] Instead of following the instructions, however, the

---

48   Xu Huizhu 徐慧珠, '黑吃黑? 大清算? 3台南人柬埔寨遭槍殺 家屬報案盼查死因' (Black Eat Black? Big Clean-Up? Three People from Tainan Were Shot Dead in Cambodia), TVBS, 29 August 2022; '疑争柬埔寨诈骗利益, 台湾新竹两大帮派起冲突互开10余枪, 嫌犯焚车逃逸! ' (Suspected of Fighting for Scam-Related Interests in Cambodia, Two Gangs in Hsinchu, Taiwan, Clashed and Fired More Than Ten Shots at Each Other. The Suspect Burned His Car and Fled!), 海峡新干线 (Strait New Line), Douyin channel, 2 September 2022.

49   This story was recounted by Gao Renhe, a retired senior criminal police officer in Taiwan, on a news programme on Taiwanese television. '台人黑吃黑! 爆柬埔寨詐騙3命

man called a van and sent the freshly arrived staff to a rival compound before vanishing into thin air. It was soon discovered that the rival gang had bought the people at a rate of US\$23,000–25,000 per person. The first gang put a huge bounty on the traitor. Eventually, they caught him: first, they filmed as they tortured him to death in front of other gang members; then they dumped his body.

Further complicating this issue, some triad-linked actors have also been involved in rescuing people from the industry. Relatives of trafficked individuals are often unable to secure their release by simply engaging with law enforcement or government officials. This is especially the case for people from Taiwan, which does not have formal diplomatic or law enforcement relationships with the countries where the scam compounds are located. In several reported cases, these family members have sought help from people with triad connections.[50]

Zhang Anle, also known as White Wolf (白狼 *bailang*), a former leader of the United Bamboo Gang, has been one of the best known and most controversial characters in this regard. Now head of the Chinese Unification Promotion Party (中華統一促進黨 *zhonghua tongyi cujin dang*), which he established in 2005, he claims to have retired from the underworld. Stories describing how he used his connections to secure the release of people in scam compounds abound in Chinese-language media. Taiwan's *Mirror Media*, for instance, reported that in one case he used alleged connections with the Cambodian military to assist the rescue of five people.[51] Voice of Democracy reported how Zhang helped to secure the release of another Taiwanese man, who had been trafficked to Cambodia and then to northern Laos.[52] While this has earned him some praise from the public, it has also attracted the attention of Taiwanese law enforcement,

案　前刑警: 凌虐致死丟草叢' (Taiwanese Black Eat Black! Three Murders in Cambodia. Former Criminal Policeman: Tortured to Death and Thrown On), 三立新聞網 (SETN), 15 August 2022, youtube.com/watch?v=ombmH1nKlBs.

50　Liu Wenyuan 劉文淵, '外交救援緩不濟急白狼出手　黑幫大老竟調動柬國軍隊搶人 (Diplomatic Rescue Is Slow and Urgent, White Wolf Takes Action, Gang Leader Mobilises Cambodian Army to Take Away People), 鏡週刊 (Mirror Media), 18 May 2022.

51　See, for instance, '台湾青年被骗去柬埔寨"卖身", "白狼"张安乐惊险救援过程曝光' (Taiwanese Youth Was Deceived into 'Selling Himself' in Cambodia, Here's 'White Wolf' Zhang Anle's Thrilling Rescue Process), 搜狐 (Sohu), 19 August 2022; '张安乐出手从柬埔寨诈骗集团救回五名台湾人' (Zhang Anle Rescued Five Taiwanese from a Cambodian Fraud Syndicate), 镜周刊 (Mirror Media), 18 May 2022.

52　Jintamas Saksornchai and Cindy Liu, 'Scam Workers Relocated from Cambodia to Laos, Myanmar', Voice of Democracy, 24 October 2022.

which accused him of 'playing both angel and demon': according to them, while the United Bamboo Gang has played a role in rescuing some people, it is simultaneously one of the main groups allegedly selling Taiwanese citizens into the scam industry in Southeast Asia.[53]

Kidnappings

Another route into the scam compounds is kidnapping. This became more common during the COVID-19 pandemic, when travel was restricted, making recruitment increasingly difficult. This was particularly the case in Cambodia.

As the country's casino industry expanded rapidly in the late 2010s, areas in which casinos were concentrated soon became associated with high incidences of violence and other crimes. Many casino operators utilised security teams led by gang-affiliated individuals, who dealt with unruly patrons but also enforced debt collection, among other tasks. However, after the ban on online gambling in August 2019 and the obliteration of tourism caused by the pandemic, a wave of casino closures occurred, leaving many of these debt collectors unemployed and seeking new ways to make a living. As one of our informants who worked in a scam compound told us: 'Debt collectors are used to fancy lives, and the only skill they have is violence. So, when they found themselves out of the casinos, they resorted to kidnapping people for the scam companies.'

Through the COVID-19 pandemic, some of these gangsters resorted to kidnapping Chinese residents and selling them to scam compounds to make a living. They generally operated independently, building connections with multiple companies and selling their services to the highest bidder. One interviewee told us a story about his former supervisor in a scam company who had taken seven workers out for dinner, planning to sell them to another company. He contacted a group of gangsters in advance and arranged a hijacking. However, when the gangsters appeared, they seized the supervisor along with the men he was planning to sell, and sold them all to yet another company that had made a better offer. Information gathered from informants indicates these kinds of incidents

---

53   Li Yujin 李昱菫, '救困柬埔寨台人? 張安樂遭批「神鬼分飾二角」怒告刑事局' (Rescue Taiwanese in Cambodia? Zhang Anle Sues the Criminal Bureau after Being Criticised for 'Playing Both Angel and Demon'), TVBS, 16 August 2022.

remain relatively frequent in Cambodia, even though the targets of kid-nappings these days seem to be mostly people who owe debts, for instance due to gambling losses, or those who are already involved with the scam industry.

Transfers between Compounds

No matter how they enter the compounds, once inside, scam workers can always potentially be sold between different operators. A Vietnamese recruiter active in Bavet, Cambodia, described this process as 'redeeming' workers, with a company taking less skilled or efficient staff off the hands of another one for a lower price.[54] According to this recruiter, the price for a Vietnamese worker in Bavet in 2022 was around US$1,000, compared to US$3,000 in more established hubs such as Sihanoukville. This is a developed market, with rates dependent on several factors, including a worker's current location, nationality, linguistic skills, and ability. According to our interviewees, skilled Chinese workers in Sihanoukville in 2022 sold for as much as US$10,000–15,000, while others who could not speak Chinese cost around US$3,000–5,000; in some parts of Myanmar the price for Chinese speakers could be double this amount, presumably due to the challenges and expense of getting them there.

Either because they cannot afford it or because they want to keep their hands relatively clean, some scam compounds try not to get directly involved in human trafficking and kidnappings, preferring instead to take in workers who have joined voluntarily or are sold by other compounds. In these cases, they usually offer appealing commissions, called tea fees (茶水费 *chashuifei*), to brokers from other compounds who claim to offer people who have joined their workforce voluntarily. Before moving forward with the hire, they conduct interviews with both the compounds selling the workers and the workers themselves. According to some of our interviewees who went through this process, the interviews usually focus on whether the worker joined the industry willingly and if abuse was involved at any point. But according to the testimonies we collected, those who were forced to take part in these interviews were intimidated into pretending willingness to work in the scam industry.

---

54   Keeton-Olsen and Nguyen, 'How Cambodia's Scam Mills Reel in New "Cyber Slave" Workers'.

Routes

So far, we have covered the main channels through which people end up in the scam compounds but not the physical routes they take in their journey. Once recruited, workers need to be transported to the location where they will be working. Depending on their circumstances and where they are travelling from, they may travel by themselves or in a group with fellow recruits via regular channels. In some cases, they may be smuggled or trafficked across (sometimes multiple) international borders.

In many reported cases, those who have been tricked into the work realise that something is amiss only when they are already well on their way to the scam compounds. As Alice recounted to us:

> I arrived in Phnom Penh by plane in late June. A person picked me up from the airport and brought me to a hotel. After a few hours, someone else came up saying that he would drive me to the company. I got in the car. After one or two hours, I asked why we hadn't arrived yet. He said that the company was in Sihanoukville and there were still two hours to go. I looked it up on the map and realised the place was very far, a coastal city. They drove for a long time, and I felt it was a bit strange, because I texted the person who introduced me to this work, but he had blocked me. The entire four-hour drive was through some rural and less developed places. I felt like I was being kidnapped and started panicking.
>
> Once I arrived in Sihanoukville, I found it full of casinos, online gambling venues, hotels, and KTVs [karaoke parlours], so it felt weirder and weirder. Then I arrived at a compound called Huangsha Casino. There was a large fence at the gate to prevent people from entering, with many security guards around. After entering, I still did not see the boss I was supposed to meet, so I panicked. They put me into a small room. Inside the room were bunk beds, and some people were sleeping in them. Then they broke the news to me that I was not there to be a secretary, that I had been trafficked to do online gambling. The person who had picked me up at the airport had just sold me for US$25,000.

These days, many of those who travel through legal channels first fly to Thailand and then are brought to neighbouring countries by land. As news of the industry has spread far and wide, this is one way for recruiters to avoid arousing the suspicions of their targets. But not all those who have been recruited into compounds in Southeast Asia are able to travel through legal channels. As awareness of the problems associated with online gambling and scam operations in Southeast Asia spread in 2020, the Chinese government stepped up border controls for citizens travelling to countries known to host these operations and, although the document was never published, China's Ministry of Culture and Tourism reportedly circulated a blacklist of destinations for which travellers were subject to additional scrutiny before being permitted to depart.[55] To make things more complicated for prospective migrants, starting in May 2022, to enforce their zero-COVID policy, the Chinese authorities began to 'strictly limit' unnecessary outbound travel.[56]

Many of those recruited into the industry had never left China before, and with Chinese citizens applying for a new passport now needing to declare which countries they planned to travel to and provide documents proving why the trip was necessary, obtaining a passport for destinations such as Cambodia, Myanmar, Laos, or the Philippines became increasingly difficult, if not impossible. Even those Chinese citizens who already possessed travel documents faced hurdles. After purchasing flights to these countries, some received calls from the local police enquiring about the purpose of their trips. Once they arrived at the departure airport, border guards stopped them to ask questions about their planned activities in the destination country, asked to see return tickets, and, if they were travelling for work, demanded that they produce documents proving the work was legitimate. If the officers found the situation suspicious, they refused permission to leave the country.

These travel controls were integrated into the Law against Telecom and Online Fraud, passed in September 2022, which formalised Chinese immigration authorities' powers to impose exit bans on those travelling to overseas hotspots if suspected of being likely to engage in telecom or online fraud once abroad.[57] Since then – and even after the Chinese government lifted its zero-COVID policy in December 2022 – there have been

55   Takeshi Kihara, Takashi Nakano, and Tomoya Onishi, 'China's Foreign Casino Ban Risks Snake Eyes for Vietnam and Rivals', *Nikkei Asia*, 7 September 2020.

56   'China to "Strictly Limit" Unnecessary Overseas Travels by Chinese Citizens to Combat COVID', Reuters, 12 May 2022.

57   For the law, see 'Law on Countering Telecommunications Network Fraud', China Law Translate, 2 September 2022.

further reports of Chinese nationals attempting to travel to Southeast Asia being blocked by immigration at airports in China. This has also impacted people who argue vigorously that they are involved in legitimate business in the country they are travelling to.[58] Local authorities in some areas have required that travellers produce documents such as evidence of property ownership in their country of destination, work permits and contracts, and company business licences, in order to prove that the purpose of their travel is legitimate. If travel is deemed suspicious, people may be black-listed; they must then request for restrictions to be lifted and apply for a new passport. Some people report waiting weeks for clearance.

Other governments throughout the region have also been implementing measures to prevent their citizens from travelling to areas now perceived as dangerous. For instance, in the summer of 2022, Taiwan's Aviation Police Bureau started putting up warning posters and dispatching officers to its international airports to question individuals flying to Southeast Asia about their travel plans in an attempt to raise awareness about the scam compounds and prevent travellers from falling prey to traffickers.[59] Several embassies in Southeast Asia have also prominently featured travel advice on their websites, warning citizens to beware of job ads promising high salaries for vaguely described online work in the region.[60]

Unfortunately, these restrictions have not been enough; often they just make the trips more difficult and more dangerous. In the Chinese case, the country's zero-COVID policy of compulsory testing, stringent lockdowns, and travel restrictions contributed to mass unemployment.[61]

---

58   See, for instance, '出发去柬埔寨前一晚，突然接到户籍派出所电话 …' (The Night before I Travelled to Cambodia, I Suddenly Received a Call from the Household Registration Police Station), Sohu, 29 March 2023; '多人赴柬埔寨遭限制出境近2个月！网友：婚礼被迫推迟' (Many People Who Went to Cambodia Were Restricted from Leaving the Country for Nearly Two Months! Netizen: The Wedding Was Forcedly Postponed), *TNAOT*, 3 June 2023.

59   Di Yi Chongfenghao V. 第一冲锋号V, '台诈骗案逐渐离谱，男子不顾警方劝阻执意赴柬，称自己是天选之子' (Fraud Cases in Taiwan Are Becoming Increasingly Outrageous: The Man Insisted on Going to Cambodia despite the Police's Dissuasion, Claiming to Be the Chosen One), 新浪 (sina.com.cn), 22 August 2022; '家屬稱去歷練! 2台男飛柬埔寨工作' (The Family Said to Go to Practise! Two Sets of Males Fly to Cambodia to Work), Yahoo News, 17 August 2022.

60   For instance, see the warnings published by Indian embassies in Laos, Myanmar, Cambodia, and Thailand collected by Cyber Scam Monitor in its tweet dated 15 November 2022; for a warning published by the Kenya Embassy to Thailand, see Cyber Scam Monitor's tweet on 24 November 2022.

61   See, for instance, Yang Xi 杨曦, '16-24岁青年人失业率升至19.9% 国家统计

The resulting economic hardship pushed some to run unthinkable risks to find ways to cross borders and go to countries where they had never previously considered seeking employment. For instance, a Chinese restaurant owner who lost his business in 2021 told us:

> I didn't care if it was Cambodia or Colombia: I really needed a job because the whole family relies on my salary. The day after I accepted their offer, the company moved very quickly and bought me a ticket to Phnom Penh. This made me believe they were a legitimate entity with strong financial capability. However, when I got to the airport in Xiamen, I got stopped by the border police, and they kept telling me the job was fake. Of course, I had a moment of doubt, so I returned home and stayed for another two months.
>
> At that point, my children were starving. I knew the person who offered me the job for more than ten years, and I really could not afford to be unemployed anymore. So, when he asked me to go to a border city with transportation that he had arranged, I just went. To be honest, I cannot speak any language other than Chinese and have no idea of the geography; I thought where I went was Cambodia. It was when they forced me with a knife to take the small path and told me that I was in Vietnam that I realised I was being trafficked.

Large numbers of people have travelled to scam compounds in Myanmar and Laos across the long land border dividing the countries, escorted by professional smugglers, or snakeheads (蛇头 *shetou*). Although it is heavily policed, the sheer length of the border and its often rugged terrain make it impossible to stop determined traffickers moving people across. The main land routes from China to Cambodia travel through Vietnam and Laos, and chains of actors in each country shepherd recruits across borders, then transport them via a network of safe houses to their destination. Some travelling from Taiwan and China have travelled by sea, setting out in speedboats before being transferred to larger boats for the days-long journey, then handed off to smaller boats again closer to the Cambodian coast.

局：加大对年轻人就业帮扶政策措施力度' (The Unemployment Rate for Young People Aged 16 to 24 Has Risen to 19.9 per cent. National Bureau of Statistics: Increase the Intensity of Employment Support Policies and Measures for Young People), 人民网 (People's Net), 15 August 2022.

These sea routes are well known to the Chinese authorities. While the country's extensive coastline is challenging to monitor, the Chinese police have executed a number of major trafficking busts in the past few years. For instance, in November 2021 the Entry-Exit Frontier Inspection Bureau of Guangxi Province smashed a large cross-border smuggling gang suspected of organising Chinese citizens' illegal departure by sea in order to engage in criminal activities abroad.[62] Investigators found a speedboat picking people up in batches and taking them to a cargo ship: seventy-nine people were found below deck, originating from fifteen provinces around China. Over the following year, 108 connected suspects were arrested. Investigations found the gang behind the smuggling operation was not only working with overseas snakeheads, but also performed recruitment, disseminating ads over social media for well-paid overseas jobs. Investigators tracked financial flows linked to the group and during 2022 seized computers and mobile phones, leading to the arrest of gang leaders and recruiters. Sixty-nine people were eventually fined and sentenced to jail terms from nine months to eight years.

Two of our interviewees, a young couple, told us the story of how they were trafficked to Sihanoukville by sea:

> That day, two of our friends asked us to go out at sea to fish. We had already done that before, so we trusted them even though we realised that there were people we didn't know on the boat. They told us they were friends. However, after they sailed for a long time and showed no intention of stopping, we started to panic and asked them where we were going. They refused to answer until we reached a bigger boat. Those friends then pushed us onto the new boat, and people with guns immediately surrounded us. They forced us to stay below deck for seven or eight days until we reached Sihanoukville. We were so scared that they would throw us into the sea that we were completely obedient. We know they have been using the same port for parking the smuggling boat for months because later we met another couple, and they were smuggled the same way and arrived in exactly the same location.

This dangerous route made international headlines in September 2022, when a boat smuggling forty-one Chinese nationals sank off the coast of

---

62   On this case, see '突袭! 108人落网' (Raid! 108 People Were Arrested), 澎湃 (The Paper), 9 April 2023.

Sihanoukville, causing the death of at least eleven people.[63] According to survivor testimonies, the group had left Guangzhou, in China's Guangdong province, by speedboat on 11 September; six days later, on 17 September, they had boarded a second boat, accompanied by two Cambodian guides.[64] Conditions on the trip had been harrowing. On 22 September, as they encountered heavy seas and the boat started to flounder, another boat came to pick up the Cambodian guides but left the others to their fate. The stories collected by journalists in the wake of the tragedy repeated the usual refrain: the survivors had been left unemployed by the pandemic and were desperate, then someone had come along promising them employment.[65]

An Increasingly Diverse Workforce

As we put the final touches to this book in late 2024, we are witnessing some concerning developments in the recruitment strategies of scam operations. First, as the crackdown on online scams and related activities has intensified in mainland China, scam businesses are increasingly reluctant to let their hard-acquired workforce go. According to a police officer involved in investigating online scam cases in Gansu province who has been quoted by Chinese media, the crackdown means that the cost of recruiting personnel has increased from tens of thousands of yuan to hundreds of thousands: 'Once they fall into the hands of a fraud gang, they will not let these people go home easily unless they earn their money back with interest.'[66]

Second, as the industry has grown it has diversified its targets, which in turn has increased the need to find workers from a range of countries. As we mentioned earlier in the book, international organisations have recorded people of over forty nationalities trapped in Southeast Asia's scam compounds.[67] We ourselves have witnessed how the industry today

63   Reuters, '7 Bodies of Cambodia Boat Sinking Victims Found on Vietnam Beach', *South China Morning Post*, 30 September 2022.

64   'Hopes Fade for 23 Chinese Nationals, Missing after Boat Sank off Remote Cambodian Island, as Dramatic New Video Shows Rescue Attempts', *Khmer Times*, 24 September 2022.

65   Ibid.

66   Hu Weijie 胡伟杰 and Cui Jiaqi 崔嘉琪, '境外诈骗, 回国亨受?' (Commit Fraud Overseas and Return Home to Enjoy?), 新华网 (Xinhua), 12 June 2023.

67   United Nations Office on Drugs and Crime (UNODC), 'Casinos, Cyber Fraud,

is less reliant on Chinese workers and has become more diverse, with more survivors hailing from farther away. Thousands of Indonesian and Vietnamese workers are present in scam operations across the region, targeting their compatriots back home with online gambling promotion and scams. Individuals from Malaysia, the Philippines, Laos, and Myanmar are also present, as well as people from South Asia and Africa. While some countries have been proactive and determined in trying to assist citizens trapped in the compounds, others have shown a disappointing lack of concern. As the workforce further diversifies, people from further afield may not even have an embassy in the country where they end up, making assistance all the harder to find.

Third, as the adult population in China and other Southeast Asian countries becomes more aware of the existence of the scam compounds and the ways people get tricked into them, younger people are increasingly likely to fall victim to the industry. Cases of minors from the region tricked into scam operations are on the increase. The 2023 report on efforts to tackle the industry published by China's Supreme People's Procuratorate, referred to earlier in the book, noted that the number of minors prosecuted in connection to online fraud was just 1 per cent of the total.[68] This represented a 68 per cent increase on the previous year, however, and examples of minors being lured or trafficked abound in the Chinese press. In March 2023, a Shanghai media outlet covered the case of a fifteen-year-old boy from Sichuan province who had been missing for a month after crossing into Myanmar for a promised 'high-paying job'.[69] In the same month, Chinese media also widely reported the story of four students from a vocational school in Hefei, Anhui province.[70] In May, Along, an anonymous Chinese blogger who has made a name for himself in covering these issues, reported that he had received a request from a

and Trafficking in Persons for Forced Criminality in Southeast Asia', UNODC website, September 2023, p. 10.

68   '检察机关打击治理电信网络诈骗及其关联犯罪工作情况 (2023年)' (State of the Prosecutors' Efforts to Combat Telecommunication and Online Fraud and Related Offences (2023)), Supreme People's Procuratorate website, 30 November 2023.

69   '四川15岁少年失联：家属称系被骗至缅甸，警方已介入' (A 15-Year-Old Boy from Sichuan Disappeared: His Family Said He Was Deceived into Myanmar and the Police Have Intervened), 澎湃 (The Paper), 23 March 2023.

70   '偷渡缅甸的4名合肥学生安全回国，缅甸警方：经网友引诱出境' (Four Hefei Students Who Entered Myanmar Clandestinely Returned Home Safely. Myanmar Police: They Were Lured out of the Country by an Internet Friend), 大众网 (Dazhongwang), 21 March 2023.

Chinese family to help find their sixteen-year-old son who was missing in northern Myanmar.[71]

In 2024, we ourselves came across several disturbing cases involving minors trafficked to Southeast Asia. One of them, a fifteen-year-old girl from Yunnan province, was introduced to a man through a childhood friend. Even though he was fully aware of her youth, the man pursued a romantic relationship with the girl and eventually convinced her to travel to his workplace, in Laos's Golden Triangle. Blindly in love, she agreed to go to a city near the border with Vietnam, where someone picked her up. Having never been outside China, the girl believed she was heading to Laos; only after days of travel did she realise that she had been brought to Cambodia. Once in Sihanoukville, she received help from an unexpected quarter: her snakehead. Upon hearing that the plan was to bring her to a notorious compound further down the Cambodian coast and having realised her young age, the man contacted the bosses at another compound in the vicinity, who agreed to pay US$7,000 to redeem the girl from the scammers who claimed to have bought her. Such help was not selfless, as the girl would soon learn when one of the men attempted to take advantage of her. Only the intervention of a Chinese businessman in Cambodia, who was known for helping people escape from the compounds, got her out of this ordeal.

All we have discussed so far allows us to draw a couple of important conclusions. One is that the variety of channels into the online scam industry reflects the diversity of the people who end up ensnared by it. While once dominated by ethnic Chinese people, the workforce of the online scam compounds is now becoming increasingly diverse in terms of country of provenance, skills, age, and gender. This means that any attempt to sketch a profile of the typical victim of forced criminality in the industry is likely to be an oversimplification. As we have seen in the Introduction, many observers have adopted a narrative that 'cyber slaves' are generally better educated and more skilled than traditional victims of modern slavery. But official data and our own surveys show that many survivors from mainland China – the backbone of the industry for many years – are young, with a relatively low level of education, and most often from disadvantaged

---

71   Along 阿龙, '四川16岁少年被骗佤邦诈骗园区，有人知道他在哪里吗？' (A 16-Year-Old Boy in Sichuan Was Cheated into a Fraud Park in Wa State: Does Anyone Know Where He Is?), 阿龙闯荡记 (Along's Adventures), 3 May 2023, mp.weixin. qq.com/s/fwqL93nKDk3WMRIc0vRApw.

backgrounds. The truth is that, thanks to advancements in the technology available to scam operators, the industry attracts and relies on all sorts of people, and there is no such thing as a typical victim.

This brings us to another uncomfortable conclusion about current prevention strategies, which are largely based on raising public awareness about the industry. It is true that, as knowledge of the scam compounds spreads due to increasing media coverage and government-led awareness-raising efforts, recruitment is becoming harder than it was for scam operators. On the other hand, as the lingering economic impacts of the COVID-19 pandemic – which, in many cases, have occurred on top of decades of neoliberal and predatory economic policies – have left behind a legacy of widespread immiseration, many, especially those from younger generations, are likely to continue experiencing limited employment prospects and to remain prime targets. Recruitment dynamics might shift over time, with operators adjusting the balance of coercion versus rewards in order to attract their staff, but as long as viable alternatives remain scarce, people will remain vulnerable to the lure of the industry.

3

Inside the Scam Compounds

Allen had never left his hometown in China before, but he was young and wanted to see the world, so when someone he knew offered him a position at a Chinese restaurant in Sihanoukville he jumped at it. It did not matter to him that the COVID-19 pandemic was then at its height, making travel complicated, nor had he any qualms about quitting his job. Little did he know that this would be the beginning of a six-month ordeal that would see him detained and tortured in one of the Cambodian city's scam compounds. This was how Allen described the place to us:

> The compound is huge, and you need a special pass to get in and get out. Every building is occupied by a scam company, and some companies share canteens. In the building where I was, the gate was guarded by two security guards armed with guns and electric batons, and you had to swipe your card to enter. There are some small supermarkets and restaurants on the ground floor, while the first floor is a large open space that could potentially accommodate hundreds of people. The second floor is the training room for newcomers. The third and fourth floors are occupied by scam rooms [诈骗专用房 zhapian zhuanyongfang], each one of which is dedicated to a different country or a specific type of scam, such as pig butchering, impersonating law enforcement, and so on. The fifth floor and those above it are dormitories.

To restrict the mobility of a large portion of their inhabitants, most scam compounds are structured as complex self-contained communities. A single compound is usually overseen by a property manager (物业 *wuye*) and contains numerous scam companies, shared canteens, brothels, clubhouses, clinics, pharmacies, and services of all sorts, ranging from restaurants to hair salons. Where compounds are attached to licensed public-facing casinos, online workers are kept separate and do not mix with casino staff, remaining generally invisible to the public. The smaller operations often look like standard apartment buildings with unusually strict security measures, such as high walls with barbed wire and guards posted at gates, to prevent people from escaping as much as to stop unauthorised people from entering.

Although they are not always formally registered as such, scam operators are often referred to as companies (or, more specifically, online investment companies, 网投公司 *wangtou gongsi*), which is why in this book we often adopt this terminology. Testimony from our interviews revealed that these companies are structured like many other business entities, including departments dedicated to human resources (狗人事 *gourenshi*) and operations (that is, scams or 狗推 *tuigou*). They also often include teams responsible for logistical support (后勤 *houqin*), to take care of the basic tasks that make running scam operations possible, such as formatting the phones and computers used for the scams, and liaising with outside actors and contractors. While structure and operations will differ across companies, and there may be overlaps between the different roles, the general picture elaborated below was recounted to us by several of our interviewees.

Human Resources

According to one of our interviewees, a man who voluntarily chose to work for a scam company in Sihanoukville, managers in human resources departments tend to have close ties with the owners of the business or are professionals recruited through formal channels. These managers can enter and exit the compounds freely. Our informant believed most of them are aware of the illegal nature of the industry they operate in but often compartmentalise, holding on to the belief that their part of the work is unrelated to the crimes that are committed all around them. Their main task is to help the company to recruit staff and to offload workers who cause trouble or perform badly to other companies. For this, they often receive a base salary, with bonuses of varying amounts per worker acquired.[1] They are also the ones behind the mass of recruitment ads posted on social media platforms and in charge of liaising with social media influencers, brokers, and smugglers to recruit potential workers.

The human resources departments are also responsible for the daily management of those working in the scam company. According to a Chinese law enforcement officer we spoke with, later confirmed by two other interviewees, if a worker runs away, human resources managers are held responsible to recoup what the fugitive supposedly owes to the company. These fees begin to accrue when a worker is bought from another company. Employees are told they must work until the fee paid for them has been reached and, even in cases where people enter a compound willingly, they are generally bound to work for a specific period. In one example reported in the Myanmar press, a scam worker in Shwe Kokko in Kayin State explained how he signed a six-month contract with a salary of THB25,000 per month (roughly US$725).[2] If he were to break the contract, he would have to pay a fee equal to his salary for the remaining time. For example, if he were to quit after two months, he would have to pay THB100,000 for the outstanding four months. These fees often become part of the ransom that is demanded in exchange for a worker's freedom, although the relevant figures are often arbitrarily inflated. To minimise the risk that employees will try to leave, human resources managers prefer workers who willingly choose to sign contracts. For those who need persuading, managers promise generous compensation and rewards (see below). Indeed, many of our interviewees reported that human resources managers were very friendly, at least at the beginning.

After providing an initial assessment of each newcomer's skills on basic matters such as typing and communication (including their capacity to flirt), human resources managers usually collaborate with managers in the scam department to train the new recruits on scam strategies for several weeks. Allen had to take more than eight hours of classes per day for a couple of months on how to conduct pig-butchering scams. According to his testimony, trainers would randomly check whether recruits had

1   See, for instance, Danielle Keeton-Olsen and Lam Nguyen, 'How Cambodia's Scam Mills Reel in New "Cyber Slave" Workers', Rest of World, 10 November 2022.

2   'A Day in the Life of a Shwe Kokko Scammer', Frontier Myanmar, 1 June 2023.

learned what they were supposed to, and if they did not receive an adequate answer, would mete out punishments such as frog jumps or running up and down stairs multiple times. Such punishments continue after training is completed, and rescued workers have spoken of being made to stand out in the blistering sun of Myanmar for hours as punishment for failing to hit quotas.[3] There were also incentives. For instance, as he obeyed the rules and learned quickly, Allen was given back his personal phone after only one week.

Scam companies produce their own training materials, many of which can be found circulating in online messaging platforms such as Telegram. Apprentice scammers who cannot type quickly or are clumsy but willing to comply with the tasks required of them are asked to copy and paste from a predetermined script. One such phrase book was discovered by the Shenzhen police during a raid on a scam operation in 2018.[4] Entitled 'Phrases for Love, Friendship, and Gambling', the book features on its cover the slogan: 'Keep it strictly confidential; implement it strictly; happiness is achieved through effort!'[5] The content includes specific instructions on how to attract 'customers' and effectively convince them to invest. The book, which appears to have been updated quite often as the cover notes that this is 'version 3.23', includes chapters with titles such as 'Chatting Skills', 'How to Make People Happy through Conversation', and 'Great Opening Lines'. It also features some 'tips':

1. Chatting seems easy but to conduct a good conversation is actually very difficult. It requires us to have strong flexibility when facing different types of customers. We need to improve our logical thinking and increase our knowledge. Our personal experience might limit the conversation, but we need to make an effort and consult other colleagues.
2. You need to make the customers feel happy and comfortable during your conversation. You can politely refuse unreasonable requests from

---

3   Yohana Belinda, 'How an Ojek Driver Became Entangled in a Thai "Pig Butchering" Scam, Pt. 1', *Jakarta Post*, 26 January 2023.

4   '看过《恋爱秘籍》，你会发现"心上人"可能是抠脚大汉 …' (After Reading 'Cheats of Love', You Will Find That Your 'Sweetheart' May Be a Big Guy Who Picks His Feet …), 搜狐 (Sohu), 29 June 2018.

5   Incidentally, the last sentence is a catchphrase associated with Xi Jinping. See '幸福都是奋斗出来的' (Happiness Is Achieved through Effort), 百度百科 (Baidu Baike).

the customer, but the goal is to create dependency. You have to make him feel empty if you do not text him back.

3. At the beginning, you must show your feminine characteristics such as gentleness, supportiveness, empathy, etcetera. Show solicitude whenever it is appropriate, make him fall for you. (For instance: do not drive after drinking; good morning, don't forget to wear more clothes since it is cold outside; remember to eat meals at regular times; take care of your health; etcetera.)

Scam companies have created diverse personas and strategies targeting people with different identities and sexual orientations. For instance, in 2019 the Weibo account of the Criminal Investigation Bureau of China's Ministry of Public Security published excerpts from another phrase book that included an appendix that focuses on exploring the 'characteristics' of gay people, 'leftover women' (剩女 *shengnü*, a common derogatory term that refers to women over thirty years of age who remain unmarried), and those who might be called incels in English (饥渴男 *jikenan*, literally 'hungry and thirsty men').[6] One common feature shared by these target groups is that they may be, or perceive themselves to be, socially marginalised, a factor which the manual encourages scammers to capitalise upon.

According to one of our interviewees who had been held in a scam compound in Sihanoukville, team leaders would punish trainees who made poor progress memorising scripts by forcing them to copy the contents of the handbook between ten and twenty times. A handwritten copy of a chapter entitled 'How to Start an Enticing Conversation' published by Chinese media read:

Do not use a simple emoji to open your conversation because it shows no sense of need from your side. Even though she is a cold fish, there is still a little girl in there.

If a girl shares many selfies with a peace gesture, you could open the conversation saying: 'You look so cute when you are doing the peace sign in your photos.' How can a girl say no to a guy who pays attention to details such as her poses?[7]

---

6 Weibo post by the Criminal Investigation Bureau of China's Ministry of Public Security, dated 23 May 2019, m.weibo.cn/status/4375089426171934.

7 '杀猪盘诈骗团伙话术本曝光 内容令人大开眼界' (The Story Book of the Pig-

After they are properly trained, most recruits are brought into the operations department. However, those people who are consistently more trouble than they are worth, due to inability or unwillingness to work, are either returned to their family in exchange for a substantial ransom or sold on to other companies that might still find a use for them. As we saw earlier in the book, there is a thriving market in the trade of these workers.

Whether workers are sold to another compound, pay a ransom to leave, or complete their contract period, the human resources department will facilitate or coerce them into signing an employee separation agreement detailing their payout and compensation (赔付 *peifu*). Far from being moot, this signature – along with the existence of a contract stipulated upon arrival – has significant implications for survivors in that it makes it even more difficult for them to be acknowledged as victims of human trafficking. These contracts are often interpreted as proof of their consensual labour relationship with the scam company, with the result that any subsequent complaint can be reframed as an ordinary labour dispute – a narrative that local authorities, as we have seen, are often eager to adopt. Additionally, human resources managers will confiscate or wipe workers' phones to ensure that no evidence of the scam company is retained or shared, along with other evidence that might confirm they were deceived or coerced.

It is worth noting that, rather than using their own human resources department, some scam operators outsource recruitment to agents (代理 *daili*). Each agent independently recruits through their own network and takes the responsibility for all associated costs, including transportation, accommodation, and food within the scam compound. According to an article in *China Prosecution Daily*, such agents can take up to 30 per cent of the profits their team generates for the company.[8]

Butchering Fraud Gang Was Exposed, and the Content Was Eye-Opening), 大性感 (Daxinggan), 23 April 2021, web.archive.org/web/20210620103808/https://www.daxinggan.com/archives/59784.

8   '还原境外电诈真相：一个"总代理"把几十名同乡引上犯罪路' (Restoring the Truth of Overseas Online Fraud: A "General Agent" Led Dozens of Fellow Villagers to Commit Crimes), 检察日报 (China Prosecution Daily), 14 November 2023.

Operations

With multiple rows of tables equipped with monitors and keyboards, in offices that look similar to call centres, the scam department is tasked with coordinating and conducting scam activities. According to a survivor testimony collected by Chinese-language media, the section of the Cambodian scam compound where this worker had been held used a three-level structure, with a clear division of labour: first, 'fishing' for targets; second, 'catching' the target and obtaining information; third, 'butchering' the target.[9] Figure 1 draws from information about a scam company in Myawaddy, Myanmar, recounted to us by a man who had worked there in 2022, and adds more detail to the hierarchy. At the top sits the head of department (狗庄 *gouzhuang*), who monitors the overall activities of the division. Under them are the core managers (主管 *zhuguan*); in this case eleven people were in charge of managing team leaders, motivating employees, teaching scam techniques, and tracking important targets (so-called customers, or 客户 *kehu*). Next are team leaders (组长 *zuzhang*), who in this case totalled thirty-eight people, each in charge of teams of seven to nine. These team leaders were responsible for training newly recruited scammers, enforcing discipline, and tracking possible targets. Finally, at the very bottom are the scammers (狗推 *goutui*, or 菠菜 *bocai*).

Newly trained workers are assigned different tasks. If they do not show much aptitude for scamming, they may be asked to do activities that do not require strong interpersonal skills. For example, one of the lowest-level jobs is to send out thousands of messages to cell phone and messenger accounts. Any who reply along the lines of 'I think you have the wrong number' will receive a follow-up message from the scammers, who try to initiate a conversation. Those who engage are marked as potential targets and passed on to more capable upstream scam workers. In operations targeting Chinese people, new workers may be assigned the role of cultivating WeChat (养微信 *yang weixin*), an important and ongoing task. Due to strict regulatory rules, WeChat and QQ accounts that frequently post gambling or fake investment information, or are simply suspicious, are blocked. To avoid being blocked, each account must be actively used

---

9 '出逃者讲述电诈园区的日与夜：囚禁、套路和自救' (A Fugitive Tells the Day and Night of the Scam Zone: Captivity, Routines, and Self-Help), 红旗新闻 (Red Flag News), 21 June 2023.

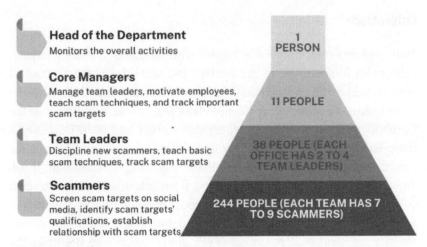

Figure 1: Structure of a scam department, based on the real case of a scam company in Myawaddy, Myanmar, in 2022.
Source: The authors

for more than half a year and several 'friends' have to verify the user. Scam companies therefore set up special teams to use the accounts daily, so that they appear legitimate.

A significant volume of personal information, comprising sensitive details including names, contact information, residential addresses, and other private data, is actively traded on platforms such as Telegram. This information is used for more targeted fraud. In these lists, individuals are categorised by their background, including factors that might impact the scammers' approach, such as pregnancy, international-student status, and their business type and size, among others. Based on such details, scammers refine their approach, employing tailored scripts and speech patterns to maximise the efficiency of their strategy (we will discuss this in more detail below). According to some of our informants, scam work is often divided into heavenly scams (天推 *tiantui*) and earthly scams (地推 *ditui*) depending on whether scammers have access to such a list. Those that already have a list of contacts are conducting the former; those engaged in the latter must search out and develop their own client base via the bulk messages described above, or by approaching people on social media, dating apps, and other platforms.

Other Units within the Compound

While the two key departments discussed above are at the core of the scam companies, these operations depend on other units or teams that take care of other supporting or logistical tasks, including so-called phone-brushing (刷机 *shuaji* – resetting and reprogramming phones), equipment maintenance, and IT support. Property managers also play an important role in ensuring that everything runs smoothly. They are responsible for taking care of the day-to-day management of the compound, and deal with attracting tenants, collecting rents, and maintenance issues related to the buildings and grounds. Property managers recruit and oversee local staff, such as security guards and cleaners, and deal with the authorities, in terms of both meeting official requirements for business operations, as well as liaising informally with their contacts in local state bodies and law enforcement.

In larger scam compounds, there is also a wide range of services that are run at the compound level. These include canteens, clubs, and other businesses managed by *cainong* (菜农, literally 'vegetable farmers'). These spaces can be rented out to business operators, and posts can be found online advertising units for rent in scam and online gambling compounds.[10] In many cases, however, these *cainong* are relatives or friends of the owners of the compound or scam company, and can take advantage of the labour of the people trapped in the compounds. For instance, because of his poor performance, one of our interviewees, a Chinese man, was assigned to work as a kitchen hand in a restaurant inside the compound in Sihanoukville where he was trapped. When he asked the owner of the business to help him escape, he was reported to the boss of one of the companies within the compounds, who turned out to be a relative of the restaurant owner. This resulted in the man being locked in a small room and tortured for three days.

The clubs in the compounds are staffed by young women who provide sexual services to managers and scammers as a reward for good

---

10 See for example this post on a popular Chinese-language forum in Cambodia, advertising a 'business for rent in a prime location' suitable for a restaurant, bar, KTV, or other type of business, located at Lixin Harbour City, which it describes as 'the safest online investment area', with 30,000 housed there and in surrounding compounds: '西港黄金旺铺招租' (Sihanoukville Gold Shop for Rent), 柬单网 (Jiandanwang), 8 August 2018, web.archive.org/web/20240105160849/https://share.58cam.link/wap/thread/view-thread/tid/390470.

performance. Many media reports have documented that women have been tricked into this work after being offered bar, karaoke, or customer service jobs, and, like those coerced into scam work, they face violence if they refuse. These women are extremely difficult to contact so it is often very challenging for anti-trafficking groups to locate and help them.

Remote Illicit Infrastructure

As we mentioned in the Introduction, scam operations would not be able to operate if it were not for the existence of an 'illicit infrastructure' composed of people with IT expertise available for remote hire.[11] These external service providers develop and maintain the apps and platforms used to perpetrate scams or, most commonly, simply rent out or sell existing tools that they have already created and provide training on how to use them. Ads for these services can easily be found in message groups, especially on Telegram, where people offer these types of services, as well as troves of personal data, and hacking tools.

Even relatively basic tools can wreak a lot of damage. For instance, in early 2024 hundreds of thousands of people in the United States received text messages saying that the United States Postal Service was trying to deliver a parcel but needed more details, including their credit card number, with links to websites where the information could be entered.[12] A US-based security researcher whose wife had been targeted managed to find the name of a Chinese-language Telegram account and channel, which appeared to be selling a kit scammers could easily use to create fake websites. Eventually, he also tracked down the group behind it and found that their targets had entered 438,669 unique credit card numbers into 1,133 domains used by the scammers.

In another example illustrating the importance of this illicit infrastructure, in October 2023, cybercrime experts at the United Kingdom's Revenue and Customs helped to bring down a 'prolific fraudster' in Indonesia who sold scamming software to criminals across the world.[13] In one

11   Ben Collier, Richard Clayton, Alice Hutchings, and Daniel Thomas, 'Cybercrime Is (Often) Boring: Infrastructure and Alienation in a Deviant Subculture', *British Journal of Criminology* no. 61, 2021, pp. 1407–23.

12   Matt Burgess, 'USPS Text Scammers Duped His Wife, so He Hacked Their Operation', *Wired*, 8 August 2024.

13   'HMRC Collaborates with International Agencies to Arrest Cybercriminal Selling Website Phishing Kits', UKNIP 247, 30 October 2023.

year, the thirty-six-year-old man had posted over 3,000 ads promoting his illegal spoofing software on social media channels and crime forums for up to US$250. The software mimicked genuine webpages of major international businesses and institutions, including banks, tax authorities, and government webpages in the United Kingdom, Canada, United States, and Australia. In August 2023, Chinese police arrested a gang in Shandong province that had illegally registered and sold 3 million WeChat IDs in batches for telecommunication fraud and online gambling, making over CN¥10 million in profits (US$1.4 million).[14] They did so by taking advantage of contacts within communication companies in China, mid-level managers who had allegedly registered over 80 million phone numbers for the purpose.

Illicit infrastructure is also essential for money laundering. Anthropologist Chen Yanyu has documented in detail the complex process that unfolds after someone takes the bait and invests in a fake financial product.[15] First, scam operators will coach them to invest money, claiming they have privileged information that enables them to predict trends, but also warning that the investment will be profitable only if it is made within a short window of time. Once the target agrees to proceed, the scam operator will send a message to a Telegram group run by a third party acting as a guarantor (the so-called gateway, 通道 *tongdao*), explaining the currency and amount of money about to be remitted by the scam target. Brokers at the gateway will then send the details to another group, known as motorcades (车队 *chedui*) to procure the details of a bank account or crypto wallet to send the money to. After the motorcade group provides the account information, the gateway will send the appropriate details and trading rules back to the scam operator. Money launderers call this type of matchmaking transaction (撮合交易 *cuohe jiaoyi*) process 'moving bricks' (搬砖 *banzhuan*).

Gateway companies play a fundamental role in ensuring that transactions work smoothly in an illicit market where legal rules do not apply and there is no recourse in case something goes wrong. Considering the size of the market, they can make huge profits in the process. For instance,

---

14   '运营商内鬼被抓！搞8000万个手机号注册账号售卖，用于电信诈骗、网络赌博 …' (The Operator's Insider Was Caught! Sell 80 Million Registered Mobile Phone Accounts for Telecom Fraud and Online Gambling …), 每日经济新闻 (Everyday Economic News), 22 August 2023.

15   Chen Yanyu, 'Moving Bricks: Money-Laundering Practices in the Online Scam Industry', *Global China Pulse* 3(1), 2024.

in July 2024, UK blockchain analytics firm Elliptic revealed that one such company based in Cambodia had transactions to the value of at least US$11 billion going through their platforms.[16] Later reports identified even larger amounts flowing through this platform, with its marketplace handling over US$49 billion in crypto transactions between 2021 and 2024. Although not all of these transactions could be linked to criminal activity, the blockchain analysis firm Chainalysis stated the platform was used by 'a wide array of illicit and risky counterparties'.[17]

Motorcades are equally essential. They are involved in what are known as running-points platforms (跑分平台 *paofen pingtai*), that is, complex networks of people selling or loaning their bank accounts and security keys, national ID, and mobile phone numbers, and setting up or allowing their businesses to be used to receive illicit funds.[18] These motorcades build and curate portfolios of such details, often paying other parties paltry amounts for the use of their accounts, which are then used as mules for illicit transactions.

The use of mule bank accounts is extensive, and police actions in various countries have targeted people who have opened accounts and sold their information to organised crime groups.[19] In 2020, Chinese officials estimated that the support structure for facilitating money flows to and from overseas scams and gambling employed 5 to 6 million people, and in the first nine months of that year alone laundered over US$150 billion.[20] A 2023 report from *South China Morning Post* covered the arrest of over 450 people, mostly for allowing criminal syndicates to use their accounts to

---

16   'Huione Guarantee: The Multi-Billion Dollar Marketplace Used by Online Scammers', Elliptic Research website, 10 July 2024.

17   '2024 Crypto Crime Mid-year Update Part 2: China-Based CSAM and Cybercrime Networks on the Rise, Pig Butchering Scams Remain Lucrative', Chainalysis website, 29 August 2024.

18   'China's Crackdown on Online Fraud Continues', Cyber Scam Monitor, 30 June 2023.

19   For example, in January 2023, Singapore police announced it had arrested 411 people suspected of being scammers or money mules linked to 1,500 cases costing victims US$13 million: 'Police Investigate 411 Scammers and Money Mules in Island-Wide Enforcement Operation', Singapore Police Force website, 2 January 2023. In October 2023, Thailand's Anti–Money Laundering Office estimated 200,000 to 500,000 bank accounts could be mule accounts; see 'Up to 500k Bank Accounts Possibly Used for Fraud', *Bangkok Post*, 19 October 2023.

20   Zhang Yuzhe and Denise Jia, 'Cover Story: How Illegal Online Gambling Launders $153 Billion from China', Caixin Global, 21 December 2020.

move money.[21] A Hong Kong police official said the backgrounds of the suspects included 'jobless residents, people from low-income families, students and domestic helpers', indicating that fraud groups target people likely to be in need of extra cash – creating another group of complicit actors who in many cases are not hardened criminals but are driven to break the law by financial difficulties or simply taking the opportunity to make a quick buck.

In some cases, these mule account holders are professionals; in others, they are just people who have responded to ads on social media and are paid a small amount for handing over their information. In others again, the owners of mule accounts are victims themselves. Local media have documented how Myanmar migrant workers in Thailand have been forced by employers and agents to open bank accounts that were then used by others to launder money from illegal online gambling and other illicit sources.[22] In China, scam operators recruit individuals burdened with debt as mules by tricking them into borrowing from fraudulent 'lending institutions' set up specifically for the purpose.[23] Scammers promise these people a hassle-free process, then convince them that they can expedite the loan-approval process by enhancing their bank statement. This involves depositing and withdrawing funds provided by the scammers into the bank account to create an illusion of stable income and reasonable expenses. The funds are then taken back by the scammers or sent elsewhere, with their origin obscured. It is easy for indebted individuals to fall for this as the process promises hassle-free credit and does not require them to spend any additional money, but we also heard of several cases in which scammers not only recovered their own money but also wiped out the bank accounts entirely.

As widespread as the practice of using such proxies is, one Taiwanese district prosecutor told media that these mule accounts are still not

---

21   Clifford Lo, 'Hong Kong Police Arrest 458 People in 17-Day Crackdown on Money Laundering Syndicates Handling HK$470 Million in Crime Proceeds', *South China Morning Post*, 25 August 2023.

22   'Myanmar Workers Face Jail in Thailand over Bank Account Abuses', Dawei Watch, 22 July 2024.

23   Wuhan Anti-Telecom and Online Fraud Centre, '"恐吓+诱骗""刷流水+洗钱", 拿捏不住就别轻易网贷' (Intimidation + Deception and Bank Statement Enhancement + Money Laundering, Don't Easily Take Online Loans if You Can't Handle Them), Tibet Autonomous Region Internet Illegal and Bad Information Reporting Centre website, 2 August 2023.

adequate to move the tremendous volume of revenue generated through online scams, and fraud groups have therefore begun colluding with bank staff.[24] In 2023, this led to raids on seven branches of major Taiwanese banks. With the volume of revenues linked to scams increasing, when traditional banks are used, transfers are likely to exceed limits. This raises problems for victims when they attempt to transfer money, and also for fraudsters when they seek to move their ill-gotten gains. By colluding with bank workers, fraud rings can raise the transfer limits on specific accounts to avoid transfers being blocked or attracting attention.

In many cases, scam and online gambling operators require their targets or players to pay using cryptocurrencies. These are sent to wallets which mix the proceeds with digital currency from other sources, then transfer them through chains of digital wallets to obscure their source.[25] Although challenging to trace, investigators have been able to track digital wallets linked to online scams in Southeast Asia, and law enforcement agencies in several countries, including the United States, have taken action in several cases. For example, in December 2023, US authorities seized half a million dollars held in the Binance account of a Chinese national based in Thailand. He had been subject to a Reuters investigation identifying a crypto account in his name that had received over US$90 million, of which at least US$9.1 million was identified by a blockchain analysis firm as linked to pig-butchering scams.[26]

---

24   Pei-hua Lu, Chan-Hua Yang, and Wenrong Chang, 'Taiwan's White-Collar Fraud Infiltrating Banks', *Commonwealth Magazine*, 30 November 2023.

25   In particular, several sources have reported on how the cryptocurrency Tether is commonly used for laundering money from scam operations. See, for instance, 'Pig Butchering Scams: What the Data Shows', TRM Labs website, 7 February 2023; Zeke Faux, *Number Go Up: Inside Crypto's Wild Rise and Staggering Fall*, Currency, New York, 2023, chs 18 and 19. In November 2023, following an investigation by the United States Department of Justice, Tether voluntarily froze approximately US$225 million in USDT tokens in wallets linked to an international human trafficking syndicate in Southeast Asia responsible for a global pig-butchering romance scam; see 'Following Investigations by Tether, OKX, and the U.S. Department of Justice, Tether Voluntarily Freezes 225M in Stolen USDT Linked to International Crime Syndicate', Tether website, 20 November 2023.

26   Tom Wilson and Poppy McPherson, 'U.S. Seizes Crypto Linked to Southeast Asian Investment Scam', Reuters, 13 December 2023.

Scam Techniques

The infrastructure set out above enables a wide range of scam techniques. During our interviews with former compound workers, we identified several common strategies. These were corroborated in media coverage from various countries and reports from state and law enforcement agencies around the world, which also revealed other scam techniques that our interviewees were not exposed to.[27]

Pig butchering is an innovative type of scam at the intersection between traditional romance and investment frauds that emerged in the Sinophone world in the early 2010s.[28] There are numerous variations on this technique, but generally it involves scammers – the pig butchers – posing as wealthy, attractive people. They create fake profiles and find their targets (what they refer to as 'pigs') on social media, via wrong-number messages, or using illegally procured datasets.[29] After striking up a conversation, they gradually work to gain the trust of their targets by seeming caring, sending gifts, and, in some cases, interacting with them for weeks or even months. These two early stages of the scam are commonly known as 'finding pigs' (找猪 *zhaozhu*) and 'feeding pigs' (喂猪 *weizhu*). Once the target is on the hook, the 'pig-grooming period' (养猪时期 *yangzhu shiqi*) begins. At that point, the scammers recommend fake investment products or steer their targets to cryptocurrency or foreign-exchange investment platforms

---

27   See, for instance, China's Ministry of Public Security's Bureau of Criminal Investigation, '公安部刑侦局公布：十类高发电信网络诈骗手段及防骗提醒' (Release by the Criminal Investigation Bureau of the Ministry of Public Security: Ten Types of Common Telecommunication and Online Scam and Relevant Protection Strategies), Public Security Bureau of Chongqing City website, 10 April 2019; China Anti-Fraud Centre, '防范电信网络诈骗宣传手册' (Handbook to Guard against Telecommunication and Online Fraud), HSBC website, 2021.

28   See Cross, 'Romance Baiting, Cryptorom and "Pig Butchering"'; Fangzhou Wang and Xiaoli Zhou, 'Persuasive Schemes for Financial Exploitation in Online Romance Scam: An Anatomy on *Sha Zhu Pan* (杀猪盘) in China', *Victims and Offenders* 18(5), 2022, pp. 915–42.

29   Researchers have criticised the propagation and validation of the term 'pig butchering', an animal metaphor, in light of its implications for the dehumanisation of victims of online fraud across various discourses. For an example of this critique, see Jack M. Whittaker, Suleman Lazarus, Taidgh Corcoran, 'Are Fraud Victims Nothing More Than Animals? Critiquing the Propagation of "Pig Butchering" (Sha Zhu Pan, 杀猪盘)', *Journal of Economic Criminology* no. 3, 2024, pp. 1–8. While we agree with this critique, we chose to report the language used by the scammers to highlight exactly the process of dehumanisation that takes place in these types of fraud.

that often mimic legitimate sites and apps but are in fact controlled by them. The targets will be shown how to invest and, through the scammer-controlled app, they will see their investment steadily increase in value. Often the scammers will allow them to withdraw early gains to build their confidence, then will coach them into making increasingly large investments. 'Pig-butchering time' (杀猪时刻 *shazhu shike*) generally comes when victims want to cash out or start to get suspicious. When that happens, scammers lock them out of the app and vanish.

A variation is the so-called task scam – known in Chinese as 'fish butchering' (杀鱼盘 *shayupan*).[30] Scammers posing as recruitment consultants contact potential targets through social media platforms or mass messages, then explain to their marks how to earn commissions by submitting pre-written reviews on spoof websites for a fee. The victims are told they are doing this to increase website traffic for the company. Again, to build confidence, these reviewers earn some money at the beginning. After trust is established, the scammer then introduces the idea of earning higher rates by aggregating reviews and appraisals of valuable products in sets they call merges. To be able to publish these merges, users are asked to pay a deposit in cryptocurrency. What they are not told is that the terms and conditions include a tiered membership rewards system that binds the amount of commissions they can receive to their level of investment in the scheme. To access the commissions, they are required to upgrade their membership level – which can cost thousands of dollars, but in the eyes of the target can unlock the large amounts of commission they have accumulated. Eventually, it becomes clear to victims they are locked in a cycle of paying in to cash out; many walk away, leaving the scammers to claim whatever the targets have invested.

A third type of scam is more elaborate and involves the impersonation of law enforcement officials. One day, a friend of one of the authors, then a young Chinese graduate student in the United Kingdom, received a call from someone claiming to be from the Chinese Embassy in London. She was told that she was in trouble and the Shanghai Municipal Public Security Bureau wanted her cooperation. Surprised and wary, she checked the number that had popped up on her screen and it matched that of the embassy. The call was transferred to a second person claiming to be from

---

30   This type of scam is discussed in detail in Andy Brown, Valentina Casulli, and Ling Li, 'Task Scams: A New Wave of Online Fraud', Humanity Research Consultancy briefing, October 2023.

the Shanghai police, who informed her that she was among the suspects in a serious case involving forged passports and money laundering. He warned her not to notify her family or friends because anyone who knew about the situation could be accused of harbouring a criminal. Soon after, another alleged police officer contacted her on Telegram, sent her what he claimed was an arrest warrant, and video-called her to collect her testimony. For almost two months, she had to report her thoughts and activities to this fake officer every day. Once she was completely subjugated and had become dependent on him, he told her that if she wanted to prove her innocence, she had to transfer CN¥500,000 (roughly US$72,500) to a designated 'safe account' so that the police could escrow the money until all suspicions about her were cleared. After she did so, the scammers vanished.

Another acquaintance of one of the authors, a Chinese woman living in Cambodia, received a phone call in 2022 claiming to be from a special investigation department of the Chinese police. He knew her name and previous place of work, and claimed to know where she lived. He informed her he was in Cambodia on a special investigation and wanted her to answer his questions. Being wary of such scams, she requested his identification number, which he declined to provide. She asked him to tell her what department he was from so she could call back herself, to which he responded by warning her not to make things complicated for herself. When she continued to insist that he share his identification number, he eventually hung up. Police and state agencies in Australia, Canada, and the United States have issued warnings to Chinese communities in their countries, as have various Chinese embassies.[31] Although this type of scam appears to have initially targeted mostly Chinese nationals, it is now being reported all across Asia and has resulted in millions of dollars of losses to victims.

Other types of scams are more straightforward, such as luring often inexperienced investors to put their money into buying or exchanging

---

31 For an example of warnings from Canadian police, see 'Public Advisory: Fraud Alert, Toronto Chinese Community Targeted in Fraud Scheme', Toronto Police Service website, 13 December 2023; from the Australian government, see 'National Anti-Scam Centre Warns of Spike in Scams Threatening Chinese Students', National Anti-Scam Centre website, 21 September 2023; from the United States, see 'Chinese Police Imposters Incorporate Aggressive Tactics to Target U.S.-Based Chinese Community', Federal Bureau of Investigation website, 3 January 2024; and from the Chinese Embassy in the United Kingdom, see 'Chinese Embassy in UK Warns of Telecom Fraud', Xinhua, 9 June 2018.

cryptocurrencies on phony platforms by offering artificially high rates. These scams can involve one-on-one interaction between the scammer and victim or may be more sophisticated. In some cases, scammers create an online chat group and tell its members – which include accomplices of the scammer – about a promising fake investment. Again, they often let the target earn some profits to build trust and then, once they have extracted as much as they can (or when a member grows suspicious), they lock out the target and keep the funds. This is an age-old scam, but previously would have been executed in person, through things such as investment seminars, where scam team members would scatter themselves among a group of curious potential investors. Now it has gone online.

Another way to extract funds is by flooding dating apps with fake profiles that are used to induce targets into participating in intimate chats or video calls, then threatening to share the screenshots or videos with relatives and friends or to upload them online. This type of scam hit headlines in August and September 2023, when Indonesia deported 153 Chinese nationals caught up in raids of operations that extorted over Rp20 billion (Indonesian rupiah, equivalent to US$1.3 million) from victims.[32] These operators had lured their targets into compromising situations, encouraging them to expose themselves in chats and video calls; the scammers then blackmailed them with threats that they would publish the images and videos.

While many of the scams that have featured in media reports involve significant amounts of money, sometimes in the hundreds of thousands of dollars, and can involve months of grooming the victims, many operators instead implement small-scale scams at large volume. For example, a 2023 article from *Nikkei Asia* reported that over a third of surveyed Filipinos said they had been victims of e-commerce scams.[33] This involves offering low-priced products on mainstream online marketplaces to entice victims. After a purchase is made, the seller contacts them via a chat app and persuades them to make their payment via a separate digital payment platform, but never sends the purchased item. The same survey found a

---

32   Criminal Investigation Bureau of the Ministry of Public Security, '153名跨境裸聊敲诈的犯罪嫌疑人从印度尼西亚被押解回国' (153 Criminal Suspects Who Committed Cross-Border Nude Chat Blackmail Escorted Back from Indonesia), *China Daily*, 21 September 2023.

33   Ramon Royandoyan, 'Philippines Emerges as Asia's Epicenter for Online Shopping Scams', *Nikkei Asia*, 18 December 2023.

high prevalence of the scam across East and Southeast Asia. In Singapore, parcel-delivery phishing scams have risen exponentially. Here the victims receive a text or email saying they need to make an additional payment for the delivery of items they have bought.[34] When they click the enclosed link, they are sent to a site mimicking a real delivery company. After they enter their personal data, the information is then harvested and used to make unauthorised transactions using their bank or credit card details.

Predatory loan scams have also become pervasive, and feature commonly in Indian media reports, although the method has spread globally. Scammers attract victims by placing ads on social media for easy, no-questions-asked loans. In some cases, the loans are straightforward scams, with victims told to first deposit some funds before their loan can be cleared – money that the scammers simply steal. In others, even after repayment, the fake loan companies continue to harass and intimidate people with demands for exorbitant fees and interest they never agreed to. A more sophisticated version that received increased attention in 2023 instructed loan applicants to download an app that secretly accesses the data on the victim's phone, harvesting photos and other personal information. Compromising material is used to blackmail the target, and scammers also harass the contacts of the original victim, claiming they were listed as guarantors for the loan.[35]

In addition to these more common types of scams, the industry is constantly evolving in unexpected and sometimes truly bizarre ways. For instance, in February 2023, the Hong Kong police issued an alert about a fraud targeting animal lovers.[36] A vice president of a fashion company was duped out of digital currency worth HK$6 million (roughly US$770,000) after responding to an online post about the sale of a kitten by someone in Thailand. She was first asked to pay delivery costs and some other fees, then later told the kitten had died during delivery, but that she would be entitled to insurance compensation. Asked to pay an administration fee up front in cryptocurrency, the woman subsequently transferred

---

34   Carmen Sin, 'Victims Lose $560,000 to Parcel Delivery Phishing Scams in 11 Months This Year: Police', *Straits Times*, 19 December 2023.

35   Devesh K. Pandey, 'Enforcement Directorate Chargesheet Recounts Misery of Victims in Chinese Loan App Case', *The Hindu*, 18 March 2023; Catherine Ngai, 'Predatory Lending Apps Claim Victims across Asia', Bloomberg, 13 December 2023.

36   Clifford Lo, 'Hong Kong Fashion Company Vice-President Loses HK$6 Million in Bogus Kitten Sale, Prompting Police Alert against Online Pet Scams', *South China Morning Post*, 7 February 2023.

HK$6 million worth of Bitcoin across forty transactions before she realised that she had been scammed.

Another peculiar technique targets overseas Chinese students. As in the police-impersonation scams described above, in this case, after convincing their targets that they or their family are under investigation for financial crimes, the scammers persuade the students to stage their own kidnapping and document it with photos and videos. They then use these materials to extort ransoms from their family members. For example, in October 2022, two students in their early twenties living in Singapore were contacted by fake police officers who said they were under investigation for spreading misinformation, one about monkeypox and the second about COVID-19 in Guangdong.[37] They were told they would have to assist in investigations and instructed to travel to Cambodia to conduct 'missions'. Once in Phnom Penh, they were told to stay in separate hotels, cease all communication with family and friends, and record videos of themselves pretending to be kidnapped for the purpose of scam education and investigations. The fake kidnapping videos they filmed were sent to their parents with ransom demands totalling CN¥2.8 million (US$390,000). Cambodian police located them before any ransoms were paid.

Occasionally, these scams develop into authentic kidnappings. In one truly horrific case that occurred in the summer of 2023, a twenty-three-year-old Chinese student in New Zealand received a call claiming to be from the Chinese consulate. She was told the consulate had received a complaint that someone was sending harassing texts from a phone number registered with her ID.[38] She was instructed to file a police report and the call transferred to the 'Chinese police department'. The fake police asked for her ID number and told her that there was a file on her and she was also being investigated in a transnational money-laundering case. The scammers sent various official-looking documents to her, including an arrest warrant. She was told that she could avoid investigation if she cooperated as a witness and travelled to Cambodia to identify the people involved.

---

37   Ian Cheng, 'Two Victims of Staged Kidnap Scams Found in Cambodia after Travelling from Singapore', Channel News Asia, 28 October 2022.

38   For the following account, see '中国女孩在柬埔寨遭绑架后获救' (Chinese Girl Rescued after Getting Kidnapped in Cambodia), 西港日记 (Sihanoukville Diary), 17 August 2023, mp.weixin.qq.com/s/R2wyviAOrQ2nubERegvcuw; '发声: 我是被骗子骗到柬埔寨，不是网恋！' (Voice: I Was Tricked into Cambodia by a Scammer, It Was Not Online Dating!), 西港日记 (Sihanoukville Diary), 18 August 2023, mp.weixin.qq.com/s/fdFH_-RNzAJMNqCO9VeeoQ.

After arriving in Cambodia, she was taken to Bavet, near the border with Vietnam. Once there, she was tortured, with a video showing in graphic detail how she was tied and beaten, then shocked with an electric baton, before, during, and after having a finger cut off with a meat cleaver. The kidnappers then sent the videos to her family to extract a ransom and threatened to sell her to people in Myanmar if they did not pay, where her kidney would be extracted for sale. A few days later, her family sought support from Chinese nationals in Cambodia, who reported the case to the Sihanoukville provincial military police. The police organised a rescue operation that eventually led to her release.

Whatever approach is used, skilled scammers are adept at capitalising on the emotions of their victims. As one of our interviewees, a former scammer from mainland China, told us:

> The scam is about finding the weaknesses of a human being. The goal is to find out what you need the most and fill that gap. It can be about your work, business, family life, or anything about your desire for emotional support. The scammers take their time to record your life, everything, every detail about your life. For instance, they will mark down that your marriage is not happy, or there is a problem in your business, or you have a bad relationship with your family; there is always some problem in one's life, and they will take time to identify it, analyse it and provide the support accordingly. Then they gain your trust.

Perversely, as the news of cyber slavery has become mainstream, we have even heard about scammers who, when confronted, have drawn on the stories of trafficking and forced labour in the industry to exact the target's sympathy and financial support. In one remarkable instance reported by the Chinese media in 2024, a forty-year-old Chinese woman fell in love with a Chinese scammer who claimed to be detained by a scamming ring in Myanmar.[39] Even though she had been cheated out of CN¥100,000 (US$14,000) by him, she believed his story that he was being forced to meet a quota. She assisted him in moving funds extracted from other scam victims to help him earn enough to secure his release, so that they could be together in China. A subsequent victim filed a complaint and the woman's account details were identified during the police investigation,

39   Yating Yang, 'China Woman Falls for Scammer despite Losing US$14,000, Helps in Fraud so Can Be Together', *South China Morning Post*, 12 June 2024.

leading to her being charged, put on trial, and given a suspended prison sentence.

While the techniques used by scammers are already highly sophisticated, the emergence and accessibility of new artificial intelligence (AI) tools is creating more opportunities. In the last couple of years, media reports have documented scams facilitated by deep-fake technology, where software is used to mimic the face or voice of someone known to the scam target. In August 2023, police in Hong Kong arrested six people for using an AI face filter to apply for online loans from financial institutions using information from stolen identity cards.[40] In mainland China, similar tricks have been used to dupe people into lending money, using face and voice filters to masquerade as a friend of the target.[41] Additionally, generative AI tools can make it easier to send out phishing messages using duplicate or fabricated backstories and trails of digital activity to make fake identities seem more believable.[42] According to the head of the financial and economic crime unit at Europol, with large language tools such as ChatGPT, 'you can write thousands of tailored messages in different languages with different targets, different stories, and you can do that with your laptop from wherever'.[43]

The Compound Labour Regime

How much of the wealth extracted by scam operations trickles down to frontline scammers? According to our interviewees and various other accounts, scammers earn a commission for each successful fraud, usually a percentage of the total sum. Bonuses can be lucrative, and the rules are often posted in public areas as a reminder to all staff. In a scam company located in Mong Pawk, Myanmar, in late 2019 recruits were guaranteed a basic salary of CN¥5,000 (roughly US$720) during their first month of training.[44] From the second month, the basic salary fell to CN¥3,000

40   Clifford Lo, 'Hong Kong Police Arrest 6 in Crackdown on Fraud Syndicate Using AI Deepfake Technology to Apply for Loans', *South China Morning Post*, 25 August 2023.

41   Yang Zekun, 'Authorities Warn Public against AI Fraud', *China Daily*, 26 May 2023.

42   Quinn Owen, 'How AI Can Fuel Financial Scams Online, According to Industry Experts', ABC News, 12 October 2023.

43   Lisa O'Carroll, 'AI Fuelling Dating and Social Media Fraud, EU Police Agency Says', *Guardian*, 9 January 2024.

44   He Chengbo 何承波, '被骗到缅甸搞诈骗 我从枪口下死里逃生' (Tricked to Go

(US$430), supplemented by performance bonuses based on the number of new targets each worker attracted. For instance, if a scammer could get eight new customers and generate more than CN¥100,000 the same month, their basic salary would be raised by CN¥1,000 (US$145) and they would also receive a 9 per cent performance bonus the following month. A staff member who managed to generate between CN¥30,000 (US$4,400) and CN¥50,000 (US$7,300) in monthly revenue could get a 7 per cent commission; for between CN¥400,000 (US$58,000) and CN¥500,000 (US$72,600) of revenue, the bonus would be 12 per cent. Anyone generating CN¥500,000 in a month was promised the latest iPhone as a reward.

One of our interviewees who had been held at a compound in Poipet, a town on Cambodia's border with Thailand, provided us with further insights into how the internal promotion process inside a scam company works:

> A person is promoted by his team leader if he shows his ability to earn money. Normally, [as a team leader] he would be in charge of a team of nine people; his goal is to teach the team members and improve their performance. They will set performance targets, which he has to report to the manager above him. A good example goes like this: 'This month, I will scam CN¥5 million, and I will ensure I reach this target for two or three consecutive months.' This way, the company will see your leadership ability and your talent in scamming. And after he continues to bring profits to the company for months, he can be promoted from team leader to core manager (主管 zhuguan) and then from core manager to managing director (经理 jingli). And this position is almost the highest you can reach; if you are a managing director, you will be in a team with a real boss.

Even though these commission schemes and bonuses might seem appealing on the surface, the labour process inside scam companies is designed to exploit first-line workers ruthlessly. Regardless of whether they join the operation willingly or unwillingly, these workers' relationship with the company invariably begins with a debt, as their company will have paid

to Myanmar to Do Scams, I Narrowly Escaped at Gunpoint), 新浪新闻 (sina.com), 23 August 2021.

money to bring them to the compound (for instance, for flight tickets, visas, and work permits, or to pay brokers and smugglers). Although the basic monthly salary can go some way to repaying these debts, the managers of the scam operations levy additional charges for accommodation, food, water, and all sorts of other expenses.

In one example covered by Chinese media, a company in Cambodia charged workers for everything they used inside: toilets, chairs, keyboards, the portion of floor they occupied and 'consumed', and even the 'seaside air' they breathed.[45] Consequently, no matter how long they work, their debts can continue to grow, and full repayment is often impossible unless they are consistently able to land high-value scams. To make things worse, the price of basic goods in the compounds can be three to four times what they would cost outside. For instance, one interviewee who worked in a compound in Sihanoukville told us a small bottle of Coca-Cola was sold for US$5 (five times the regular price), and the compound clinic charged US$50 for paracetamol tablets. Where workers are not allowed to leave the compound, they are effectively a captive market.

The work is extremely demanding. One interviewee recounted that in the compound where he worked in Sihanoukville, workers had to deal simultaneously with more than ten phones from seven a.m. to midnight or, if the targets were in the United States, from one a.m. to four p.m. There were no breaks during office hours and no weekends off. A militaristic style of management often pervades the compounds. Every team would begin and end their shift by shouting aloud slogans such as: 'With a click and clack on a keyboard, you earn ten thousand taels of gold, get deposits from customers, and obtain another high salary' (键盘一响，黄金万两，客户入金，再创高薪 *jianpan yi xiang, huangjin wan liang, kehu rujin, zai chuang gaoxin*); or: 'Two hands typing on a keyboard can earn you billions in gold; work hard on marketing and you will win. Go for it!' (双手敲出亿万金，推销要拼才会赢，加油! *shuangshou qiaochu yi wan jin, tuixiao yao pin cai hui ying, jia you!*).[46] Frontline workers must report to the team leader for permission to take toilet breaks and are punished if they take too long. One person who spent time as a scammer in a compound in Wa State, Myanmar, told us that in his company each person was given

---

45   For this bill, see Zhou Tutu 周土土, '柬埔寨"严打": 4天捣毁63个窝点, 诈骗团伙连夜转移' ('Strike Hard' in Cambodia: 63 Dens Were Destroyed in Four Days, and the Fraud Gangs Moved Overnight), 腾讯 (qq.com), 1 November 2022.

46   These slogans were mentioned by one of our interviewees.

three toilet and cigarette breaks per day, each of which could not exceed eight minutes.

Workers are under intense pressure to meet their performance indicators. Tao, a young Chinese man who spent time working as a scammer in a compound in Kandal province, Cambodia, told us that every month he had to generate US$10,000 in revenue for the company, and every day had to attract two or three new targets and send out a certain number of messages. At the end of the month, a celebratory gathering was held to announce what had been achieved in the previous four weeks. On these occasions, 'excellent-employee certificates' (优秀员工证书 *youxiu yuangong zhengshu*) were awarded to the workers who had met their quotas and scammed the highest amounts. These model employees then took the stage to share their experiences, discuss their chats with targets, and brag about how victims walked into their traps, went bankrupt, or even committed suicide after realising they had been scammed. 'It was like a method of brainwashing, to push our moral limits,' Tao said. He continued: 'The excellent employee would get monetary awards, promotions, and, sometimes, the privilege to temporarily exit the compound. If you were one of them, they would buy you good food and take you to gamble or even pay for prostitutes to let you taste their rich life.' For those who could not meet targets, life became a nightmare. They were beaten, subjected to electric shocks, and in some cases even had their nails extracted. 'We could hear the screams continuing until midnight,' Tao said. 'They made sure you understand that you do not want to be the next one to end up in the punishment room.'

Sleeping arrangements also reflect this need to enforce discipline, with all workers being accommodated on the premises. Allen's room in his compound in Sihanoukville had four bunk beds, and the curtains were permanently drawn so that people could not see in from the outside. To prevent escapes, windows were barred (a common situation in scam compounds, and one of their recognisable features), and the company combined staff from different hierarchical levels in one room. Allen, for instance, shared a room with a deputy manager, a team leader, and two staff members who had voluntarily joined the enterprise. 'They watched us newcomers day and night. There was basically no hope to get out,' he told us. To prevent workers from bonding with each other, they are also often moved from one room to another. Only money can buy some rare comfort. One of our interviewees told us that he was charged US$800 a month for a private room for his pregnant partner, who had been trafficked with him to a compound in Sihanoukville.

While compounds host people from several different countries and ethnic backgrounds, cross-ethnic solidarity appears to be scarce. Just like in other workplaces in Southeast Asia, where Chinese and local workers toil side by side but often eat, sleep, and socialise separately, the managers of the compounds skilfully exploit ethnic and linguistic cleavages among their staff.[47] In many cases, workers of different ethnicity are kept in different offices and dormitories. Even when they are able to mingle, language barriers, racial prejudice, and suspicion often keep them apart. In our interviews, former scam workers from mainland China repeatedly expressed jealousy towards their foreign counterparts because the latter could count on support from their embassies and governments while the Chinese felt abandoned. They also envied other groups which they perceived to be more cohesive and united. For instance, Liu, in his early thirties, spent eight months trapped in a compound in Poipet, Cambodia. He told us:

There were many people from Thailand in our compound, and we were targeting customers in the United States. We didn't communicate with the Thais because we didn't know whether they were monitoring us. Maybe they were scared of us too because the boss was Chinese, and they thought that all of us had come there voluntarily.

One day, the manager locked all the Chinese staff inside in dark rooms and told us to keep quiet. My team leader told me it was because the Thai government had forced the police in Poipet to cooperate with a raid on our compound. Although it was a raid, they had an agreement to take away only Thai nationals.

Even though we could hear people running all around, we could not even shout for help because the security guards were with us with their batons. We were so jealous of them getting rescued that easily. You know, I feel Chinese were less united in the compound. If you talked with anyone, they would tell you stories about how Vietnamese staff organised among themselves and escaped together. This would never happen to us Chinese workers: we don't trust anyone around us, and we don't know how to work as a team.

47   See, for instance, Ivan Franceschini, 'As Far Apart as Earth and Sky: A Survey of Chinese and Cambodian Construction Workers in Sihanoukville', *Critical Asian Studies* 52(4), 2020, pp. 512–29.

Paradoxes

This chapter has shown how scam compounds and the companies located therein are highly hierarchical structures based on a complex division of labour, which points to the corporatisation process that the online scam industry has gone through in the past few years. It has also exposed the blatant paradox that underpins these operations. On the one hand, scam groups take advantage of the latest technological advancements that a global illicit infrastructure has to offer, in terms of dedicated toolkits, AI tools, automatic translation software, phony crypto exchange platforms, and so on. This allows them to perpetrate increasingly sophisticated scams. On the other, scams remain grounded in the extreme exploitation of a workforce achieved through a combination of control over workers' living arrangements, militaristic discipline, and enticement through bonuses and rewards, all enhanced through segregation along ethnic and other divisions. Ultimately, it is the work of many toiling in conditions akin to modern slavery that sustains the industry.

This type of labour is at the same time visible and invisible.[48] Even though they are subjected to heavy surveillance and control, the victims of forced criminality in the online scam industry remain constantly connected to the outside world through the internet. Many are even able to contact their families and friends. In some cases, they beg for help; in others, they lie about their situation, knowing that there is very little that people back home could do to help, and that if they told them the whole story they would just feel powerless and miserable. In this sense, they are very visible. At the same time, they are invisible in at least two regards. First, while their online presence continues to be manifest, they are physically hidden behind the walls of the compounds, out of reach of those who are trying to help them. Second, their whole personality is annihilated in the scam process, cancelled under the layers of obfuscation required by the emotional and identity work involved, where men pretend to be women, the poor act as if they were rich, and people communicate in languages of which they may not know a word.

The compounds themselves embody this paradoxical relationship between seen and unseen. While supposedly secretive and well-guarded

---

48 For a thorough discussion of the concept of 'invisible work', see Erin Hatton, 'Mechanisms of Invisibility: Rethinking the Concept of Invisible Work', *Work, Employment and Society* 31(2), 2017, pp. 336–51.

crime bases, most of these structures stick out like sore thumbs in the surrounding landscape. Many of the scam compounds have been mapped, and many of those who pay attention to this sector, including law enforcement, nongovernmental organisations, and local journalists, know where they are. Yet these facilities continue to operate as areas of exception, as if shrouded in a cloak of invisibility. This is the paradox to which we turn in the next chapter, where we explain the role of the local and transnational players and enablers who make the existence of the compounds possible.

4

Players and Enablers

COVID-19 upended his life. William used to own a successful halal food import-export company in China, but during the pandemic business rapidly slowed down until he had no choice but to close shop. Desperate, he started looking for new opportunities until, in March 2021, he landed a job interview in Dubai. Excited about the possibility of a fresh start, he jumped at the chance:

> My primary goal was to get a new contract, but I also wanted to earn some pocket money before returning to China. I saw a job offer as marketing manager on 58 Tongcheng [a Chinese job-hunting website], and that suited me well since I knew the Dubai market, had a relevant education and professional background, and could speak good English. We did an online interview that was very professional, and it really felt authentic to me. Once I got there, the human resources person was friendly and informed me immediately that I would get the position. Several days later, the same person told me that she had sent a car to pick me up for a health check before the hiring process moved forward. I didn't have any doubts until I realised the car was heading directly into the desert.

When William asked what was going on, his escorts threatened him with a gun and forced him to hand over his phones and passport. After a while, they reached a compound:

We were in the middle of nowhere, and there was a real community inside the compound. It included fifty to sixty companies, and they shared a dormitory and jointly covered the property management fee (物业费 *wuyefei*). This fee was for protection: if the police came to inspect, the companies would get notified one day before and hide all the people who had been sold like me. They even paid locals around the compound to watch out for escapees. One roommate ran away and met someone who pretended to be a police officer. This person sent him back to the company and I never saw him again.

William's captors told him that if he wanted to regain his freedom, he would have to come up with US$40,000. If he tried to escape, they would kill him and bury his body in the desert.

William's experience speaks to some common characteristics of the scam compounds. First, it highlights the intrinsic international mobility of these operations. William soon discovered that the operation that had bought him had relocated from the Philippines to the United Arab Emirates barely one month earlier, to avoid law enforcement. As we have seen, this remarkable ability to relocate rapidly, sometimes transnationally, is a notable characteristic of the industry. Second, it shows that the compounds are not self-contained, insulated realities; rather, they integrate into their local environments, including the surrounding communities, which start to supply daily necessities and services. For instance, to get local people on side and keep them from reporting the compounds to the police, the managers provided job opportunities to them, but largely kept them separate from workers trafficked from China and elsewhere. In addition, money flowed to local businesses, with restaurants inside and around the compound charging above-market rates as they were marketing to affluent managers from the scam operations.

As noted earlier, rather than simply being parasitic alien entities that take root in otherwise healthy host societies, scam compounds become deeply embedded in their surroundings and can exist only thanks to the tolerance, cooperation, or even active support of a broad range of stakeholders, both local and foreign. The compound ecosystem carves out a place within pre-existing political and societal conditions, exploiting unregulated spaces and weak law enforcement, identifying and collaborating with corrupt actors, and partnering with local elites. At the same time, they embed themselves in local communities to varying degrees and, while bringing a host of social problems, can generate employment and revenues in the surrounding areas.

Entrepreneurs and Transnational Crime Groups

In Southeast Asia, scam operations are overwhelmingly run by ethnic Chinese groups. Malaysian, Myanmar, Indonesian, Thai, and Vietnamese groups are also well established, frequently, but not always, operating in partnership with Chinese counterparts. There are also reports of South Korean and Japanese actors involved in the regional cybercrime ecosystem. Individual scam operations can vary in size, and the groups behind them include smaller crime groups as well as larger networks that may operate across various sites. However, behind the facilities that host these operations – the scam compounds at the centre of this book – are often large, well-resourced companies led by entrepreneurs from across East and Southeast Asia who have planted themselves into the local business landscape. In some cases, they have built up a presence in the country over years, often obtaining local citizenship (in some cases alongside multiple other citizenships). Acquiring additional nationalities is not necessarily illegal and is not uncommon. It can help foreigners avoid restrictions on owning land and remove the need for a company to include a local shareholder, where the law requires this. Yet this is also used by people seeking to evade scrutiny by law enforcement, aid the movement of illicit funds, and increase their ability to travel around the region and beyond, visa free.

Several companies that have been linked to the regional scam industry have developed large, diversified business portfolios. One such entity is the Zhengheng Group. Zhengheng's founder has been in Cambodia for over fifteen years, starting in online services and human resources, and later expanding in to property development. He became a Cambodian citizen in 2016. Zhengheng developed the Long Bay real estate project in Koh Kong, which is a secure site known to house online operations linked to numerous rescues of people who have been detained there and forced to perpetrate scams.[1] Although, again, this compound appears well protected

---

1   See for example Danielle Keeton-Olsen and Mech Dara, 'Rescue Reveals Scam Compound at Koh Kong's UDG', Voice of Democracy, 24 August 2022.

from local law enforcement actions, in December 2023 the company was sanctioned by the United Kingdom 'because it has facilitated or provided support for or obtained benefit from activity that violates the right to be free from slavery, not to be held in servitude or required to perform forced or compulsory labour' by forcing people to work as scammers.[2] When confronted with the reports of criminal activity taking place at the Long Bay site, Zhengheng has denied responsibility and blamed the criminal activity on a company that leases part of the property.[3]

Another example of these transplanted elites who have been implicated in the industry is Dong Lecheng. Born in Yunnan province, close to the border with Myanmar, Dong was a major player within the frontier economy. Coming from the Jingpo subset of the Kachin ethnic group, he had strong connections spanning the border areas, and built his wealth and political connections upon this foundation.[4] He had had brushes with the law in China for his involvement in casinos in Myanmar that facilitated both in-person and telephone gambling for Chinese clients, and was later implicated in corruption cases involving various Yunnan provincial officials, yet he always managed to emerge largely unscathed.[5]

Obtaining Cambodian citizenship in 2014, Dong was the architect of the Jinshui compound in Sihanoukville, although when it became famous for the online scam and gambling operations it housed, he claimed he had already sold the buildings.[6] His company website published several photos of personal meetings at the home of former prime minister Hun Sen, and on one occasion he paid for a chartered plane to take the latter to a UN meeting. He also hosted delegations at the Yunnan headquarters of his company on more than one occasion, with Cambodian senators, ministers, police, and military figures joining, along with their family members. Dong became less visible as controversy around his projects

2   HM Treasury, Office of Financial Sanctions Implementation, 'Financial Sanctions Notice: Global Human Rights', UK government website, 8 December 2023.

3   Jack Brook and Runn Sreydeth, 'Company Linked to Scams, Human Trafficking Ousted from Cambodia Property Awards', CamboJA website, 26 July 2024.

4   Elanah Uretsky, 'Tracing China's HIV Epidemic: A Story of Cross-Border Geopolitics', University of British Columbia's Open Collections, 2017.

5   Liu Pei 刘培 and Lü Yinling 吕银玲, '"边境王"帝国垮塌 豪车豹子号车牌覆盖"云N11111"到"云N99999"' (The Empire of the 'Border King' Collapsed. The Licence Plates of the Leopard Luxury Cars Went from 'Yun N11111' to 'Yun N99999'), 风暴眼 (Eye of the Storm), 16 December 2022; see also 'Jinshui', Cyber Scam Monitor, updated 23 April 2023, web.archive.org/web/20230704093225/https://cyberscammonitor.net/profile/jinshui.

6   'Jinshui', Cyber Scam Monitor.

grew, and by late 2022, reports were circulating that his empire was in financial trouble.[7] He was sanctioned by the United Kingdom in 2023. In November 2023, Dong's Jingcheng Group posted a notice on its WeChat account stating that it had filed for bankruptcy, and soon after its account was deleted.[8] Whoever is currently in charge of it, at the time of writing in late 2024 the Jinshui compound remains active, and rumours about the takeover of various other projects previously linked to Dong were circulating.

She Zhijiang is another character who embedded himself in Southeast Asia. Born in China's Hunan province, She – who has gone by various aliases over the years – first built up his fortune in online gambling in the Philippines, then sought to expand to Cambodia and Myanmar.[9] In 2017, he received Cambodian citizenship and adopted a Cambodian name. He was at one point involved in the Long Bay project mentioned above, but his then business partner has said the relationship did not work out.[10] He is much better known for the work of his company, Yatai International Holding Group, which developed the infamous Yatai New City in Shwe Kokko, a village close to the scam hub of Myawaddy in Myanmar.

She's initial strategy was both to loop local powerbrokers into the development and to present the project as aligned with the strategies of the Chinese Party-State. He networked extensively, building his profile and appearing on magazine covers, and on a handful of occasions even attending events where high-level Chinese officials were present. In the case of the Yatai New City the strategy worked, and, with a company owned by the Kayin Border Guard Force taking a 20 per cent stake, construction of the project moved fast.[11] She was a consummate promoter of the project, and emblazoned it with the branding of China's Belt and Road Initiative (BRI), seeking to present it as a legitimate development and leading some to believe it had Chinese state backing. The project quickly became mired in controversy, however, initially with accusations that it was building

7   Liu and Lü, 'The Empire of the "Border King" Collapsed'.

8   Cyber Scam Monitor, tweet dated 24 November 2023.

9   Plato Cheng, 'Shwe Kokko Special Economic Zone/Yatai New City', People's Map of Global China, 18 August 2022.

10   Jared Ferrie, Martin Young, and Tobias Andersson Åkerblom, 'Gambling Tycoon's Partners Abandon Him as Extradition to China Looms', Organized Crime and Corruption Reporting Project website, 27 July 2023.

11   Naw Betty Han, 'Shwe Kokko: A Paradise for Chinese Investment', Frontier Myanmar, 5 September 2019.

beyond its approved boundaries and grabbing land from local people, and later that it was in fact a massive hub for online crime.[12]

With controversy around the project growing, the Chinese Embassy in Yangon attempted to address the reputational harm caused by the project, and issued a statement in 2020 saying it was 'a third-country investment and has nothing to do with the BRI'.[13] Very soon after, Chinese business news outlet Caixin reported that She was a fugitive and had been on the run since 2014.[14] Yatai vigorously denied these reports, but in August 2022 She was arrested in Thailand under a Chinese arrest warrant for operating illegal casinos, and at the time of writing in late 2024 he remained in a Thai jail, fighting his deportation back to China.[15] She was also included in the 2023 UK sanctions against cybercrime-linked actors and entities, alongside his business partners Saw Min Min Oo and Saw Chit Thu of the Kayin Border Guard Force. Despite all this, the Yatai New City compound continued to operate.

While some senior industry figures have risen to prominence, many remain unknown, and pinpointing bosses and key investors is extremely challenging. As Sheldon X. Zhang and Ko-lin Chin have written, a 'new generation of non-traditional Chinese criminals' has emerged over the past few decades, a cohort they describe as 'enterprising agents [who] have no identifiable organizations, no rigid structure, no clearly defined deviant norms and values'.[16] With hundreds of compounds scattered across multiple countries and varied geographies within those countries, it can be assumed that these types of actors have proliferated. Yet the involvement of people associated with triad groups has also been well documented, although it is unclear how expansive their role is across the industry. Two individuals in particular stand out: Wan Kuok-koi (whom we briefly encountered earlier in the book) and Alvin Chau.

---

12   Karen Peace Support Network, 'Gambling Away Our Lands: Naypyidaw's "Battle-field to Casinos" Strategy in Shwe Kokko', Progressive Voice Myanmar website, March 2020.

13   Embassy of the People's Republic of China in Myanmar, '中方支持缅方依法依规处理"亚太新城"问题' (China Supports Myanmar in Handling the 'Yatai New City' Issue in Accordance with Laws and Regulations), Huanqiu, 25 August 2020.

14   Tang Ailin, Fan Wenjun, Liang Shuting, and Han Wei, 'A Fugitive Chinese Busi-nessman's High-Profile Bet in Myanmar', Caixin, 27 October 2020.

15   AFP, 'Chinese Gambling Kingpin Taken into Custody in Bangkok', Bangkok Post, 13 August 2022.

16   Sheldon X. Zhang and Ko-lin Chin, 'The Declining Significance of Triad Societies in Transnational Illegal Activities: A Structural Deficiency Perspective', British Journal of Criminology 43(3), 2003, pp. 469–88, at p. 485.

Wan Kuok-koi, better known as Broken Tooth, is the former head of the Macau branch of the 14K triad. After serving more than fourteen years in prison, he emerged from jail in 2012 and focused his attention on building up connections and a portfolio of businesses in Southeast Asia. Broken Tooth's penchant for self-promotion has made him well known: a few years ago, he went as far as to produce an autobiographical movie, even though he was reportedly deeply unhappy with the result, which was insufficiently grandiose.[17] Via social media channels and local media, he has spent the last decade promoting various regional business ventures, including a line of beer, the launch of a new cryptocurrency that never materialised, and a groundbreaking development in Myanmar that would become the notorious Dongmei scam park.[18]

While the scope of Broken Tooth's role in the broader industry is uncertain, Dongmei Park remains operational, and several media reports, including a 2023 *New York Times* piece, have documented the brutal conditions within.[19] The alleged one-time protégé of Broken Tooth, Alvin Chau was also for a time linked to both online gaming and casino junkets operating in Cambodia and the Philippines, and he had ties to several actors in Cambodia with direct links to the scam compounds.[20] Chau was arrested in China in 2021 and later jailed for eighteen years for a host of offences related to illegal gambling and organised crime.[21]

Local Elites

The largest scam operations are generally those that have most effectively managed to develop connections with local elite power structures willing to act as their protective umbrellas. They may be major landowners who rent space to foreign developers, or joint-venture partners in

17   Federico Varese, *Mafia Life: Love, Death and Money at the Heart of Organised Crime*, Profile Books, London, 2018, pp. 137–40.

18   Justice for Myanmar, 'The Karen Border Guard Force/Karen National Army Criminal Business Network Exposed', Justice for Myanmar website, 22 May 2024.

19   Isabelle Qian, '7 Months inside an Online Scam Labor Camp', *New York Times*, 17 December 2023.

20   United Nations Office on Drugs and Crime (UNODC), 'Casinos, Money Laundering, Underground Banking, and Transnational Organized Crime in East and Southeast Asia: A Hidden and Accelerating Threat', UNODC website, January 2024.

21   Grace Tsoi, 'Alvin Chau: Macau Gambling Kingpin Jailed for 18 Years', BBC News, 18 January 2023.

the developments themselves. These linkages are sometimes identifiable in corporate documents, and when more informal links exist, investigators have been able to piece together evidence of relationships and fill in gaps through open-source intelligence methods, scouring company press releases, media reports, social media accounts, and other sources.

For instance, Cambodian senator Kok An has been connected to multiple compounds in Sihanoukville, one carrying the name of his Crown company brand, with security guards posted outside wearing uniforms with the logo of his water company emblazoned upon them.[22] He has also been linked to other known scam sites in Sihanoukville and, although he may not have formal connections to them, he was front and centre at the opening ceremonies for compounds that his late son-in-law, Rithy Samnang, and his brother, Rithy Raksmei, are closely tied to.[23] The *New York Times* heard from local police and officials that Senator Ly Yong Phat owned properties in Koh Kong where people were known to be held, and they found the same in northern Oddar Meanchey province.[24] In late 2023, the senator became a permanent member of the ruling Cambodian People's Party's Central Committee.[25] He was sanctioned in 2024 by the United States for his alleged links to human trafficking linked to the cyberfraud industry.[26] In Pursat, one of the largest compounds in the country was developed through a joint venture by Chinese investors and Try Pheap, a tycoon and former adviser to Cambodia's previous prime minister Hun Sen.[27] All of these compounds have avoided significant law enforcement action, and remain operational at the time of writing.

---

22   Mech Dara, Cindy Liu, and Danielle Keeton-Olsen, 'Victims Allege Sihanoukville Precincts with Ties to Major Businesses Are Sites of Scams, Torture, Detention', Voice of Democracy, 18 February 2022.

23   See 'Kaibo', Cyber Scam Monitor, 6 November 2022, web.archive.org/web/20230323150103/https://cyberscammonitor.net/profile/kaibo; and 'K99 Group Triumph City', Cyber Scam Monitor, 23 April 2023, web.archive.org/web/20230704093705/https://cyberscammonitor.net/profile/k99-group-triumph-city.

24   Sui-Lee Wee, 'They're Forced to Run Online Scams. Their Captors Are Untouchable', *New York Times*, 28 August 2023.

25   'CPP Further Elects 23 Permanent Members of the Central Committee', Fresh News, 10 December 2023.

26   Press release, 'Treasury Sanctions Cambodian Tycoon and Businesses Linked to Human Trafficking and Forced Labor in Furtherance of Cyber and Virtual Currency Scams', US Department of the Treasury, 12 September 2024.

27   Mech Dara and Cindy Liu, 'From Timber to Human Trafficking: Rescued Victims Allege Major Scam Operations in Tycoon's SEZ', Voice of Democracy, 17 November 2021.

The rise of illegal online industries in the Kokang Self-Administered Zone in northern Myanmar displays the role of local elite actors even more starkly. Under the rule of the Kokang Border Guard Force, there was little separating the zone's business, state, and military elites, which were effectively one and the same. As discussed in Chapter 1, the online industries ballooned in this area in the late 2010s, and local actors played a central role in their implementation. Although the latter rented space to foreign companies in their compounds and casino complexes, they also held direct ownership stakes in these operations. The four families who dominated the Kokang zone own and control the major conglomerates that operated its illicit industries, with executives and management holding important government positions, as well as senior roles in the police and military.[28] With the dominant business elites controlling the border, regulation, and law enforcement, and also having a well-armed militia on hand, a perfect environment existed for foreign scam operators to take root, although the status quo was turned upside down by the military offensive that erupted in the area in October 2023, leaving the industry in disarray, for the time being at least.

While the fates of those mentioned above have been mixed, where fortunes have suffered this has been largely due to external factors – international sanctions and arrest warrants, bankruptcy, and armed conflict – not because of the actions of law enforcement in the places where their criminal activities are actually located. While compound operators have supreme power within the confines of their operations, they cannot operate at scale without building relationships with local political and economic elites.

---

28   In December 2023, China issued arrest warrants for members of three of the four families. This included the Bai family: Bai Suocheng is former chairman of Kokang region; Bai Yingcang is the captain of a Kokang militia, deputy director of the Economic Development Bureau, and chairman of the Cangsheng Sci-Tech Park; and Bai Yinglan is chair of the Xinbaili Group. Three members of the Wei family were also subject to warrants: Wei Huairen, the head of a border battalion supervision committee; Wei Qingsong, a member of the same border committee; and Wei Rong, the chair of conglomerate Hengli Group. Finally, three members of the Liu family were pursued: Liu Zhengxiang, director of Kokang Urban Development Bureau and chair of Fulilai Group; Liu Jiguang, director of the Kokang Health Bureau and executive director of Fulilai Group; and Liu Zhengmao, general manager of Fulilai Group. In January 2024, six of the wanted individuals, including the heads of three of the Kokang crime families, were arrested by Myanmar authorities, handed to Chinese police, and put on chartered flights to China.

Local State Actors

The complicity of local state actors in the host countries is fundamental to ensure that scam compounds can be established and remain in operation. In Cambodia, the media have extensively reported on the inability or unwillingness of local law enforcement to police the compounds. At best the authorities have turned a blind eye to these operations, which, as we have seen, are often easily identifiable from outside, with their tall walls topped with razor wire, patrolled entry points, and barred windows. In many cases, confronting these operations may be too risky or challenging for local police and administrative authorities. Reporters asking local officers about well-known and often problematic compounds have often been told that these facilities effectively exist outside the law. When investigating the discovery of a body in 2022 at a hotel situated at the heart of a major compound in Sihanoukville, a local police officer told Voice of Democracy: 'These places don't allow us to go in ... When we get information, we investigate and question others.'[29] The previous year VoD had spoken with a commune chief responsible for an area in Cambodia's Pursat province where a huge online compound is located. Again, he was in the dark. Although he believed there to be as many as 2,000 people inside, he was quoted as saying: 'I do not know what they are doing, and I also have doubts about it too ... I do not know what kind of business they do to earn, because I do not see them going outside and they only stay inside the buildings. I have nothing to say.'[30]

Even after the Cambodian government announced its crackdown in 2022, officials reported that compound managers resisted their inspections. Four months after the announcement of the crackdown, the director general of the Department of Immigration said: 'There was non-cooperation, mostly at sites of illegality ... They did not allow us to go in, and when authorities arrived, they shut the door and stopped us from getting inside.'[31] Despite having the legal authority to conduct inspections, the department admitted it 'took a soft approach, understanding that the employers were investors', and due to the potentially serious consequences,

29   Mech Dara, 'Body Found Hanging in Sihanoukville's Alleged Slave-Compound Area', Voice of Democracy, 18 March 2022.

30   Mech Dara and Cindy Liu, 'From Timber to Human Trafficking: Rescued Victims Allege Major Scam Operations in Tycoon's SEZ', Voice of Democracy, 17 November 2021.

31   Mech Dara, 'Authorities Admit They Were "Soft" on Foreign-Labor Compounds', Voice of Democracy, 23 January 2023.

they would raid such operations only if they received instruction from 'the leaders'. When the *New York Times* investigated Cambodia's scam compounds in 2023, reporters visited two sites allegedly linked to the powerful ruling party senator Ly Yong Phat. They spoke with a senior police officer who said he was aware of what was going on in a major compound in Koh Kong province, and that many people had asked to be rescued. However, he said it was impossible to get inside without special permission from the Ministry of Interior because of who owned the property.[32]

While some officers and officials may genuinely be unable to take action against these criminal activities, even when they take place directly in front of them, there is also ample evidence indicating that others are enjoying the benefits of the industry. A common refrain in the coverage and testimonies of people who have escaped the compounds is that there is a direct line of communication between police and compound managers. In several cases, when reports reached the police, they immediately informed the compound managers, often giving them time to take countermeasures – including harming the people who were seeking rescue.[33] A property manager of a scam compound in Sihanoukville once openly boasted to us about this: 'After the crackdown, the authorities told us to install rescue hotlines inside the compound. Of course, we did – each building has one on the first floor, as you can see. But don't worry, the calls go directly to the police we have connections with.'

The consequences for people trapped inside are dramatic. One of our informants, a young man surnamed Li, was sold by a friend to the Jinshui compound in Sihanoukville in 2022. Having lived in Cambodia for some time, he knew what awaited him, and managed to contact a rescue team within a week. Team members immediately contacted a law enforcement officer in Sihanoukville, who then informed Li that the police would go to remove him from the compound the next day. When the time came, police officers showed up as planned. However, when Li asked them to retrieve his passport and personal phone from the company, they pretended not to understand his English and dragged him out of the compound. From there, they took Li directly to the immigration bureau, where another nightmare began:

---

32   Wee, 'They're Forced to Run Online Scams'.

33   See, for instance, Mech Dara and Andrew Haffner, 'A Friend's Journey Attempting Rescue from Alleged Slave Compound', Voice of Democracy, 24 May 2022; Keeton-Olsen and Dara, 'Rescue Reveals Scam Compound at Koh Kong's UDG'.

The immigration officers accused me of illegally entering the country because I didn't have a passport. I tried to explain that I was a victim, but they wouldn't listen.

Even worse, on the second day I saw the manager of the scam company waiting for me in the interrogation room. He shouted at me in Chinese that they would torture me so hard because they had to pay US$13,000 to get me back and said that he hoped I had enough money to pay off my life.

I begged the immigration officer to charge me with illegal immigration and let me stay in jail. But again, they pretended they could not understand me. They simply asked me to sign a document written in Khmer without giving me any explanation. I was forced to put my signature there and then leave with those scammers.

When Li was brought back to the scam company, he was beaten viciously while his captors filmed the whole process. They then sent the video to his family, demanding a ransom. When the family's money transfer fell short of the demanded amount, they stripped Li naked, hit him on the genitals, and locked him in a dark room for three days. Not only did the police fail to help, but they also exposed him to further violence and triggered yet another transfer. He was later sold to another compound, and again subjected to repeated violence. At that point, Li managed to get in touch with the police in his home province in China, who reached out to their counterparts in Cambodia to ask that they rescue him. However, as the situation dragged on and the torture continued unabated, he could not bear it any longer and decided to escape by himself. On the run, he arrived at a hospital and begged the doctors to help him find a car to Phnom Penh, but the staff were too scared of the scam companies and refused to assist. Eventually, he flagged down a car on the street and told the driver that he would pay him US$100 if he brought him to the capital.

On-the-ground reporting, again from VoD, exposed the role of provincial law enforcement in the case of a Taiwanese man held at the Long Bay compound in Koh Kong. In this case, the man's father travelled from Taiwan to the location where his son was held. Provincial police told him: 'If he wants to leave, he has to pay the money because he has not finished his work contract' – directly supporting the system of fees and forced labour we describe above, which is central to maintaining the compound workforce. The father later found out that hours after he spoke to the police, his son, who was still being held in the compound, was interrogated by his captors, who had somehow obtained photographs of documents that his father had given to the police earlier that day. He eventually negotiated a US$7,500 payment to extract his son, without police assistance.[34]

A 2022 ProPublica report observed a similar dynamic, with reporters recounting the story of a man they had spoken to; he had been held in a Sihanoukville compound and contacted the provincial governor over Facebook, who referred him to the police. Again, the compound managers were informed, and the man and his brother were forced to make videotaped confessions that they had not been trafficked or held against their will, before being sold.[35] Notably, in the *New York Times* article cited earlier, Thailand's then deputy national police chief told reporters of planned joint raids in Cambodia being derailed by their Cambodian counterparts.[36]

There is abundant evidence of Cambodian officials consorting with stakeholders of scam companies and compounds, and there is a trove of photographs circulating on the web and on social media of officials attending ground-breaking ceremonies, opening events, and parties, and standing alongside industry operators, including a few who have gone on to be arrested or left the country, and some who are subject to international arrest warrants. Companies linked to the scam compounds also frequently make cash and in-kind donations to local police and other government agencies. For instance, K99 Group, a gambling junket operator which owns properties that have been implicated in online scams and forced labour, has made considerable donations to government and security forces.[37] These included donations of vehicles and supplies to the national and provincial gendarmeries (which are involved in law enforcement operations targeting scam compounds) and the Sihanoukville city jail (which houses people arrested for crimes related to these compounds). The company has also made donations to the Cambodian Red Cross in Sihanoukville and at the national level.[38] Those linked to the compounds are active in donating to

34   Keeton-Olsen and Mech, 'Rescue Reveals Scam Compound at Koh Kong's UDG'.

35   Cezary Podkul, 'Human Trafficking's Newest Abuse: Forcing Victims into Cyber-scamming', ProPublica, 13 September 2022.

36   Wee, 'They're Forced to Run Online Scams'.

37   See, for instance, Cindy Liu and Jack Brook, 'Kidnapped, Beaten and Ransomed in Post-crackdown Sihanoukville', CamboJA News, 1 May 2023.

38   See 'K99 Group Triumph City', Cyber Scam Monitor, updated on 23 April 2023,

humanitarian causes, and the Cambodian Red Cross, which is chaired by Bun Rany, the wife of former prime minister Hun Sen, is a common vehicle for this type of transaction.[39]

These dynamics are not unique to Cambodia. In the Philippines, immigration officials have been censured for facilitating travel in and out of the country by people who are destined, willingly and unwillingly, for illegal online scam and gambling operations.[40] Highlighting both the influence of industry actors and their access to law enforcement, it emerged in October 2023 that the Philippine national police was investigating reports that its officers had served as 'escorts' for Chinese online gaming operators.[41] This followed revelations from a former police chief who said that motorcycle cops were clearing the way for the passage of executives' luxury cars through heavy traffic. Not long after this, the interior and local government Secretary called for an investigation into the police chief of Pasay City and the commander of a sub-station in the area of an earlier raid on an online gambling company that was believed to have been involved in criminal activities.[42] In the words of the Secretary: 'It is highly improbable to think that an entire six-story building essentially dedicated to criminal activity, involving almost 600 potential victims, could somehow escape the notice of the local Sub-Station Commander.'

The complicity of state actors in the industry was further demonstrated in sensational style in March 2024, when a raid on the gambling hub Zun Yuan Technology in Bamban municipality, Tarlac province, uncovered an expansive network of actors and implicated the town's mayor. Initiated after a Vietnamese man escaped and informed the police, the action led to the rescue of hundreds of people from at least six countries.[43] Law enforcement

---

web.archive.org/web/20230704093705/https:/cyberscammonitor.net/profile/k99-group-triumph-city.

39   '"Crackdown" Six Months On (Part 2)', Cyber Scam Monitor, 30 June 2023, cyberscammonitor.substack.com.

40   'Immigration Chief Calls for Coordinated BI, Airport Authority Probe into Human Trafficking Scheme', Rappler, 30 November 2022; William P. Depasupil and Bernadette E. Tamayo, 'DoJ Orders Probe on Recruitment Scam', Manila Times, 1 December 2022.

41   Joviland Rita, 'PNP-HPG Probes Report on Cops Escorting "Chinese POGO Operators"', GMA News Online, 12 October 2023.

42   'Abalos Wants Pasay Police Officials Probed over Raided POGO Hub', ABS-CBN News, 29 October 2023.

43   Joann Manabat, 'Authorities Raid POGO Compound in Tarlac over Alleged Human Trafficking', Rappler, 13 March 2024.

interviews with workers revealed the location was hosting not only online gambling, but also scam groups.[44] With police investigating the ownership of the compound, documentation emerged indicating the town's mayor held a stake in the project, and later examination raised questions as to whether she was even Filipino, with evidence indicating that she had been born in China and had acquired a Filipino passport illicitly.[45] The compound had already been raided one year previously but was simply rebranded and continued without interference, despite the fact that it sat mere metres away from the city hall and municipal police station.

Surrounding Economies and Communities

The kingpins behind the scam compounds are able to establish and grow their business by building links with local elite actors and capitalising on systemic corruption in host countries, integrating themselves into local power structures in the process. While often walled off from their surroundings, the compounds also play an important role within local economies and communities.

Land and property owners are among the main local beneficiaries of the compound economy. In Cambodia, for instance, foreign nationals are allowed to own buildings but not the land on which they are built, which means that the owners of the compounds in the country must lease land from a Cambodian individual or entity, or establish a company majority-owned by a Cambodian citizen (alternatively, they can obtain Cambodian citizenship, which is eminently possible, but expensive). As we discussed earlier in the book, this provision is one of the reasons why at the time of writing in late 2024 Sihanoukville is still studded with unfinished buildings: local landowners refused to change the terms of their leases when the local economy contracted in 2019, leaving foreign investors unable to pay their rent and causing them to have their properties seized or simply abandon their projects.

In some cases, Cambodian nationals have built hotels and office buildings with the express intention of renting them to incoming investors,

---

44   Aaron Recuenco, 'From Offshore Gaming to Love Scam: Link of Some POGOs to Online Scamming Activities Discovered', *Manila Bulletin*, 14 March 2024.

45   'Gatchalian Urges Guo Hua Ping a.k.a. Alice Guo to Unmask POGO Kingpins', Senate of the Philippines 19th Congress, 2 July 2024.

many of whom are hungry for properties that can be converted for online operations. Likewise, established hotels and casinos found they could make much more money by simply renting their premises to online companies than by running their own business.

In the Philippines, the explosion of online gaming operators that started in 2016 led to a boom in office construction, but the contraction of the industry during COVID, raids, and the threat of the industry being banned led to an exodus of operators and consequently a surfeit of vacant office space. One major real estate services provider estimated that the Philippine offshore gaming operators – the state-licensed online gambling operations discussed earlier in the book – occupied around 656,000 square metres of office space in 2023, down from 1.3 million at the 2019 peak.[46] The glut of available office space inevitably led to a drop in rental prices. This hit land-lords, but also state revenues in the form of taxes, electricity charges, and gaming licence fees – all sources of income which proponents pointed to in their ultimately unsuccessful arguments against an online gaming ban.

In Myanmar, as discussed in Chapter 1, after the Kayin Border Guard Force issued a notice in May 2024 instructing foreign online workers to leave Myawaddy, operators reportedly began to move south. *Frontier Myanmar* reported from Payathonzu town in August 2024 that an influx of Chinese nationals had already started to arrive.[47] *Frontier* spoke with a restaurant owner who had started learning Chinese and hired two Chinese-speaking staff, as well as a cleaner at a hotel who described the influx as 'a gold rush for the hospitality industry'. Local people had already begun leasing their land and properties to Chinese online companies.

In some areas, compounds have become an engine for the local economy, as they need constant supplies of food and other necessities for the communities that reside within them. Restaurants, retailers, and hordes of delivery workers serve those who are able to come and go and receive orders from people trapped within. These companies are often owned by Chinese nationals, but we have also seen Thai, Indonesian, and Vietnamese businesses establish themselves around compounds through-out Southeast Asia, in addition to locally owned stores. Entering into a business relation with a compound can be very profitable. As the Chinese

46   Viviana Chan, 'POGO Office Space Demand Still Remains Far from Pre-COVID Levels: Colliers', Asia Gaming Brief, 20 September 2023.

47   Naw Betty Han, 'South for the Winter: Myanmar's Cyber Scam Industry Migrates', *Frontier Myanmar*, 29 August 2024.

owner of a restaurant in Bavet, Cambodia, a major hotspot of the online industries in Cambodia, told us: 'It's almost a guaranteed profit for us. We have to pay the compound 30 per cent of our earnings, but they make sure that the workers can only order from those of us who have established a connection.'

Although fraught with problems, including poor working conditions and often unpaid wages, the building boom in Sihanoukville that was fuelled by the online industries generated thousands of construction jobs. More recently, on a visit to a border scam hub in Kandal in June 2024, we witnessed frenzied construction work going on at several new compounds, which were flanked by makeshift camps housing hundreds of Cambodian workers, along with dozens of roadside stalls selling packed meals for the workers, clothes, toys for their children, and various other items. Although the camps in which these mostly itinerant labourers were living were extremely rudimentary, the expansion of the online industry in this area is clearly creating jobs. The security guards that controlled the external entry points to the already operational compounds were all Cambodian, and local workers could be seen moving in and out freely, some wearing cleaning uniforms and some likely working for the online operations themselves. We also spoke with researchers examining the economy around Bavet. There, in the surrounding communities, many people have ceased farming, or at least diversified their incomes by providing services such as manufacturing furniture or working as security, janitorial, and maintenance staff for the compounds.

Aside from the obvious concern that the industry feeding these economies is based on exploitation and extortion, it is also a double-edged sword. Typically, the compounds have entered new spaces and rapidly injected capital into the surrounding area. However, the moment demand from the compounds slows, ceases, or is disrupted, the people and businesses benefiting from them find themselves in trouble – as happened in Sihanoukville in the wake of the 2019 online gambling ban and the crackdown on the scam compounds in the fall of 2022. After two compounds on the outskirts of the city were raided in April 2024, local media reported how Cambodians who worked in the facilities but had not yet been paid went inside to take wine, food, refrigerators, and motorcycles.[48] One local seller was quoted as complaining: 'How can we sell and who will I sell to because

---

48   Mech Dara, 'Over 700 Chinese to Be Deported after Dramatic Sweep at Two Sihanoukville Resorts', CamboJA, 6 April 2024.

now it's very quiet. No one received any payment because they arrested the Chinese people … Many who bought my things owe me a lot of money, but what can I do about it?' When the industry slows down, the surrounding economies that have reconfigured to serve them are left bereft.

Beyond these economic ties, there is a darker side, as discussed at the outset of the chapter in the case from Dubai. Here, William told us that local residents were paid to look out for escapees from the compound. We have heard similar stories from other countries. As one of our interviewees, a young Chinese man who was sold to three different compounds in northern Myanmar within one year, told us:

> It is not possible to escape. The scam companies would send people to capture you, and on the way to the border there is always the possibility of running into traffickers sent by other compounds who would lure you by saying that they would help you get back to China, get your money, and then sell you again.
>
> Besides, local Burmese will also take you back to the compound and get paid for it. This is because Burmese people also depend on the scam compound to live, for instance working there as cleaning ladies, cooks, or waiters. These jobs are usually offered to the locals and salaries are higher than what they would normally be. Also, the locals inform the compound when the Myanmar military is coming to inspect or there is anything new happening in the vicinity. One victim I knew told me that when he tried to escape, some Burmese people saw him and started throwing stones at him.
>
> Another thing is that on your way back, as you will pass through many cities in Myanmar before you finally get to China, the chance of you meeting a trafficker is just too high.

In another instance, one of our informants, a young Chinese man from Guangdong province whom we will call Nan, was trafficked in 2023 to a scam compound in Laos's Golden Triangle Special Economic Zone (GTSEZ). Since he did not know how to type, the managers put him to work as a waiter in a KTV within the premises, and after several months released him. Finding himself stranded in a foreign country with neither documents nor money, Nan resorted to begging for food in the street, until one day he encountered a local who spoke some rudimentary Chinese. Under the pretence of offering him a job to help him get back on his feet, the man convinced Nan to get in a car. He later realised the driver worked for a human trafficking group and he subsequently found himself in another scam compound in Bavet, Cambodia.

The Elephant in the Room

Our discussion so far has not touched on one actor that some commentators have suggested is involved in the online scam industry: the Chinese Party-State. As the scale of the industry came into public view, a common criticism emerged that China was not doing enough to combat it, which was interpreted by many as indicating some level of complicity. While it could be argued that China did not react quickly or forcefully enough, the country's government has been much more active than many observers have given it credit for. Recently, the authorities have become much more public about the actions they have been taking over the past few years, but prior to this, relevant reporting was mostly in the Chinese language, meaning it was largely not on the radar of the wider world. Chinese-language reports can be found going back several years detailing police investigations, cross-border law enforcement cooperation, arrests, and deportations. Chinese embassies have been issuing warnings to their citizens about the perils of the industry for years, while extensive law enforcement action has been targeting the parts of the industrial chain located within China. Amendments to the criminal law increased punishments for illegal overseas gambling and a new law on online fraud was recently adopted.

Concerns have similarly been raised that powerful kingpins with alleged links to the Chinese Communist Party have been allowed to operate without interference. Questions certainly need to be asked as to why notorious crime figures, including Zhao Wei and Broken Tooth (Wan Kuok-koi), have been able to operate so openly. Broken Tooth is a vocal supporter of the party, often expressing support for core positions such as the One China Policy. Yet taking such public positions is not unusual for overseas businesspeople of all stripes, and this alone would not result in any special treatment. Zhao Wei's position is likely bolstered by his important networks within the region, specifically his likely connections to senior levels of the Lao government, but also armed groups in northern Myanmar that control territories along China's border. Yet, as discussed in Chapter 1, Chinese law enforcement actions have been targeting Zhao's GTSEZ for the past few years, with a dramatic uptick in August of 2024 indicating that any tolerance for his activities has diminished. Action has been taken against other regional crime figures, including most prominently She Zhijiang and Alvin Chau, and several other leaders have been apprehended or are being pursued, which is one reason why so many have acquired additional nationalities for themselves and their family members in countries such as Cambodia, where they can rely on protection from their well-connected partners.

Further fuelling the theory that the Chinese state has some level of involvement in the industry, opportunists have in some cases framed their developments as integral parts of China's BRI, most famously She Zhijiang in the case of his Yatai New City. As noted above, this led to the Chinese Embassy in Myanmar dismissing the connection, and China is now seeking the return of the long-time fugitive from a jail cell in Thailand. This hijacking of the BRI brand was not uncommon in the 2010s, when it was used by various actors, both legitimate and criminal, to add a veneer of legitimacy to their projects, regardless of whether they had any form of state backing. As a result, and as casinos and crime in Sihanoukville began to dominate the news in the 2010s, various reports began equating the rise of crime and even human trafficking into the online industry with China's landmark foreign policy initiative.[49]

To stick to the example of Sihanoukville, it is definitely the case that Chinese development finance and investment, strongly backed by both governments, enhanced the city's connectivity, and strengthening ties between the countries led to a formidable increase in Chinese tourism. Both facilitated an influx of all types of Chinese business. But investment into casinos, hotels, and illicit business came from private investors, and while some have employed BRI rhetoric in their promotional materials, this is not evidence of endorsement. In 2017, China's State Council issued guidelines for overseas investment that reiterated a longstanding prohibition on Chinese enterprises investing in gambling and put limitations on investments in hotels and real estate.[50] Much of the capital that flowed into

49   'The Aftermath of the Belt and Road Initiative: Human Trafficking in Cambodia', China Labor Watch website, 19 August 2022.

50   State Council of the People's Republic of China, '国务院办公厅转发国家发展改革委商务部人民银行外交部关于进一步引导和规范境外投资方向指导意见的通知, 国办发〔2017〕74号' (General Office of the State Council Forwards the National

places such as Sihanoukville was therefore likely not formally recorded in China, and many real estate investments likely utilised cash that was generated outside of China, in some cases through illicit activities.

Many of the reports linking Sihanoukville's unravelling to the BRI were based on misunderstandings of the local context. Principal among these mistakes was the fundamental confusion between the city of Sihanoukville and the Sihanoukville Special Economic Zone (SSEZ). Sihanoukville is the capital of Preah Sihanouk province; the SSEZ is an industrial zone located outside the city limits, in neighbouring Prey Nob District. However, numerous reports presented the city and the SSEZ as one and the same. This is more than a semantic quibble, as the effect was to equate the SSEZ, which was indeed branded a showcase BRI project by China and Cambodia, with the neighbouring city and its social ills. For example, one report from Germany stated: 'Many of the compounds and criminal syndicates are linked to the southern port town of Sihanoukville, which became a special economic zone under the Belt and Road Initiative agreement between China and Cambodia.'[51] A report from the US research organisation C4ADS went a step further: 'Belt and Road Initiative investments, including Sihanoukville SEZ, ostensibly espouse the goal of progress for local communities and countries. However, in this case, that progress greatly harmed the local populations with increasing crime rates, higher rents, overwhelmed infrastructure, suppression of the local culture, with locals cut out of the profits.'[52] In reality, the SSEZ predates both the BRI and the rise in Sihanoukville crime by many years, but as this narrative was put forward and widely repeated, it became commonplace to see reports linking the scam industry to the initiative by the Chinese government.

These arguments are further undercut if we take a step back and look at other countries in the region. Indonesia is a major BRI partner, hosting billions of dollars of investment in infrastructure and strategic industries, much of which carries the BRI branding. Yet the scam industry did not establish itself there; instead, scams targeting and staffed by Indonesians

Development and Reform Commission, Ministry of Commerce, People's Bank of China, and Ministry of Foreign Affairs on Further Guiding and Regulating the Direction of Overseas Investment [2017] No. 74)', State Council website, 4 August 2017.

51   Enno Hinz, 'Cambodia: Human Trafficking Crisis Driven by Cyberscams', Deutsche Welle, 12 September 2023.

52   Coby Goldberg, Max Kearns, Henry Peyronnin, Ben Spevack, and Sofia Vargas, 'Zoned Out: A Comprehensive Impact Evaluation of Mekong Economic Development Zones', C4ADS, Washington, DC.

are located largely in mainland Southeast Asia. Conversely, the Philippines, which has had a complicated relationship with China in recent years due to maritime territorial disputes, is not a key node of the BRI, yet it is the place where overseas Chinese online gambling first exploded. While China is the dominant source of investment in Cambodia, Laos, and Myanmar, it is neither the BRI nor any other state intervention that created the expansion of the scam industry – it is the geographical convenience and permissive local environment that drew in criminal actors.

It could in fact be argued that the industry has been extremely damaging to China's attempts to roll out the BRI and bolster its international image. Notwithstanding the often sloppy reporting, it cannot be denied that the industry is dominated by Chinese actors, and failures to crack down on it early and publicly further fuelled speculation that the state was at worst complicit and at best unconcerned. This is compounded by the fact that many construction projects for casinos, hotels, and real estate projects linked to the industry were awarded to Chinese state-owned enterprises (SOEs).[53] Some of these enterprises may have been oblivious to the end use of the properties and others may have adopted a don't-ask-don't-tell approach, but either way state-owned firms have probably benefited from illicit capital. As contractors, their involvement in a project ceases when they have delivered the facilities they were hired to build, but SOE banners could be seen over many construction sites that later became scam compounds. With SOEs scrambling for overseas construction contracts, their banners can still be seen hanging on buildings whose investors are known to be involved in illicit industries. While this leaves important questions to be answered, it points more towards a lack of corporate due diligence and state oversight than state support for the industry.

Obfuscations

Ultimately, the criminal groups that run scam operations are just the tip of the iceberg when it comes to the cyberfraud industry. If scam compounds can exist and thrive, this is only thanks to the protection guaranteed by their protective umbrellas in the local elite and state. They also depend on the cooperation of the surrounding communities

---

53   See, for example, Cyber Scam Monitor's entries for Jinshui, Kaibo, and Long Bay.

to ensure that their operations are sustained. This pushes back against the idea of the scam economy as a parasitic external entity that preys on vulnerable localities. This misconception is at the core of many assumptions about the compounds as exclusively foreign entities that operate in a void. Crucially, it also feeds into obfuscation by host-country state actors seeking to paint the problem as something external and beyond their knowledge. The compounds can be better interpreted as yet another instance in which powerful and dynamic local elites have been able to collaborate with shady international actors to reap profits – in this case by appropriating the labour power of hundreds of thousands of workers, in some cases toiling in conditions of modern slavery, to scam unfortunate targets worldwide.

5

Getting Out

'I have been waiting for too long. I cannot bear this life any longer, and they might find out anytime that I am talking to you. I will jump from the third floor tonight, please come and help.' This message was sent in early 2023 by a young Chinese man we will call Jack, to one of the authors who was then a volunteer in a Chinese rescue group in Cambodia. At that time, the team members were receiving dozens of distress messages every day, and their main task was to guide their interlocutors to report their situation through the formal channels or, if official rescue was impossible (as it almost always was), to assist by arranging for transport and shelter if they were able to escape by themselves.

Jack had been trafficked to a scam compound in Cambodia's Pursat province at the end of 2022. After realising what he had got into, he had immediately tried to contact the police back in China and the Chinese Embassy, but the police informed him they had no jurisdiction in a foreign country and the embassy did not even pick up the phone. It was a police officer in China who referred the case to the rescue group, which then spent almost one month unsuccessfully looking for a local police representative to help. As the situation dragged on, Jack was beaten several times due to his poor work performance. Scared and frustrated, he eventually decided to orchestrate his own escape.

As scam compounds are usually enclosed by high walls topped by barbed wire and their gates are heavily guarded, many of those trapped inside have no choice but to jump from outward-facing windows. Aware of this, compound managers usually install bars on most windows, adding another layer of security to their facilities – and one more hurdle for those wishing to leave. On the night of his escape, Jack lied to his supervisor that he wanted to spend a few more hours in the office (which was located on the lower floors of the building) to nail down a target. Around one a.m., as the security guard dozed, he climbed out of the window, closed his eyes, and jumped into the void, landing on the lawn below.

The members of the rescue team who were waiting for him nearby were equally nervous. They knew that a safe landing was just the first step of the escape and that, regardless of the injuries he might have sustained in the fall, Jack still had to get to the pick-up point where they were waiting for him. They did not dare get any closer to the compound, because they had heard that a member of another rescue team had been chased by armed guards during a previous operation.

After briefly losing consciousness, Jack woke up to searing pain in his legs and later found out he had broken both his ankles. Fearing that his supervisor might soon realise that he was gone, he hobbled to a hidden corner and sent his location to the team. As they could get no closer, Jack had to crawl for a hundred metres to meet the driver in a safe place. He begged them to take him to a nearby hospital, but the rescuers had to refuse as they knew that the scam compound had extensive connections with local businesses and were worried somebody might inform on them. On his way to the Phnom Penh safe house, Jack could see that the manager of the scam operation had already posted that there was a bounty of US$20,000 on his head and was threatening to cut off his hand if they caught him. He immediately deleted his Telegram account and threw away the SIM card.

How to Get Out

People trapped in the scam compounds who want to get out generally have three options. The first is to get their relatives and friends to put together the money that the criminal groups demand as ransom. This is no ideal choice, as the amount can reach into the tens of thousands of dollars and there is no guarantee that the criminals will not pocket the funds and then still sell the person to another operator.

The second is to slip a message out to ask for help. Unlike many victims of traditional forms of modern slavery, the people trapped in the scam compounds remain connected to the outside world through the internet. Even though they are heavily monitored, this means that they can occasionally sneak out distress messages to relatives, friends, journalists, embassies, or host-country authorities. For instance, some people trapped in scam compounds in Cambodia have sought help from local and national authorities by leaving messages on the Facebook pages of the prime minister, the minister of interior, or the governor of the province they were in. They can also attempt to contact their embassies or dedicated hotlines set up by the government – Cambodia's Ministry of Interior, for instance, has been running such a line since September 2022.[1]

Even this solution is far from ideal. When people trapped in the compounds manage to attract official attention, there are numerous reports of this worsening their predicament. As discussed earlier, in many cases where people have alerted local police, information gets back to compound managers, giving them time to erase evidence. The young man surnamed Li, sold by a friend to a compound in Sihanoukville in 2022 and mentioned in Chapter 4, presents us with one such instance. As he told us:

When I reached Along [an anonymous Chinese blogger with a long history of reporting on scam companies], I was desperate. He asked me whether I dared to use my real name and ID number when I reported to the police because it would add credibility to my case and also attract more attention. I agreed. It was because I really did not want to do scams, but also because I could not bear the physical punishments anymore.

I thought that with Along's help, both local and Chinese police would acknowledge that I was a victim and treat me as such. However, the second day, the rescue I expected did not come. Instead, the manager shouted at me: 'How dare you even think of getting away? Are you looking for trouble?' Several guys dragged me into the dark room, where they stripped me, handcuffed me, and beat me with wires and batons. I was left there like a corpse for three days.

---

1   'Cambodia Sets Up Hotline to Report Illegal Detention', Vietnam+, 31 August 2022.

There are several reports in which relatives of individuals trapped in scam compounds in Southeast Asia recount how they were stonewalled by local authorities and law enforcement, even after obtaining support from diplomats from their home countries or by journalists and media. For instance, on 8 August 2022, the Embassy of the Philippines in Cambodia sent a letter to two senior Cambodian police officials, stating that it had received 'another urgent request' for police assistance from citizens being forced to work as 'online scammers' at Long Bay.[2] They had had their passports seized and were being prevented from leaving without paying a fee. The letter included the specific floor and room number where the detainees were being held and requested the release of the four men.

When journalists from Voice of Democracy followed up with provincial police almost two weeks after the letter was sent, the case was still being dealt with, and the provincial police claimed to have requested national-level support.[3] The provincial police spokesman even confirmed to reporters that foreigners from two or three countries had already requested help to get out of the compound in the past. However, in a follow-up report a few days later, VoD quoted the provincial police spokesperson as saying: 'This case is done. The team went down to check that location and found out that they had left even before we got there.'[4] He went on to deny that any detention had taken place: 'There was no detention of the four. They came to work and now left.' The investigation was over.

The third option is to seek help from unofficial actors. Given the limited official assistance available to individuals trapped in the scam compounds, civil society has stepped in to fill the gap. Existing nongovernmental organisations with a history of working on human rights, human trafficking, and modern slavery throughout Southeast Asia have scrambled to make sense of this new industry and adapt so as to help the survivors. For instance, in Cambodia, a handful of local human rights NGOs began to assist the most vulnerable survivors on a case-by-case basis, providing them with medical support, basic supplies, and assistance in applying for

2   Ban Na 班纳, '菲律宾大使馆: 菲公民被困七星海长湾娱乐场内一家网投公司，请求柬当局解救' (Philippine Embassy: Filipino Citizens Are Trapped in an Online Investment Company in the Long Bay Casino of Qixinghai and Request the Cambodian Authorities to Rescue Them), 柬中时报 (Cambodia China Times), 19 August 2022.

3   Mech Dara, 'Philippine Embassy Urges Rescue from UDG, Americans Rescued in Sihanoukville', Voice of Democracy, 22 August 2022.

4   Mam Sampichida, 'Filipinos Who Sought Rescue in Koh Kong Not There When Police Arrived', Voice of Democracy, 26 August 2022.

repatriation funding. In Myanmar, organisations specialised in assisting those who have been trafficked for the purpose of sexual exploitation organised their own rescue groups and coordinated with psychologists in China to provide mental health care to ease the trauma of compound survivors. Later, international NGOs and agencies started paying attention to the situation in the compounds, providing financial support to local organisations and creating or repurposing platforms where policymakers and representatives of local civil society could discuss the issue. Some used their contacts in government and law enforcement to share information on specific operations and pushed for authorities to investigate sites on which they had obtained intelligence or from where they had received rescue requests.

While most attention has been focused on the role of international groups, it was Chinese actors who first came to the fore to launch efforts to rescue people trapped in the scam compounds. These included associations of Chinese businessmen based in Southeast Asia and survivors who, once out of the compounds, decided to stay behind to assist those still inside.

The Cambodia–China Charity Team

One prominent example of how Chinese civil society overseas came to be involved in assisting people trapped in the scam compounds can be found in Cambodia. For a while, individual Chinese businessmen in the country had been actively helping members of the Chinese community in distress, raising money for those who fell sick or had accidents and could not afford hospital bills. To boost and formalise these efforts, in September 2021, the Chinese Commerce in Cambodia Association (中柬商业协会 *zhongjian shangye xiehui*) formally established the Cambodia-China Charity Team (中柬义工队 *zhongjian yigongdui*), a volunteer group composed of Chinese nationals from various walks of life based in the Southeast Asian country.[5]

The team became increasingly visible in Chinese-language media as a leading force behind the attempts to rescue people from scam compounds

---

5 '中柬义工队正式成立！为同胞互助开辟新渠道' (The Cambodia-China Charity Team Is Formally Established! It Will Open Up New Channels for Fellow Compatriots to Help Each Other), NetEase, 15 September 2021.

in late 2021 and early 2022, mostly thanks to the tireless outreach efforts of its leader Chen Baorong.[6] Chen's story is nothing short of remarkable.[7] Born in China's Hubei province in 1973, he began a wandering life after losing his parents at the age of fifteen, working all over the country to make a living. In 2002, he travelled to Cambodia to try his luck as one of the earliest Chinese gold diggers in the country, investing in a remote gold mine. After decades of doing business in Cambodia, he started to do charity work. For instance, he told us how in 2013 he heard that the owner of another gold mine had offered high salaries to lure some Chinese workers to Cambodia. Not only had he then reneged on his promise and failed to pay the workers, but he had also kept twenty-eight of them in captivity with no food or water after they tried to leave. Contacted by one of these workers, Chen reported the case to the Chinese Embassy, which referred it to the Cambodian police. He then bought flight tickets for these people to return to China. This was Chen's first encounter with the abuse of Chinese workers in Cambodia.

His introduction to the online scam industry came much later. In November 2020, he encountered three young Chinese men in Phnom Penh. They were dishevelled and in considerable distress. When he approached them, they told him that they had just escaped from a scam compound. The stories they told him shocked him so much that he arranged for them to stay at a hotel owned by a friend, and again bought their tickets to China with his own money.[8] After that, Chen began looking out for similar cases, which seemed to multiply by the day. When he heard about

---

6   '中柬商会刘阳秘书长主持中柬义工队成立大会' (Secretary-General Liu Yang of the China-Cambodia Chamber of Commerce Presided over the Founding Meeting of the Cambodia-China Charity Team), 创头条 (Chuang Tou Tiao), 19 November 2021; Lirenbusong 离人不送, '中柬慈善委员会授牌仪式暨中柬义工队迎新分享会圆满召开' (The China–Cambodia Charity Committee Awarding Ceremony and the Cambodia–China Charity Team Welcome Session Were Successfully Held), 人在东南亚 (People in Southeast Asia), 24 January 2022.

7   Except for the passages where another source is indicated, the story of Chen Baorong recounted in these two paragraphs is based on two sources: '他，在柬埔寨拯救了300多个中国同胞的家庭' (He Saved the Families of More Than 300 Chinese Compatriots in Cambodia), 柬单网 (Jiandanwang), 5 February 2022, mp.weixin.qq.com/s/dL_TDnoIJm89fGCl28UbtQ; '中柬义工队队长讲述"血奴"事件背后：高薪诱惑、熟人骗熟人' (The Leader of the Cambodia–China Charity Team Tells the Story behind the 'Blood Slave' Incident: The Temptation of High Salary, Acquaintances Deceiving Acquaintances), 喜马拉雅 (Ximalaya Podcast), 24 February 2022.

8   Zhan Yan 詹钘, '困在柬埔寨诈骗公司的中国人：交了30万赎金却被转卖, 完不成业绩被电击' (The Chinese Trapped in a Scam Company in Cambodia: They Paid a

someone trapped in a compound, he usually helped them to contact their families and the police back in China. Gradually, word spread about his work and more people in Chen's social circles began to offer a hand in this unofficial repatriation process.

At that early stage, these efforts were not organised and largely depended on Chen himself. In June 2021, a new case that made waves among the Chinese community in Cambodia pushed Chen and his collaborators to rethink their approach. That month, a Chinese woman called Deng was found wandering in the streets of Sihanoukville in a state of confusion.[9] It was later discovered that she had arrived in Cambodia almost one year earlier, after accepting what she believed was a good job, but was instead sold into the scam industry in Sihanoukville. Unwilling to do online scams, she was subject to sustained sexual and physical violence, and then sold to company after company. Based on our interviews with actors involved in her rescue, it was her case that triggered the strategic rethinking that in September 2021 led to the creation of the Cambodia–China Charity Team. According to one core member of the team:

> It was said that it was Chen Baorong who rescued Deng from a scam compound, but no one really knows how he did it. It was also hard to get the truth from Deng, largely due to her mental state. Even after we settled her down, she would still run off from time to time and we wouldn't notice. Hence, it required much more attention and assistance than in other cases that Chen had encountered before. Many people in Sihanoukville started helping, crowdfunding some money to send Deng to Phnom Penh, where they arranged accommodation and psychiatric treatment for her. Others helped her connect with her family in China and assisted her with getting the proper documents and a ticket back home. Chen and these people were all saying that they should help these victims in a more systematic way. This is how the Cambodia-China Charity Team came to be.

Ransom of 300,000 but Were Resold and Were Electrocuted after Failing to Complete Their Performance), Government of Linbi County website, 17 February 2022.

9   Along 阿龙, '我叫邓媛，被肆意殴打，恐吓威胁，语言凌辱，侮辱强奸！' (My Name Is Deng Yuan, and I Was Beaten Arbitrarily, Threatened, Verbally Abused, Humiliated and Raped!), 阿龙闯荡记 (Along's Adventures), 27 September 2021, mp.weixin.qq.com/s/b-L42O1qimWcuv-7PMFKrQ.

After the establishment of the Cambodia-China Charity Team, Chen's work changed substantially. Where he had previously been acting primarily as an individual, with the foundation of the charity team he could now count on a formal organisation to assist him. The first significant change was that with more people in the team, it became possible to gather distress messages in a systematic way. Instead of relying on Chen's personal connections to hear about cases, the charity team began to run hotlines to receive messages from people trapped in the scam compounds, or from their families and friends. They also started methodically to monitor social media for appeals for help.[10]

Another significant change occurred at that point, with Chen and the team beginning to organise rescue operations. The team would investigate the cases brought to their attention, thoroughly gathering information such as how the person had arrived in the country, whether they had a passport, their name, age, ID number, and specific location.[11] After ascertaining the situation, they would adopt one of two main strategies. The first was to seek assistance from state actors, such as governors of the province in which the person was held. Official support was especially important in cases where people were trapped in the larger fortified scam compounds. Nevertheless, since such help was rarely forthcoming, on most occasions the team still found itself relying on Chen's personal connections with trusted Cambodian police contacts, as well as the property management staff working in some of these compounds. The second strategy, which was much more dangerous, was for Chen himself to go into the compounds and attempt to negotiate the release of the people trapped inside, while other team members remained outside to watch the exits, in case the company tried to transfer the people somewhere else.

After a rescue operation, the team would look for ways to send the survivors back to their homes in China. At the beginning, they received support from some Chinese airline companies who assisted them in

10   Han Xin 韩鑫, '柬埔寨获救同胞逾百人：总理、省长、民间组织、记者共同出马' (Cambodia Rescues More Than 100 Compatriots: Prime Minister, Provincial Governors, Civil Society Organisations and Journalists Jointly Took Action), 搜狐 (Sohu), 16 November 2021.

11   Chen Man 陈曼, '中柬义工队队员揭露柬埔寨人口买卖利益链，中国人在当地成"行走的美金"' (Members of the Cambodia–China Charity Team Reveal the Profit Chain of Human Trafficking in Cambodia, Where Chinese People Have Become 'Walking Dollars'), 河南一百度 (Henan100), 21 February 2022.

repatriating survivors.[12] But after the Chinese authorities began implementing the zero-COVID policy in March 2020, China's Civil Aviation Administration drastically limited the number of flights allowed in and out of the country.[13] The cost of flight tickets skyrocketed, and travellers now also needed to shoulder the costs of extensive periods of quarantine both before and after travelling, so many repatriation plans had to be postponed indefinitely. This caused considerable distress to the survivors, some of whom were in a precarious condition due to the physical and mental abuse they had suffered in the compounds.

In addition to the rescue work, between 2021 and 2022, stories started being shared on WeChat news accounts about bodies of deceased Chinese people accumulating at pagodas in Phnom Penh. In April 2022, it was reported that over eighty corpses were being kept at two pagodas in Phnom Penh. A list published in one article included the names of sixty-three people being stored at Tuek Thla pagoda. The bodies came from seven different provinces, but there were forty-three from Sihanoukville alone. Some had been at the pagoda since 2019.[14] The pagodas charge a daily fee for storing bodies, and repatriating human remains costs money, so many families in China were unable to afford the cost to bring back their deceased relatives, and corpses continued to accumulate.

To help deal with this macabre load, Chen turned to his connections, including the Chinese owner of a bar in Phnom Penh. Known by many as Motorcycle Uncle (机车大叔 *jiche dashu*), he had become famous among the Chinese community in Cambodia for travelling on a motorbike and performing philanthropic acts, such as bringing goods to orphanages and delivering food during the pandemic.[15] Motorcycle Uncle raised funds and helped organise the cremation of the bodies of Chinese nationals who had passed away in Cambodia, and the repatriation of their ashes.

---

12   Zhan Yan, 'The Chinese Trapped in a Scam Company in Cambodia'.

13   Civil Aviation Administration of China, 'Notice on Further Reducing International Passenger Flights during the Epidemic Prevention and Control Period', International Cooperation and Service Center website, 26 March 2020.

14   Along 阿龙, '金边德克拉寺庙一份63具未处理的遗体名单！' (A List of 63 Unprocessed Remains at the Teuk Thla Pagoda in Phnom Penh!), 搜狐 (Sohu), 21 March 2022; 'Longing to Return to Their Homeland: Over 80 Chinese Deceased Still "Unclaimed" in Cambodian Morgues', *Khmer Times*, 4 April 2023.

15   '39岁机车大叔：在善行中挤掉悲痛的自己' (39-Year-Old Motorcycle Uncle: Squeeze Out Your Sorrowful Self in Good Deeds), 柬单网 (Jiandanwang), 20 December 2021.

The people whose bodies accumulated during this period likely died from numerous causes, including accidents and ill health, but we know that some perished in or after escaping from the compounds.[16] Motorcycle Uncle and others continue to play this role to this day, and in July 2023, after a man who had escaped from a compound in Sihanoukville committed suicide, they paid for the funeral and for the man's father to travel to Cambodia, to attend the ceremony and retrieve his son's remains.[17] In this case, the man had been showing suicidal tendencies and had talked with a Chinese journalist just days before his death, telling him he was terrified that the compound managers would find him. Ultimately, he succumbed to his trauma.

Throughout the pandemic years, the team kept up with its rescue work. Among the many considerable challenges they faced was the risk that bounty hunters or other brokers would find the survivors and sell them back to the compounds. To avoid this, they found a safe space to lodge the people in their care temporarily, until they could be repatriated. For this, they turned to Li Jie, another Chinese businessman who had arrived in Cambodia in 2019 and was running a guesthouse not far from Phnom Penh's international airport. As a member of the charity team, Li began providing the facilities of his Great Wall Hotel – more than twenty rooms on five storeys – as a temporary shelter free of charge.[18] Since Li never asked for any money from the survivors, the daily expenses caused him huge financial pressure and he eventually let the receptionists and cleaners go and took on these roles himself.[19] Other Chinese residents donated various necessities to help him support the survivors. For instance, Sister

---

16   Along 阿龙, '小伙在西港意外死亡，家属频繁接到贷款催收电话？' (A Young Man Died Unexpectedly in Sihanoukville, and His Family Received Frequent Loan Collection Calls?), 阿龙闯荡记 (Along's Adventures), 22 July 2022, mp.weixin.qq.com/s/i22Mn7JSwEnPPCzMXl4JcQ.

17   '从园区逃出来后 他最终还是选择了自杀' (After Escaping from the Compound, He Finally Chose to Commit Suicide), 柬单网 (Jiandanwang), 31 July 2023; Huang Yan 黄岩, '从园区逃出来后自杀的他 今天火化了' (Man Who Committed Suicide after Escaping from the Park Cremated Today), 柬单网 (Jiandanwang), 12 August 2023.

18   Li Yiming 李一鸣, Chen Kaiyue 陈锴跃, and Xie Ziyi 谢紫怡, '难以逃离的柬埔寨西港"中国城"：被绑架被倒卖，被威胁"沉尸海底" …' (It Is Difficult to Escape from Sihanoukville's 'Chinatown' in Cambodia: Kidnapped, Resold, and Threatened to Be 'Sunk to the Bottom of the Sea' …), Career Engine, 1 April 2022.

19   Brother Meng 猛哥, '我在柬埔寨开宾馆，专门收留被凌辱虐待的中国人' (I Opened a Hotel in Cambodia to Take In Chinese People Who Have Been Abused), NetEase, 22 December 2022.

Pang, a woman from Sichuan who had come to Cambodia in 2019 to start a restaurant business, offered free meals and launched crowdfunding initiatives for people in particularly hard circumstances.[20] Other Chinese businesspeople attempted to offer jobs to survivors, but they were rarely successful as people who had emerged from the compounds tended to distrust anyone.[21]

Chen and his collaborators focused their activities on Chinese nationals and put considerable emphasis on this patriotic angle. Chinese-language articles reporting on the team's operations include phrases such as 'pride of the Chinese community' (华人之光 *huaren zhi guang*)', 'compatriots in need' (苦难同胞 *kunan tongbao*), or 'fellow-countryman feeling' (同乡之情 *tongxiang zhi qing*). Amid this patriotic rhetoric, the charity team helped both mainlanders and people from Taiwan. Yet, according to one informant from Taiwan, in some cases where Taiwanese people were rescued from the compounds and brought to live side by side with mainlanders in the shelter, geopolitical tensions intruded, with constant quarrels and verbal abuse due to different political standpoints about cross-strait relations among the residents.

Around that time, frictions started to emerge within the team. Interviewees recounted to us that the group had to be sensitive to the concerns of the business association that it sat under, as well as its membership. The team's publicity focused on philanthropic work and non-sensitive public-awareness work, such as disseminating information about COVID-19 vaccinations and assisting Chinese families facing severe financial difficulties in Cambodia, while the rescue work remained in the background.[22] According to one of our informants, this was a deliberate decision, as management of the Chinese Commerce in Cambodia

20   PanasiaLife 泛亚生活, '西港胖姐专访: 坚守西港的叛逆中年少女' (Interview with Sister Pang in Sihanoukville: The Rebellious Middle-Aged Woman Who Sticks to Sihanoukville), Sohu, 12 June 2020; Along 阿龙, '剃刀边缘-东南亚闯荡记' (The Razor's Edge: Travelling in Southeast Asia), 阿龙闯荡记 (Along's Adventures), 8 October 2021, mp.weixin.qq.com/s/oTiMX7tfKRVwavGhkyS3Qw; Huang, 'Man Who Committed Suicide after Escaping from the Park Cremated Today'.

21   Han Xin 韩鑫, '原网诈人员回归社会, 中国老板鼎力救助' (Former Internet Fraudsters Return to Society, Chinese Bosses Vigorously Rescue Them), 柬单网 (Jiandanwang), 27 February 2022.

22   On 'disseminating information about COVID-19 vaccinations' see Lirenbusong, 'The China Cambodia Charity Committee Awarding Ceremony and the Cambodia-China Charity Team Welcome Session Were Successfully Held'; on 'assisting families facing severe financial difficulties', see Fang Nan 方南, '谁说在柬埔寨的中国人都是坏

Association was concerned that the public might think they were helping scammers, regardless of whether these people had been trafficked to the compounds and forced to engage in illegal activities. This reluctance was also reflected in the association's demand, alleged by one of our informants, that the charity team focus only on cases in which people were being severely abused or where family members were willing to pay the ransom.

The picture is further complicated by the fact that the association was founded by a Chinese national with a long history of promoting multi-level marketing schemes in China, and later on, after he moved to Cambodia and acquired citizenship, dubious crypto platforms.[23] It was subsequently taken over by another Chinese-born naturalised Cambodian who has since been linked to an online compound in Cambodia and has appeared at crypto conferences in Dubai, where he is said to have relocated. Both were very visible for some years, and went out of their way to publicise their meetings with senior officials as well as donations to Cambodian state agencies, law enforcement, and the military. This led to speculation about the association's motivations in hosting the charity team. Yet despite this complicated picture, Chen and his team strongly believed that anyone trapped in the compounds deserved assistance, regardless of how they got there.[24]

All of this would soon become moot as a result of the so-called blood-slave case that we recounted earlier in the book. Late on the night of 10 February 2022, a man called Li Yayuanlun called the charity team from a hospital bed in Sihanoukville, asking for help. When they went to pick him up early the next morning, the team members saw his body was swollen due to a severe ischaemia, so they immediately took him to a hospital in

---

人? 我不服! ' (Who Said That Chinese in Cambodia Are All Bad People? I'm Not Convinced!), qq.com, 4 October 2021.

23   Liu Yiqin 刘以秦, Liu Shuqi 柳书琪, Li Biao 李彪, and Gu Lingyu 顾翎羽, '"血奴案"疑似反转，柬埔寨黑产触目惊心，大量华人卷入' (The 'Blood Slave Case' Is Suspected to Be Reversed, Cambodia's Black Industry Is Shocking, and a Large Number of Chinese Are Involved), 财经十一人 (Caijing Shiyi Ren), 28 February 2022; 'Pacific Real Estate/Golden Phoenix Entertainment City', Cyber Scam Monitor, 6 November 2022, web.archive.org/web/20230421153925/https://cyberscammonitor.net/profile/pacific-golden-phoenix.

24   '"她才14岁，却被迫在柬埔寨提供性服务长达一年! "' ('She Was Only 14 Years Old, but She Was Forced to Provide Sexual Services in Cambodia for a Year!'), 柬单网 (Jiandanwang), 24 January 2022, mp.weixin.qq.com/s/1m5HUJEEN4UI3V2C0Yi6Bw.

Phnom Penh.[25] Li claimed that in May 2021 he had applied for a security guard position in China's Guangxi province after seeing it advertised on 58 Tongcheng, the well-known job-recruitment platform mentioned earlier. When he arrived in Guangxi, he said he had been kidnapped and brought to work in a scam compound in Cambodia, where he was tortured and beaten because he refused to do what he was asked. After that, he was resold many times among several scam compounds. In one of them, he claimed, they drew his blood seven times in little more than half a year, each time in large quantities.[26] He had managed to escape in early February, and in the ensuing days was hospitalised first in a small clinic and then in a hospital in Sihanoukville, before the charity team brought him to Phnom Penh.

Late on the night of 11 February, the public WeChat account of the charity team published an angry article describing Li's experience as a blood slave.[27] The following day, the hospital reported the case to the Chinese Embassy in Cambodia, which then urged the Cambodian police to launch an investigation.[28] From that moment on, the blood-slave case started to attract widespread attention in mainland China and internationally. In China, the story began trending on online platforms, and mainstream news media also covered it, eliciting both compassion and horror from the Chinese public. Attention peaked on the evening of 22 February, when a prominent news portal in China conducted a live interview with Chen Baorong.[29] On that occasion, Chen provided a detailed

---

25   Feng Shengyong 冯盛雍, '江苏小伙在柬埔寨被多次抽血全身浮肿病危，大使馆警方已介入' (A Young Man from Jiangsu Was in Cambodia and Had His Blood Drawn Multiple Times: His Whole Body Was Swollen and He Was Critically Ill, the Embassy and the Police Have Intervened), 上游新闻 (Shangyou News), 15 February 2022; Yuan Ye, 'Chinese "Blood Slave" Rescued in Cambodia', Sixth Tone, 18 February 2022.

26   Details are fuzzy as different media reports mentioned different amounts of blood.

27   Liang Chunhu 梁春富 and Cai Zhen 蔡真, '"血奴"案反转背后：传销集团魅影闪现，牵出币圈大佬东南亚往事' (Behind the Reversal of the 'Blood Slave' Case: The Phantom of the MLM Group Appears, Bringing Out the Past Events of Southeast Asia for the Cryptocurrency Boss), Jiemian News, 2 March 2022.

28   '中国大使馆：中国公民"血奴"案正式立案，警方正协同开展侦查工作' (Chinese Embassy: The Case of the Chinese 'Blood Slave' Has Been Formally Filed, and the Police Are Cooperating in the Investigation), 柬华日报 (Jian Hua Daily), 17 February 2022; '驻柬埔寨使馆发言人就柬警方查证"血奴"案属编造事发表谈话' (Spokesperson of the Embassy in Cambodia Makes a Statement on the Cambodian Police's Verification That the 'Blood Slave' Case Was a Fabrication), Chinese Embassy in Cambodia website, 28 February 2022.

29   '凤凰网连线中柬义工队长直播视频再上热搜，更多内幕曝光！' (Ifeng.com's

overview of the latest trends in the online scam industry, describing the severity of the physical violence people received inside compounds, how young people were lured in, and how scam operators were targeting an increasingly global audience. He also offered his own experiences, discussing the challenges he had faced in providing assistance to survivors.

At that point came a twist, however. First, 58 Tongcheng claimed that it could not find any job ad that matched the information Li had described in his testimony.[30] Then, voices questioning certain details of the case grew louder. In a video shot by the charity team in the hospital on 11 February, Li is seen lying on the bed and pointing at the infusion bag above, saying that the gangsters had drawn three bags of blood that size, seven times over the previous six months.[31] Holes began to emerge in his account. Online commenters were quick to point out that it is not possible to make significant profits by selling blood, but Li had also claimed that his blood type was Rh-negative O-type blood, which is so rare that it is sometimes known as panda blood.[32] On 14 February, the director of the hospital had stated that Li had received 2,800 millilitres of blood, and netizens started to question how the hospital was able to obtain such a significant amount of this blood in an emergency, if indeed it was so rare.[33]

On 28 February, the Cambodian national police issued a statement claiming that their investigation had found that the blood-slave story was fabricated by Li and three individuals, including Chen Baorong, another charity team member, and a doctor from a hospital in Sihanoukville.[34]

Live Video: The Cambodia–China Charity Team Leader Is a Hot Search Again, More Inside Stories Are Exposed!), NetEase, 23 February 2022.

30   Shuai Kecong 帅可聪 and Chen Feng 陈锋, '58同城回应"柬埔寨血奴案": 会全力协助相关部门调查' (58.com Responded to the 'Cambodian Blood-Slave Case': They Will Fully Assist Relevant Departments in the Investigation), 华夏时报 (China Times), 17 February 2022.

31   Feng, 'A Young Man from Jiangsu Was in Cambodia and Had His Blood Drawn Multiple Times'.

32   Beijing Youth Daily, '小伙找工作被掳至柬埔寨，因拒绝诈骗而成为"血袋"' (A Young Man Was Kidnapped to Cambodia When He Was Looking for a Job: He Became a 'Blood Bag' Because He Refused to Do Scams), Sina News, 17 February 2022.

33   Kuaijixuetangshicao 会计学堂实操, '血奴案纯属编造：这位老哥就属于、偷渡去柬埔寨赌输了' (The Blood-Slave Case Is a Complete Fabrication: This Guy Was One of Those Who Smuggled Themselves into Cambodia and Lost the Gambling Game), 搜狐 (Sohu), 2 March 2022.

34   Mech Dara and Cindy Liu, 'Rescue Team Leader under Police Investigation', Voice of Democracy, 28 February 2022.

Chen was charged on four counts: 'incitement to cause discrimination', 'unlawful interference in the performance of public functions', 'unlawful use of a profession's certified documents', and 'providing false declarations'.[35] He was sentenced to two years in jail but served ten months, eventually regaining his freedom on 2 January 2023.[36] We do not know why Li embellished his story the way he did. Evidently, he did spend a lengthy time in the compounds, during which time he developed serious health problems. He may well have been tricked into the industry and held against his will, but the details he fabricated became the dominant feature of his story, with wide-reaching implications for those involved in rescue efforts for people trapped in the compounds.

Not only did the blood-slave incident provide the Cambodian authorities with new ammunition to cast doubt on survivor testimonies from the country's scam compounds but it was also a disaster for the charity. The team members and doctor who believed his story and repeated it became collateral damage as the authorities sought to make an example out of them. The group continued to work, although in a more low-key manner for a time; but without the charismatic figure of Chen at its centre, it was fundamentally weakened, especially considering that many of its operations relied on Chen's personal connections. Eventually it disbanded. Some of its members continue to be involved in rescue work, but outside of a formal organisational structure.

While the case of the charity team in Cambodia is exceptional in terms of its level of organisation and activism, figures in the business community also play an important role in other countries. For example, media reports have described escapes from Myanmar compounds as being facilitated or negotiated by Malaysian and Taiwanese businesspeople based in the country.[37] We are aware of the existence of Chinese individuals and rescue teams active in Myanmar but due to the extremely dangerous and volatile political situation they mostly take care to remain under the radar.

---

35   Mech Dara, 'Wife Says Trafficking Rescuer Sentenced to Two Years in Prison', *Voice of Democracy*, 30 August 2022.

36   Mech Dara, 'Chinese Scam Rescuer Released from Prison after 10 Months', *Voice of Democracy*, 2 January 2023.

37   See, for example, Samantha Kuan, 'Job Scam Victim Jumped from the Second Floor to Escape Syndicate', *New Straits Times*, 17 January 2023; Tsai Shu-yuan and Jason Pan, 'Beware Southeast Asia Travel after Kidnapping: GASO', *Taipei Times*, 14 August 2023.

Self-Salvation

As discussed early in the book, the industry victimises both those who are targeted by scammers and those individuals who are forced to perpetrate the scams. Even though they are ultimately victimised by the same criminal groups, there are obvious obstacles to any sort of solidarity emerging between them. Some individuals from both groups have chosen to fight back, however, and in some cases have even found ways to collaborate.

Some survivors of the scam compounds continue working to assist others who are less fortunate. While a few have joined the collective efforts of rescue teams, volunteer groups, and other NGOs, most remain independent. In this book, we have already encountered an example of this in Chapter 4 – William, the Chinese entrepreneur tricked into entering a compound in Dubai. After escaping, unable to return to China due to bureaucratic hurdles, he stayed and continued to help other Chinese nationals trapped in scam compounds in the United Arab Emirates, which eventually led to his former captors considerably raising the bounty on his head.

While people like William operate mostly under the radar, others have engaged with the media and built up a public profile. One such person is Lu Xiangri, a Chinese man who joined the Cambodia-China Charity Team when it was being led by Chen Baorong and who continued to help people trapped in the compounds even after Chen was arrested. For a while, Lu was one of the most visible of this new cohort of 'survivor leaders' who emerged from the compounds.[38] He arrived in Cambodia in 2021 upon the invitation of a friend who asked him to work at his restaurant in Phnom Penh. When the restaurant began to struggle during the pandemic, Lu decided to follow an acquaintance to Sihanoukville to try his luck there. Once there, he was sold to a compound for US$12,000, and when he contacted the Chinese Embassy, the staff told him to call the local police. He did that, and soon after his supervisor in the compound confronted him with a copy of the police report. In the end he was rescued, and once out of the compound, he joined the Cambodia-China Charity Team. Later, he also joined an NGO set up by scam victims dedicated to assisting survivors. In his words to us: 'I am a survivor too … I knew how terrible it felt inside [the scam compound], so after I got rescued, I

---

38   The following account is based on our personal conversations with Lu Xiangri.

wanted to help. If we don't save them, they will die. Someone has to help them go back home alive.'

A young Taiwanese woman named Yutang is another survivor who has chosen to maintain a public profile and continue to support other people trapped inside.[39] In April 2022, when she was still in Taiwan, she was offered a job in the call centre of an online gambling operation in Cambodia. At the beginning, she was sceptical about the legitimacy of such a job, but the recruiter said she could visit and then decide once she had seen the environment. He even offered to pay for her return flight regardless of whether she decided to stay. Yutang realised that something was wrong the moment she arrived at the airport in Phnom Penh and was welcomed by people she said looked like gangsters. These agents took her passport with the excuse of getting her a SIM card but never returned it. Then, as in so many other cases, she was sold to a scam compound, deprived of her freedom, and forced to work under constant threat of violence.

She posted distress messages on the provincial governor's social media and was eventually rescued, but after that she was again trapped, this time in immigration detention. The Cambodian police refused to identify her as a human trafficking victim, and in the end she had to pay a fine of US$4,000 to leave the country. After returning to Taiwan, Yutang decided to do what she could to help those still trapped inside the compounds. Since then, she has assisted the police in collecting the personal details of people who have disappeared into the compounds, as well as information about the locations of scam companies and the traffickers involved in the trade. Her work has helped fill gaps in the investigations of the Taiwanese police, which are complicated by Taiwan's lack of a diplomatic presence in Cambodia. Yutang has also been fighting the public perception of the victims of the compounds as greedy or naïve for falling for high-paying-job tricks, arguing instead that most of these people were pushed into the industry by extenuating life circumstances. For instance, she told the media about a young Taiwanese man who went to Cambodia because he

---

39   This account is based on Tu Fengjun 塗豐駿, '柬埔寨驚魂！「羽棠」3天就自救逃出詐騙園區 回台變身志工已跨海救10人' (Cambodia Is Shocked! 'Yutang' Saved Herself and Escaped from the Scam Compound in Three Days. She Returned to Taiwan and Transformed into a Volunteer and Has Rescued 10 People across the Sea), 中天新聞網 (CTI), 16 August 2022; Su Yuxuan 蘇育宣, '《影片專訪》30歲台女被騙去柬埔寨 親曝煉獄7日駭人內幕' (Video Interview: 30-Year-Old Taiwanese Woman Was Tricked into Going to Cambodia and Revealed the Shocking Inside Story of 7 Days in Purgatory), 中時新聞網 (China Times), 16 August 2022.

had lost everything when his house had burned down: 'He just wanted to gain enough to cover the medical costs of his family. What dream of instant wealth could he possibly hold? What Taiwan organisations could help him in those circumstances?'[40]

Scam victims have also established informal volunteer groups that can be considered part of a self-salvation movement. For instance, the International Anti Scam and Trafficking Alliance (IASA) is a group composed of a couple of dozen volunteers who run social media accounts that initially focused on exposing scams, reaching out to people trapped inside scam compounds, and coordinating with law enforcement in mainland China and other countries to try to get them out. Most of the volunteers participating in IASA's activities are former scam victims. Many of them struggled with depression after losing their life savings to these schemes and joined the group to raise awareness of online scams, which helped boost their self-esteem and combat their feelings of powerlessness. Most of them began by opening social media accounts to tell their stories or by helping the police to find evidence about certain scam compounds and trace funds. Some of these volunteers told us of the shock they felt when they discovered the appalling conditions in which the people who scammed them might have been forced to operate:

After I got scammed, I just could not believe such bad people could exist. I was furious every day. I wanted to expose this to the whole world. I wanted everybody to know about this type of scam. Then slowly, I discovered that some scammers, even though I hated them so much, were also victims; they are tools that real criminals use and abandon. At a certain level, they are even more pitiful.

Since 2021, IASA has played an important role in supporting both scam victims and survivors of scam compounds, especially Chinese nationals. In the past, its volunteers have collaborated closely with the other actors discussed in this chapter to organise and coordinate rescue operations. They have also extensively shared their experiences online to raise public awareness and provide money-tracking services for scam victims. IASA managed to establish communication channels with global law enforcement agencies and encouraged people inside the scam compounds to

---

40   For the quote, see Huang Yijing 黃怡菁, '人口販運新型態 債務奴役詐騙不成先背債' (A New Form of Human Trafficking: Debt Slavery Fraud Is Not Successful), 新聞實驗室 (News Lab), 7 September 2022.

provide information about the operations so that they could hope for more favourable treatment once they returned to China.

These activities have faced many challenges, however. The coordination of rescue operations was extremely time- and energy-consuming for their members, as they needed to be available on the phone twenty-four hours a day for people trapped in the scam compounds, who might appear online at any time of the day or night, whenever they found a small window of opportunity. Operations such as these also generated high fees in covering the costs of transportation and food for survivors, as well as possible fines from immigration detention centres. In the event of unsuccessful operations or in those cases in which a rescue proved impossible, the volunteers were left to deal with their own feelings of guilt and failure, as well as with the anger and desperation of the person trapped inside.

As a result, the turnover rate within IASA has been very high. Core members shared concerns with the authors about the sustainability of their work considering these challenges, especially the lack of operating funds. They also mentioned the need to be extremely cautious about letting new members join the group, in case scammers infiltrate their ranks to undermine their work. Eventually, after the core members received several personal threats, the group decided to cease its rescue work and focus only on exposing fraudulent websites and gathering data from victims to channel to law enforcement and the media.

Fluid volunteer groups aside, there are also groups set up by survivors that attain a more formal status, by registering as NGOs, non-profits, or consultancies. The Global Anti-Scam Organization (GASO), for instance, was set up in June 2021 by a woman who had fallen victim to a pig-butchering scam. According to a core member we interviewed, GASO operates through various means, primarily focusing on awareness-raising and investigating online scams in collaboration with law enforcement agencies. Since the organisation's establishment, it has aided the rescue of individuals from many countries in Southeast Asia. But GASO's rescue efforts focus strictly on assisting people who have been coerced or forced into fraudulent activities, which entails differentiating between supposedly real victims and those who have willingly chosen to participate in scams – a distinction that, as we have seen, is rarely clear-cut.[41]

41   Global Anti-Scam Organization, '自願搞詐騙又何來的【被騙】？' (How Can You Get 'Cheated' if You Voluntarily Engage in Fraud?), Global Anti-Scam Organization website, 26 December 2022.

Life after the Compounds

Getting out of a compound is rarely the end of the ordeal for the people trapped inside. In most cases, survivors find themselves stranded and undocumented in a foreign country where they neither speak the language nor have any personal connections. Throughout Southeast Asia, compound survivors are often treated as criminals by immigration authorities, and they are generally detained unless they agree to pay substantial fines on top of the cost of return flights and the ransoms they may have had to pay their captors.

The law should offer protection to people trafficked and forced into criminality, but this is not always the case when it comes to those who have become entangled with the online scam industry in Southeast Asia. Countries in the region have taken steps to address human trafficking through the adoption of various legal frameworks and international agreements, albeit with varying degrees of specificity regarding forced criminality. Cambodia, Laos, Myanmar, Malaysia, and Vietnam have all signed memorandums of understanding (MoUs) on human trafficking, yet these agreements do not explicitly address issues related to forced criminality. As members of ASEAN, they also adhere to regional anti-trafficking frameworks. ASEAN's 2015 Convention against Trafficking in Persons, Especially Women and Children reinforces the non-punishment principle by urging member states to consider pardoning victims of trafficking for unlawful acts directly related to their situation as captives.[42] Even though no specific offence is named, victims of trafficking for the purpose of forced criminality in the online scam sector could rely on this provision to protect themselves from prosecution for any crimes they had been forced to commit.

Domestic laws vary. For instance, Thailand – through which people escaping from compounds in neighbouring countries often transit – has passed legislation such as the 2008 Anti-Trafficking in Persons Act that aligns with the objectives to protect and assist trafficking victims as espoused in UN documents such as the Palermo Protocol.[43] Still, there are loopholes. For instance, Article 41 of the Act specifically prohibits legal

42   'Convention against Trafficking in Persons, Especially Women and Children', ASEAN website, 2014.

43   Jean-Pierre Gauci and Noemi Magugliani, 'Human Trafficking and the Rights of Trafficked Persons: An Exploratory Analysis on the Application of the Non-punishment

proceedings against trafficking victims forced into criminality, but lists only four types of offence:

> Entering, leaving, or residing in the Kingdom without permission under the law on immigration, giving false information to the official, forging or using a forged travel document under the Penal Code, offence under the law on prevention and suppression of prostitution, particularly on contacting, persuading, introducing and soliciting a person for the purpose of prostitution and assembling together in the place of prostitution for the purpose of prostitution, or offence of being an alien working without permission under the law on working of the alien.[44]

This leaves a gap in which victims coerced into committing online fraud may not receive automatic protection under current Thai law. As a Thai law enforcement officer explained to us:

> Thailand accepts this principle under Article 41, which exempts penalties as mentioned in immigration law, prostitution, labour laws, and counterfeit laws. We only include these four cases without including other types. For instance, if a person is coerced into participating in war, we do not protect that person ... With scammers, there is a growing need to invoke this principle as suggested by the US TIP ['Trafficking in Persons'] report ... but we do not have laws directly addressing it.

Similarly, Cambodia and Laos criminalise human trafficking and provide protections for victims, but lack specific provisions addressing forced criminality, especially in emerging areas such as online fraud.

In such contexts, whether individuals involved in forced criminality in the online scam industry are treated as victims or criminals and whether scam activities are included under the non-punishment principle are decisions that rest heavily on the discretion of frontline law enforcement officers and their interpretation of the law. For instance, another Thai law enforcement officer alerted us to a possible legal loophole that could work in favour of the survivors of scam compounds. Article 67 of the Thai

---

Principle', International Bar Association Legal Policy & Research Unit and British Institute of International and Comparative Law, London, 2023.

44   See the Antislavery in Domestic Legislation website, antislaverylaw.ac.uk.

Criminal Code provides for a necessity defence, which could be invoked in cases of forced criminality where individuals act under compulsion or imminent danger that cannot be avoided. Sympathetic law enforcement officers could construe this as indirectly supporting the non-punishment principle for people trafficked into the online scam industry.

Still, there is the problem of how survivors can prove that they have been trafficked and coerced into undertaking criminal activities. People trapped inside the scam compounds are generally required to sign an employment contract on arrival. This serves not only to perpetuate the pretence that scamming is a legitimate line of work that they have voluntarily entered into, but also to trap workers under the burden of additional debts and obligations (even if the validity of such contracts is highly dubious). As a result, a common point of contention between local authorities and human rights organisations when it comes to people trafficked into criminality in the online scam industry is whether these cases constitute a labour dispute or a human trafficking issue. On one side, local authorities, especially in Cambodia, often categorise survivors' reason for leaving as a contractual dispute over labour conditions. They also focus on the criminal aspect of survivors' stories, underscoring their complicity with the crime syndicates for which they worked.[45] On the other side, NGOs tend to do exactly the opposite, emphasising the suffering these people have experienced inside and framing their cases as forced labour. Besides being very distressing for survivors, this makes victim identification particularly challenging for law enforcement, as questions about where voluntary work ends and forced labour begins cannot be set aside.

The burden of proof is often an insurmountable hurdle for survivors. Almost all our informants reported that they were asked by their first responder – usually local police or immigration officers – to provide objective evidence of compulsion directly and causally linked to their trafficking situation. Few survivors can satisfy these requirements. A common tactic used by managers of scam operations is to confiscate their workers' phones, replacing them with company devices used specifically to perpetrate scams. These devices are often heavily monitored. As one survivor recounted:

---

45   See, for instance, 'Majority of Alleged Trafficking Cases Tied to Fraud Operations, Says Foreign Ministry', BERNAMA, 1 July 2024.

We were only allowed to download certain apps for scam purposes. Sometimes they let us use our personal phones to send messages to family, but the manager would be there watching us to ensure we did not leak any information about the company to the outside world. One time, they beat the person who tried to contact the police so hard in front of us … After my family paid ransom for me, they gave back my phone but cleaned everything inside. So I do not have any evidence to prove that they trafficked me.

Another survivor recounted being denied recognition as a victim because a police officer found a photo of him laughing with colleagues while in the scam compound. The police held this image as evidence that he was 'voluntarily' participating in the scam activities, despite the survivor's repeated protestations that other images documenting violence and the dark side of life in the compound had been deleted by his manager before his release.

This practice of confiscating and monitoring communication devices, combined with physical intimidation and the erasure of digital evidence, significantly hinders survivors' ability to provide proof of their trafficking experiences to law enforcement. Moreover, as reports of torture within the compounds have become more widespread, managers are displaying remarkable creativity in their methods of physical punishment. Based on the testimonies of several survivors, instead of heavy beatings, scam operators are now more likely to employ tactics such as forcing individuals to climb stairs repeatedly, hold heavy objects while standing in the sun for extended periods, and work excessively long hours. Long stints in isolation combined with food and sleep deprivation are also common. These approaches are designed to avoid leaving visible scars on the body, further complicating the process of gathering evidence.

There are cases when repatriation of survivors of the scam compounds is extremely swift, but this tends to be when a group of people has been found and extracted from a compound during raids that have come about through joint law enforcement actions. For example, in March 2024, Vietnamese border officials received more than a hundred nationals who had been detained just five days previously in a raid in Sihanoukville, Cambodia.[46] But these cases are exceptional. Normally, the victim identification

---

46 Nhu Tam, 'Vietnam Receives over 100 Citizens Accused of Gambling in Cambodia', *VNExpress International*, 14 March 2024.

and repatriation process for trafficked individuals in Southeast Asia is complex and involves several stages and actors, which vary across countries. Figure 2 shows a simplified version of how the system works in Cambodia, based on the testimonies of interviewees who went through the process.

If a survivor of a scam compound wants to be officially identified as a victim of human trafficking for forced labour and seeks repatriation through official channels without being punished for violating immigration or other local rules, they must be rescued by police. If they exit a compound on their own initiative by paying a ransom, staging an escape, or with the help of a local civil society organisation, they must report themselves to the local police. Among the survivors interviewed for this research, none of those who left the compound without police intervention had their request to have their case handled as a human trafficking victim accepted. Once such a request is denied, there are two scenarios: if the survivors still hold their passport and have committed no other crimes, they can pay an overstay fine and buy a flight back to their country; or if they do not have identification documents, they must turn themselves in to the immigration department, which will treat them as illegal migrants and place them under detention.

If the police are directly involved in the rescue or agree to handle the case as a potential instance of human trafficking, survivors undergo an initial interview by an officer in the province where they have sought help before being transferred to the Central Security Department in Phnom Penh for further interviews. Even this first step of reporting to police is never easy in a context where officials receiving rescue requests have been found to have links to the very groups involved in the alleged detention. Such situations make individuals trapped in the scam compounds wary of giving too much information to the police. As one of our interviewees explained:

> I managed to contact my family back in China, and they helped me report my situation to the local police. The Chinese police advised me to reach out to the Cambodian police for rescue and provided a website to report my case. However, when I attempted to fill out the form on the website, much of it was in a language I didn't understand … My family then connected me with a rescuer in Cambodia, but that person asked so many questions such as the identity of my trafficker, my location, and

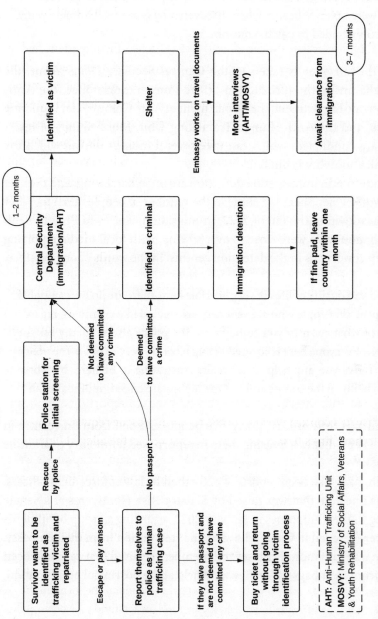

Figure 2: Identification and repatriation process for suspected foreign victims of human trafficking in Cambodia based on survivor testimonies

Source: The authors

Survivor wants to be identified as trafficking victim and repatriated

Escape or pay ransom

Report themselves to police as human trafficking case

If they have passport and are not deemed to have committed any crime

Buy ticket and return without going through victim identification process

Rescue by police

Police station for initial screening

No passport

Not deemed to have committed any crime

Deemed to have committed a crime

1–2 months

Central Security Department (immigration/AHT)

Identified as victim

Identified as criminal

Immigration detention

If fine paid, leave country within one month

Shelter

Embassy works on travel documents

More interviews (AHT/MOSVY)

Await clearance from immigration

3–7 months

AHT: Anti-Human Trafficking Unit
MOSVY: Ministry of Social Affairs, Veterans & Youth Rehabilitation

the name of my company. He said it was the only way he could contact the police on my behalf. I was terrified to disclose this information because I had seen others in my company who tried to get rescued but were severely beaten when discovered by our boss. Ultimately, my parents decided to pay the ransom.

Once the survivor is taken to the Central Security Department, the case falls under the jurisdiction of the immigration police, the Anti-Cybercrime Department, the Department of Anti-Commercial Gambling Crimes, and the Anti–Human Trafficking Unit. More rounds of interviews are conducted, which can take several months during which the survivors' mobility is limited.

Conditions in immigration detention are often harrowing, and they get even worse when there is a surge in the number of people taken in. After the crackdown of the fall of 2022, immigration centres in Phnom Penh and Sihanoukville were close to overflowing, with local media reporting on grim conditions in the detention centres. In the words of one detainee:

> Food and quality of life are very horrible here, there are no human rights to speak of. People who are sent here are treated like criminals, regardless of what country you come from. The police also regularly ask for tips … Everyone here is covered in bug bites, it's very itchy … The police won't give you any help … It's really frustrating to be here. It's worse than being in the compound … One nightmare ended, another began.[47]

Around this time at least thirty-five people escaped from one centre in Phnom Penh that was housing them in repurposed temporary quarantine facilities.[48]

There have also been reports of petty theft by law enforcement officers, such as one case that was raised by Senator Risa Hontiveros at a Senate hearing in the Philippines in January 2023 regarding a group of Filipinos who were rescued in Cambodia after an intervention from their embassy. On the way to Phnom Penh several members realised that cash had been taken from their bags while they were held at the provincial police station,

---

47   Mech Dara and Cindy Liu, 'Rescued Scam Workers Break Out of Immigration Center Amid "Nightmare"', Voice of Democracy, 8 October 2022.
48   Ibid.

and the police who had driven them also asked them for 'gas money'.[49] The next month the senator raised the issue of conditions for rescued workers again, describing the weeks-long negotiations needed to get them home as 'weeks filled with anxiety'.[50] In the Philippines itself, major raids on online gaming hubs have in several instances found hundreds of foreign workers; in the absence of dedicated facilities large enough to accommodate them, they have been held in the compound itself while investigations and immigration processing occur.[51]

These conditions were confirmed by all of our interviewees who ended up in immigration centres. Among our informants was a couple who had a baby while held in immigration detention. The mother was sixteen and already pregnant when she was trafficked by boat from China to Cambodia, where she met her new partner, who was being held in the same compound and also unable to leave. After they escaped, both were detained by Cambodian immigration police. As the man recounted to us:

> We had to sleep on the floor, and the food there was not good for my girlfriend and our unborn baby. Luckily, there was a Chinese detainee who donated a mattress to us. She told us that you could ask the guards to get anything for you if you could afford the price, which was always double or triple compared to the outside. When the due date approached, I begged the guard to let my girlfriend go to the hospital, but they just kept asking us for money. Finally, it was the rescue team who paid the fee, as well as all the charges for the delivery of the baby.
>
> But just a few days later, the immigration police locked us back in jail with our baby. My girlfriend was not able to produce any milk because she was malnourished. We were all covered with bed bugs, but when we asked for treatment, the guards again demanded tips. I really thought our baby would die soon in that environment. The Chinese Embassy never came for a visit or consultation. My girlfriend fell into depression because it felt like the entire world had abandoned us.

---

49   Michelle Abad, 'OFWs Trafficked into Crypto Scam, Then "Hostaged" after Rescue – Hontiveros', Rappler, 19 January 2023.

50   Michelle Abad, 'Weeks-Long "Negotiations" Delayed Repatriation of OFWs from Cambodia', Rappler, 27 February 2023.

51   Cyber Scam Monitor, 'Major Raids Hit Alleged Scam Hubs in the Philippines', Cyber Scam Monitor, 25 September 2023, cyberscammonitor.substack.com.

If a survivor is eventually identified as a victim of human trafficking, they are placed in an official shelter and receive support reserved for certified victims, including free food, accommodation, legal aid, and medical assistance. Further interviews are conducted by the Anti–Human Trafficking Unit and the Ministry of Social Affairs, Veterans, and Youth Rehabilitation inside the shelter. These questions are largely the same as those initially asked by the police, in a duplication of efforts that highlights a lack of coordination, or possibly mutual distrust, between agencies. If a survivor's request to be identified as a victim is rejected, they are sent to immigration detention. Here, they may face charges of illegal border crossing, visa overstays, or even fraud, if relevant evidence is found. If they can pay the fines, they may leave the country within one month.

One significant issue that has emerged from our interviews is how local law enforcement, as well as other actors involved in the process, including embassies, often proves unqualified to interview survivors who have experienced significant trauma. This applies across the board, all over the region and with a broad array of stakeholders. This results in retraumatisation and further psychological harm. This is what happened to Alice, the Taiwanese survivor who had been repeatedly raped inside scam compounds and whom we met at the very beginning of this book. When she sought help from the Cambodian police, she was interviewed by male officers who repeatedly asked for detailed descriptions of the violence to which she had been subjected. NGO practitioners told us about a similar situation involving a young woman who had been trafficked to a scam compound in Myanmar and later abandoned in Thailand due to severe medical issues resulting from physical and sexual abuse. When officers from her embassy visited her in the hospital to question her about her experience, all of them were male, which severely retraumatised her.

While in the shelter, identified victims also need assistance from their embassy to receive travel documents. The level of cooperation from consular officials varies from embassy to embassy, with some being extremely helpful and efficient, and others less so. Even after the victims get the travel documents from their embassy, they face a lengthy wait – in the case of our informants between three and seven months – for clearance from the local immigration authority before they can be repatriated. If they are lucky, NGOs or embassies with larger budgets shoulder the costs of the trip, but that is not always the reality, and it varies on a case-by-case basis.

Even at this stage, there could still be significant hurdles to repatriation. If someone is identified as a victim in the destination country, there is no guarantee they will be recognised as such in their country of origin. This is particularly problematic in the case of survivors from mainland China, as Chinese criminal law acknowledges only women and children as possible victims of human trafficking, which precludes the identification of adult Chinese men as victims of human trafficking for forced labour. If they are acknowledged as victims of human trafficking in the destination country, they might face criminal proceedings back in China anyway as their status is not recognised there – or vice versa, if they are officially acknowledged as victims of illicit detention in China (the best outcome they can hope for), this might not translate into a formal identification as a human trafficking victim in their destination country, and this might delay their repatriation considerably. The latter scenario was the experience of one of our informants, a Chinese man who was trafficked to Myanmar and managed to escape by jumping out of a car in Thailand during his transfer to Cambodia:

> My family called the Chinese police immediately after I went missing. Once I managed to contact the Chinese authorities, I cooperated extensively with them, providing names of scam bosses and helping them stop scam activities. The Chinese police identified me as a victim of illegal detention. However, after I escaped and showed the local police in Thailand this document, they insisted that I still need to go through a victim identification process, which will take months. I just want to go back home. Why can't law enforcement work together and share my information?

Even being formally acknowledged as victims of human trafficking in the source country is not always enough. We came across cases in which local immigration authorities in Southeast Asia wilfully ignored documents from Chinese law enforcement that certified that Chinese women and minors rescued from scam compounds were to be considered victims of human trafficking. This was the case for two fourteen-year-old girls from Jiangxi province who were trafficked to Cambodia in August 2024; their families spent the equivalent of over US$10,000 to pay for the freedom of the two girls, in one case tapping into money allocated for the medical expenses of an ailing grandfather. Even though Chinese law enforcement provided them with an official document certifying that they had been trafficked, immigration officials in Cambodia refused to let them leave the country, demanding instead that they pay a substantial fine on top of all the other costs related to shelter and repatriation that they had to cover out of their own pocket.

Given all these difficulties, it is perhaps unsurprising that many survivors choose either to pay the fines for violating immigration rules or to hire snakeheads to smuggle them back home. This was especially common during the pandemic period when repatriation back to China was exceptionally difficult. Even though people who lost their passports could get temporary travel papers from the Chinese Embassy, there were very few flights running, and those that were available were often exorbitantly expensive. This left many with no other choice than to resort to smugglers to get them back home. One Chinese man who supported survivors in Cambodia used to offer such services to those who stayed with him. According to two of our interviewees, he helped many to return home safely using routes through Vietnam. These people first reached Mộc Bài, on the opposite side of the border to Bavet, then travelled north by car. Once they arrived at the China–Vietnam border, they were met by Chinese police, who had been notified about the situation. The average charge for such a trip was around US$5,000.

Chinese survivors escaping from Myanmar who want to avoid the ordeal of the official victim identification system in Thailand also often resort to smugglers. Once they manage to escape the compound, smugglers will send a team to pick them up in the surrounding area and escort them to the Chinese border. While the cost of the service varies depending on where they are in the country, one smuggler we spoke to in 2023 told us that those individuals who spontaneously turn themselves in to the police when they get to the Chinese side of the border were only fined for illegal crossing in most cases. These smugglers often work closely with rescue teams and even (informally) with police officers, who refer them to people trapped in the compounds. This helps enhance the smugglers' credibility in a context in which there are multiple stories of drivers selling their charges back to the compounds. According to one of our informants, the situation changed in the wake of the crackdown launched in northern Myanmar in late 2023. At the time of writing in late 2024, the practice of demanding a fine seemed to have been discontinued, with most Chinese adults being detained for investigation and minors released once they cross the border.

Challenges and Constraints

The stories we have covered in this chapter mention just a few of those actors who have been involved in supporting people trapped inside Southeast Asia's scam compounds. Others range from politicians who have been lobbying their governments for more effective interventions to curb human trafficking to controversial underworld-linked figures, such as the Taiwanese former organised crime boss encountered earlier in the book, who helped some families get their relatives back. Journalists and bloggers have also run considerable risks to cover the industry from the ground, as have researchers and investigators who have exposed several of the actors behind the compounds. Even some white hat (ethical) hackers have been playing a role in unmasking these operations.[52] As the reach of the industry has grown, international agencies – such as the United Nations' Office on Drugs and Crime (UNODC), the Office of the High Commissioner for Human Rights (OHCHR), and the International Organization for Migration (IOM) – have also become increasingly vocal and engaged. Likewise, law enforcement agencies from around the world have been sharing information and collaborating on joint actions to investigate scam operators, seize funds, and carry out arrests.

The response to this unfolding crisis was slower than it should have been, and this was likely exacerbated by the fact that the scale of the problem really started to emerge just prior to the start of the COVID-19 pandemic. Initially, grassroots groups and individuals supporting victims struggled to get the attention of international organisations, who had not yet prioritised the issue. Today, although there is much more that can and should be done, it is encouraging to see the plight of those victimised by the industry getting the attention they deserve – including both scam victims and those brutalised by the compounds.

Yet there are numerous obstacles and factors making this already diffi-cult work even more challenging. As ever when we look into this industry, even the area of victim support has a dark side. In December 2023, Viet-namese media reported that a man had been arrested in Binh Duong province for extorting thousands of dollars from human trafficking victims

---

52   On the remarkable story of one Vietnamese hacker, see Koh Ewe, 'This Hacker Stole Data from 200M Americans. Now He's Infiltrating Scam Gangs', *Vice*, 16 September 2022; Mech Dara, Sen Nguyen, and Michael Dickison, 'Inside a Scam: White-Hat Hacker Infiltrates Cambodian Operations', Voice of Democracy, 7 July 2022.

in Cambodia after promising to rescue them. He set up a TikTok channel building a profile as a rescuer, and after two women contacted him, he requested they pay him VNĐ170 million (US$7,000) up front, followed by another VNĐ230 million (US$9,500) once in Vietnam. According to the report, when they arrived in Vietnam, he demanded their families pay the second tranche of the money if they did not want to be sold into Thailand. The police were informed and arrested the man, who said under interrogation that he had conspired with human traffickers to execute the extortion.[53] Other characters who have emerged on WeChat seem to have a dubious role in the rescue community. Several online accounts have posted dramatic accounts of rescue operations they have led into dangerous areas of Myanmar. One group in particular boasts of carrying weapons into the country, posting images of the team leader in various scenes wearing body armour, carrying a sidearm, and sometimes surrounded by heavy-duty weapons including a sniper rifle. While almost certainly fantastical, these accounts show that the attention genuine rescue groups are receiving is now so widespread that others are seeking to hitch their social media profiles to the issue.[54]

As we were putting the finishing touches to this book, accounts set up by people claiming to be able to rescue victims were flooding Chinese social media, attracting hundreds of desperate family members hoping to help individuals trapped in scam compounds across Southeast Asia. One of us entered several of these groups and discovered that many of these so-called rescuer-influencers simply act as middlemen: they charge families rescue fees and claim the credit, but then pass the cases to real rescue teams who conduct operations voluntarily (unpaid). In some cases, families paid money only to be blocked and deleted by these influencers. Such actions severely damage the trust between victims, their families, and those genuinely trying to help. As more incidents like these come to light, it has become increasingly common for rescue team members to face scepticism or even insults from victim families questioning their authenticity.

---

53   Yen Khanh and Phuoc Tuan, 'Man Poses as Rescuer, Extorts Thousands of Dollars from Trafficking Victims in Cambodia', *VNExpress International*, 25 December 2023.

54   Dong He 冬禾, '我在缅甸边境救同胞，被悬赏400万抓捕' (I Rescued Compatriots on the Myanmar Border and a Reward of Four Million Was Offered for My Arrest), 凤凰网 (Phoenix), 19 October 2023.

Various other structural and circumstantial constraints are hindering the efforts of those trying to assist people trapped in the compounds. On the structural side are the limitations of the current laws and regulations regarding forced criminality in Southeast Asia and lack of coordination among national law enforcement bodies when it comes to victim identification and repatriation. One important step forward would be for policymakers in the region to recognise the complexities of forced criminality in the online scam industry and adopt relevant legislation to fill current gaps and address loopholes. Another would be for law enforcement agencies in the region to reach a common understanding about how to apply victim identification criteria in a more consistent and transparent fashion.

Another structural constraint is the political climate that civil society organisations must navigate, not only in trafficking-destination countries such as Cambodia, Laos, and Myanmar, all of which are ruled by authoritarian regimes, but also in some source countries, especially mainland China and Vietnam. To different degrees, these governments are wary of civil society and impose often invisible red lines that many organisations cannot afford to cross. This is complicated by the fact that state actors and well-connected elites in countries hosting scam operations, including law enforcement, are often complicit in the very industry that civil society groups are at odds with. While this multibillion-dollar criminal industry has undoubtedly created a humanitarian crisis, some organisations have decided to stay away from the problem, in part due to its complexity, but also because they are wary of treading on sensitive ground; others have become involved, but need to manage their exposure carefully, and this limits their effectiveness.

Yet another structural difficulty is the lack of trust engendered by the online scam industry, which reverberates in the attitude that survivors hold towards those who are trying to help them. We have seen how survivors often have good reason to distrust local law enforcement; unfortunately, the same mistrust sometimes extends to civil society. Many of the groups offering hands-on victim support have no official status, which complicates communication with the people they are trying to help, as the latter understandably tend to be distrustful of unfamiliar entities and individuals acting independently. People from mainland China, in particular, are often hesitant to cooperate with civil society groups, questioning their motives and fearing possible associations with 'foreign hostile forces' (境外敌对势力 *jingwai didui shili*), a common refrain in the discourse of the Chinese government on the subject of NGOs working in politically sensitive fields.[55] Some victims, frustrated with the uncertainties of the rescue process, may even blame those who are trying to assist them for their predicament – something one of the authors has experienced on more than one occasion. To make things worse, this distrust cuts both ways, with civil society actors sometimes questioning the motives of those they are assisting.

Circumstantial constraints are mostly related to the scarcity of financial resources to support rescues, repatriation, and aftercare for survivors, as well as a lack of training and expertise among relevant stakeholders. Forced criminality in the online scam industry has presented law enforcement and civil society with new, unexpected challenges for which they have largely been unprepared. First, some of the new groups that have sprung up only recently lack proper training in how to operate in the field of human trafficking and modern slavery. This translates not only into a notable lack of expertise on how to engage with people who have gone through extremely traumatic experiences – a problem they share with law enforcement, as we have seen – but also into more basic mistakes such as endangering survivors by posting their personal details on social media with the idea of raising funding to help them. Second, there have been disagreements among organisations on who should be considered a victim, with some insisting that people who have entered compounds voluntarily and then end up trapped there should not be considered as such. This has driven a wedge into some rescue efforts. Third, the division of labour among the various stakeholders remains somewhat chaotic. While individuals from different organisations are often in touch with each other when dealing with specific cases, there is still a need for improved information sharing and more efficient and rational work processes to coordinate these activities.

Two additional limitations are more specific to engagements with Sinophone survivors, who still constitute the bulk of compound workforces and most often cannot speak English or any language but Chinese. Law

---

55   For a discussion of this discourse in the context of labour activism in China, see for instance Ivan Franceschini and Christian Sorace, 'In the Name of the Working Class: Narratives of Labour Activism in Contemporary China', *Pacific Affairs* 92(4), 2019, pp. 643–64.

enforcement and civil society both face considerable language barriers that prevent them from engaging with these survivors. To overcome this, many groups resort to recruiting Chinese-speaking volunteers, a solution that works in the short term when such volunteers are available but is clearly unsustainable in the longer term. Also connected to language barriers and lack of expertise is an absence of connections between actors involved in rescue attempts in Southeast Asia and civil society in mainland China. While this is an inevitable outcome of restrictive policies in China that often discourage domestic civil society attempts to work with foreign counterparts, similar attempts from the other side have also been very limited. The result is that once Chinese survivors manage to return to their homes, they are basically left to fend for themselves.

Indeed, the limited capacity to provide aftercare is possibly the most severe limitation of current civil society efforts to assist survivors of the scam compounds. For instance, after the sixteen-year-old mother we mentioned earlier in this chapter was bailed out of immigration detention, she could not find any support for herself or her child. One of the authors tried to raise some funding for them among her friends in China, but they warned her that individual fundraising could be illegal according to the country's Charity Law. When the same author tried to contact someone linked to the Chinese-led charity team in Cambodia, they offered to help the woman's partner find work in Phnom Penh to pay for their accommodation and flight tickets back to China. Despite the couple lacking proper paperwork and facing the risk of being exploited or even re-trafficked, this was the best the charity team could offer. In the end, a local NGO agreed to provide medical care and food for the family, but shelter remained a problem. The mother was in a state of severe malnutrition and suffering from depression, which required professional care and constant support from her partner. The existing shelters dedicated to trafficking and modern slavery victims in Cambodia were mostly for women only, however, and not equipped with Chinese-speaking staff.

After the couple eventually managed to go back to China, their lot did not improve. The girl had initially been trafficked after trying to run away from her violent father. At that time, she had trusted her then boyfriend when he suggested that they try to start a new life in Cambodia and she agreed to follow him, not realising that they would be smuggled by boat. After all that happened in Cambodia she had left the new partner she had met in the compound, but, without intervention from social workers and no financial support for raising her baby, had no choice but to return to her parents for help. We followed her case and helped her find a psychologist. However, after only three sessions she dropped out and sent us this final message:

> I want to thank you for what you have done for me and my child. But I don't know what I can expect in the future. My dad took the baby away, blaming me for being unable to be a mother. I am scared he will beat me again if I fight, so I think I will just go to another city to find a job. I hope this time I won't be tricked again.

Conclusion

To face a crisis that transcends national borders, transnational responses are required. Over the past few years, there have been several joint law enforcement actions made possible by bilateral or multilateral agreements and partnerships. For instance, when reports of violent crime in Sihanoukville were becoming widespread in 2018, Cambodia and China reached a formal agreement to establish a law enforcement partnership, which resulted in the opening of the China–Cambodia Law Enforcement Cooperation Office in Phnom Penh in September 2019.[1] This was the first such bilateral office set up by China in the world. The Chinese government also became proactive with Myanmar, pushing the national authorities to crack down on the online scam industry and launching several joint operations with local police in 2023, before ramping up this cooperation in the north of the country in September that year.[2] In the past couple of years, there have additionally been numerous bilateral commitments between regional police forces to increase coordination on the issue, and at the May 2023 ASEAN Summit, the leaders of the ten countries adopted a specific declaration on combating trafficking in persons 'caused by the abuse of technology'.[3]

---

1 Mao Pengfei 毛鹏飞, '中柬执法合作协调办公室在金边正式成立' (China–Cambodia Law Enforcement Cooperation Office Officially Established in Phnom Penh), 新华 (Xinhua), 28 September 2019.

2 See, for instance, 'China Ramps Up Action against Online Fraud in Northern Myanmar', Cyber Scam Monitor, 26 October 2023, cyberscammonitor.substack.com.

3 'ASEAN Leaders' Declaration on Combating Trafficking in Persons Caused by the Abuse of Technology', adopted at 42nd ASEAN Summit, 10–11 May 2023.

In the absence of any detailed and consistent disclosure on the outcomes of these various commitments, however, it is challenging to assess how effective they have truly been, especially as it is clear that the industry continues to thrive, despite various setbacks. China's law enforcement cooperation with Cambodia has been heavily publicised, yet information that can be gleaned from media reports and official Chinese documents indicates China has had far more success in cracking down on the parts of the criminal networks active within its own borders, as well as apprehending citizens when they return there. In Myanmar, despite numerous high-level engagements with the junta leadership, China's influence failed to prevent the expansion of a massive scam empire stretching from the border with Thailand to China's doorstep. The Kokang region's online scam industry was brought down, but this may not have been the case were it not for the ethnic armed organisations of the Brotherhood Alliance launching their military operation targeting the region in October 2023. The month prior, cooperation between China and Wa State authorities set in chain a series of raids which resulted in what has likely been the most successful cross-border crackdown. Thousands of Chinese nationals were handed over to China and hundreds of people from other countries were evacuated and repatriated, despite details of the operation having been leaked prior to a wave of raids, including the names of the target compounds and the times when they would be hit.[4] One of the authors even managed to obtain a copy of the schedule. Consequently, many scam operations pre-emptively moved their staff to mountainous areas, avoiding police intervention. Many others transferred to other parts of the country or hopped the border to neighbouring countries.

Under these circumstances, foreign law enforcement has focused significant effort on prevention. This is unsurprising given the enormous logistical and financial challenges involved in cross-border actions, as well as the complexity of coordinating across multiple jurisdictions and with bilateral partners that often lack the willingness or ability to crack down on activities within their own countries. During our discussions with civil society practitioners and law enforcement officials, the problem of insufficient cooperation and lack of coordination was a recurring grievance. As

---

4   Lin Huizhi 林煇智, '幕后老板中国人 很多人都是自愿 缅甸诈骗园区 为何难以整治？' (The Boss behind the Scenes Is Chinese. Many People Do It Voluntarily. Why Is It So Difficult to Rectify the Fraud Complex in Myanmar?), 联合早报 (Lianhe Zaobao), 15 October 2023.

a legal-support team member from one nongovernmental organisation told us: 'Addressing such crimes typically necessitates collaboration among law enforcement agencies spanning at least three to four countries. I have been trying to help scam victims to sue their perpetrators, but I found a common scenario in which a Chinese perpetrator residing in Cambodia trafficked a Filipino individual to deceive a US citizen, using credit cards from Dubai for money laundering.'

As we have seen, in some cases, such as Taiwan, police have attempted to stop people from travelling to high-risk areas by dispatching personnel to the airports to warn people about to embark on flights to Southeast Asia for dubious work placements. The Philippines Bureau of Immigration has released a steady stream of warnings to citizens planning to travel to Thailand, Cambodia, Laos, and Myanmar for jobs in customer service and other remote online work. In other cases, such as in mainland China, the authorities made it difficult for citizens to cross customs controls to board for a suspicious destination without a credible travel reason, with police even calling people who booked flights to travel to Southeast Asian countries to ask for details about the purpose of their trip.[5] Much effort also went into arresting recruiters and trafficking gangs, and dismantling money-laundering networks.

The Chinese government has been particularly active in seeking ways to disrupt the flow of labour and hit the sections of the scam economy that lie within its territory. Besides launching anti-scam campaigns aimed at raising public awareness of the industry, the Chinese authorities have adopted increasingly harsh measures. To list just some of the most consequential policies, in February 2021, China's Supreme Court, Supreme Procuratorate, and Ministry of Public Security jointly released a 'Notice on Urging Criminal Suspects Related to Cross-Border Gambling to Surrender', which attempted to persuade Chinese citizens involved in gambling, opening casinos, and other related crimes overseas to return to China by promising more lenient treatment if they voluntarily surrendered to law enforcement organs.[6] In December 2022, China's first Anti-Telecom and

---

5   Gu Ting, 'Booked a Flight out of China? Police Are Likely to Knock on Your Door', Radio Free Asia, 20 February 2023.

6   Supreme People's Court, Supreme People's Procuratorate, and Ministry of Public Security, ' 《最高人民法院最高人民检察院公安部关于敦促跨境赌博相关犯罪嫌疑人投案自首的通告》（全文）' ('Supreme People's Court's Notice on Urging Criminal Suspects Related to Cross-Border Gambling to Surrender' Full Text), 5 February 2021.

Online Fraud Law came into effect, requiring telecom operators, financial institutions, and internet service providers to set up internal systems for controlling fraud risks and setting out penalties, including imprisonment and fines for individuals involved in fraudulent activities.[7] In December 2024, to support the implementation of this new law, the Ministry of Public Security enforced more severe punishment measures for telecom fraudsters and those who assist them, such as people who illegally buy, sell, rent, or lend SIM cards, bank or payment accounts, digital wallets, internet accounts, and domain names.[8]

While these measures have filled legislative gaps that have been exposed by the rise of the scam industry, at the subnational level some extreme and sometimes unsanctioned methods were used to pursue people allegedly involved in illegal gambling or fraud overseas. Over the past few years Chinese police started to call the relatives of people suspected of involvement in illegal activities in Southeast Asia, and issued public announcements in their home communities threatening punishment if they refused to return within a given time.[9] These punishments included being added to a 'List of Dishonest People' (失信人员名单 *shixin renyuan mingdan*). Anyone appearing on these lists was prevented from purchasing property, using online payment platforms such as Alipay or WeChat for money transfers, and buying train and flight tickets, among many other inconveniences; as well, alleged scammers' immediate family members were forbidden from taking jobs in the public sector or joining the army, their financial credit downgraded, and their children's access to education limited. In some cases, this included cancelling their household registration (户籍 *huji*), which would prevent those on the list and their immediate family members from accessing public services.[10]

---

7   For the full text of the law, see gov.cn; for a summary in English, see Changhao Wei and Taige Hu, 'Legislation Summary: China's New Law to Fight Telecom and Internet Fraud', NPC Observer, 7 September 2022.

8   '电信网络诈骗及其关联违法犯罪联合惩戒办法' (Joint Punishment Measures for Telecommunications Network Fraud and Related Violations and Crimes), Baidu Baike, 26 November 2024.

9   Zhang Yilin 张依琳, '多地喊话! 这类人拒不回国将注销户口! ' (Many Places Shout! If Such People Refuse to Return Home, Their Household Registration Will Be Cancelled!), 中国新闻网 (China News), 10 November 2021.

10   For an example of one such policy implemented in 2023 in Xingguo county, Jiangxi province, see: '关于敦促兴国籍非法滞留境外涉诈重点人员限期回国的通告' (Notice on Urging Key People from Xingguo Illegally Staying Abroad and Involved in

Measures vary across different towns and counties, and in some hotspot areas identified for their high concentration of individuals who have entered the online scam industry abroad, some went as far as public shaming of the families of alleged scammers by daubing their houses with slogans such as 'Shame on Online Scamming' (电诈可耻 *dianzha kechi*).[11] When people do return to China, even those who are acknowledged as having been trapped in scam compounds can be subject to punishment. In December 2023, the *China Daily* reported that a man lured to northern Myanmar was sentenced to two years in prison by a court in Guizhou province after he returned and surrendered to authorities in China.[12] He had been trapped in Myanmar for three years, and had been sold several times. He was subject to physical abuse and his movement was restricted; he only escaped after paying a CN¥460,000 (US$64,000) ransom. The two-year jail sentence took into account his surrender, confession, and repentance.

Despite the widespread anger in China against those involved in online scams, some of these measures evoked public concern due to their impacts on family members who are not involved in the crimes of their relatives, as well as administrative punishments being levied on people who had after all not yet been convicted of any crime.[13] Furthermore, given what we know about the industry, it is likely that many people have been unable to return home and surrender, even if they want to. Eventually, these concerns found an echo even in the official realm. In December 2023, the Legislative Affairs Commission of the Standing Committee of the National People's Congress reviewed the issuance of local government circulars that included penalties for the family members of overseas fraud suspects and ruled that they were inconsistent with China's constitution. In their statement, they commented: 'After study, we believe that any legal responsibility

Fraud to Return to China within a Certain Time), Public Security Bureau, Xingguo, on WeChat, 10 April 2023, mp.weixin.qq.com/s/HgoqkrUDHPH83zYLs3y3Bg.

11   '电信诈骗等四大热点领域治理取得阶段性进展' (Progress Has Been Made in the Governance of Four Major Hotspot Areas in Telecommunication Fraud), 信用中国 (Xinyong Zhongguo), 20 August 2018. People's Government of Yunshishan Township, '关于进一步落实缅北电信网络诈骗人员劝返工作的通知' (Notice on Further Implementing the Work of Persuading Telecom Fraudsters to Return from Northern Myanmar), People's Government of Ruijin City website, 15 June 2021.

12   Xu Zhesheng, 'Scammed, Sold, Saved: Guizhou Man's Ordeal in Myanmar Fraud Ring Ends with Jail Time', *China Daily*, 21 December 2023.

13   Ye Zhanhang, 'Fujian District Punishes Relatives to Deter Scams, Sparks Debate', Sixth Tone, 29 May 2023.

for unlawful or criminal conduct must rest with the perpetrator him or herself and must not be extended or attributed to others; such is one of the fundamental tenets of modern rule of law.'[14]

While better rules and improved coordination between law enforcement agencies are important in fighting the online scam industry, it is not useful to focus exclusively on a legal response without understanding the root causes that allow scam operations to thrive. If the scam economy can flourish, it is because of a confluence of factors unique to this late stage of capitalism we currently find ourselves in. Our increasingly online existence and the rapid emergence of increasingly sophisticated new technologies, including artificial intelligence, that have been deployed for scamming purposes are undoubtedly an important part of the story. So is the entrenchment of corrupt elites and the globalisation of criminal groups, both perpetually on the lookout for new markets and sources of profit. But it is the predicament of those who are at the receiving end of their plunder and violence that provides us with the most significant insights into what is behind this latest humanitarian crisis.

On one hand, there is a growing supply of individuals rendered desperate by the lack of decent jobs and facing limited life opportunities – a situation exacerbated by the COVID-19 pandemic – who have been lured into the industry by the mirage of high-paying positions. Some might enter the compounds in the hope of becoming wealthy and enjoying a lifestyle as luxurious as that vaunted by their recruiters, but greed is rarely the sole motivation (and even where it is, we should interrogate the reasons behind such fascination with material wealth). On the other hand, there is an expansive pool of people who are now perpetually online, many of them also facing financial difficulties and eager to improve their lot, or simply pining for the ability to afford lifestyles and products that are marketed to them every hour of every day. Many feel lonely and isolated, leaving them vulnerable to anyone who seems to offer friendship and a sympathetic ear. While we do not seek to minimise the culpability of those who voluntarily enter into and profit from this industry, it is crucial to examine *why* they make this choice, just as it is to understand how people are tricked and forced into it. In the case of both scammed and scammers, assuming that greed is the sole motivation fails to take into account the emotionally bleak

---

14 'China's Top Legislation-Review Body Halts Local Governments' Collective Punishment of Telecom Fraudsters' Families', NPC Observer, 29 December 2023.

landscape of our societies at this stage, and the atomisation and loneliness that often characterise the human experience in our epoch.

It is exactly because of these structural conditions that, no matter how hard the authorities in some countries attempt to crack down on the industry, the scam economy has been thriving and will most likely continue to grow in the coming years. When scam operators come under pressure in some areas – as happened briefly in Cambodia in September 2022, and again in late 2023 in northern Myanmar, and in mid-2024 in the Philippines and in the Golden Triangle in Laos – they are often simply able to pack up and move to a different location. Dozens of countries can provide a suitable base for these groups, as long as they can count on adequate physical infrastructure and the protection and support of local friendly elites and complicit state actors. As we have explained, over the past couple of decades the online scam industry has leapfrogged from Taiwan to mainland China, before expanding to the Philippines, Cambodia, Laos, and Myanmar, but today fraud operations have truly gone global, with evidence of scam compounds appearing as far afield as Serbia, Turkey, Georgia, Mexico, Peru, Sri Lanka, India, and Central and West Africa. As new technologies are developed and advance, online scams are likely to become more sophisticated. In other words, the industry is here to stay.

To mitigate the immediate impacts of this industry and eventually bring it down requires joint effort from a wide range of actors, many of whom have already shown admirable dedication to the cause, under challenging and sometimes dangerous circumstances. The last few years have been a learning experience for all, from grassroots rescue groups to global law enforcement and governments. Moving forward, given the transnational and cross-sectoral implications of online fraud, it will be necessary to develop better coordination between state actors, law enforcement, international organisations, and civil society and humanitarian groups so as to conduct effective rescue operations. It will also be important to provide survivors of the scam compounds with adequate aftercare and support, including finding ways to help them reintegrate into society, as well as working with fraud victims to recover lost assets and offering them social support, including mental health services. Tech companies are failing to ensure that their services are not used as platforms for organised criminals, and urgently need to step up and address abuse to prevent the proliferation of fake job ads and the dissemination of fraudulent links and materials, as well as block channels utilised by traffickers and money launderers. Greater resources also need to be dedicated to transnational law enforcement activities targeting the industry, and crucially there must be repercussions for host-country collusion and inaction, which will otherwise continue to hamper global law enforcement efforts.

The case of Alice, the young Taiwanese woman we encountered at the very beginning of this book, reminds us of what happens if the status quo persists. Even after being rescued and temporarily accommodated in a shelter run by Chinese volunteers in the Cambodian capital, life was hard. Once she was safe, she asked local civil society organisations for legal assistance, but they declined on the grounds that they were not able to take on cases involving foreigners, which made it impossible for her to be identified as a victim of human trafficking for forced labour. Desperate, she tried to report her case to the Cambodian police but was repeatedly retraumatised by the male police officer who interviewed her, as he pushed her to provide details about the sexual violence she had been subjected to and eventually refused to open a case. On the verge of a mental breakdown, she was unable to find an organisation able to provide professional psychological support. To make things worse, due to the high number of survivors, the shelter where she was living was close to capacity and could only allocate the top floor to female victims. Alice lived locked inside her room.

While she waited to go back to Taiwan, Alice spent most of her time online. As she had asked for help through her social media accounts, her story had become common knowledge not only among her friends but also in the Chinese-speaking community in Cambodia. Many blamed her for being greedy and naïve, which caused her severe distress:

> I felt so depressed when one of my best friends called me stupid. He thought I had fallen into the trap because I wanted to be paid a lot of money without considering if I was qualified for it. I told him it was not true. During the pandemic, I had no income, and my baby's father had left me. As a single mother, I would have just grabbed any opportunity for my kid to survive.

Even after she got back to Taiwan, her life was not easy. Since the scam company had taken away all her money and belongings, she spent her first night back on the island on the street:

I arrived in Taiwan at night, and I met the police. They took my testimony but did not give me any instruction on how I could get justice or on the process of being identified as a modern slavery victim. I was lucky to get help from an organisation: they generously gave me a contract for three months as a survivor consultant, which helped me find some meaning in my life. But what about those victims who do not know such organisations exist? How can they be identified as victims and recover from the situation?

After that contract ended, the organisation attempted to find other work for Alice but it did not come to fruition. Eventually she dropped off their radar.

Postscript

Writing this book was one of the most challenging tasks any of us has ever embarked upon. The conversations, testimonies, and evidence we gathered, pored over, unpacked, and sought to process in the past three years have exposed us to some of the darkest of places. Trying to make sense of it all, in a context where the industry was both expanding at a frightening pace and simultaneously evolving in real time, was to chase a constantly moving target. Even as we put the finishing touches on the book, major developments were occurring.

In early 2025, reports emerged that a Chinese actor had been tricked into travelling to Thailand for a non-existent job only to be trafficked to Myanmar and confined in a scam compound. Although his story was not unique, and he was soon released, it captured public attention all over the world. In China, it led more than 1,880 families (as of the time of writing this postscript in late February 2025) to come together and compile an online spreadsheet listing their loved ones to petition the government to locate and free them. This mobilisation led to swift action, with the Ministry of Public Security issuing an official statement outlining efforts to address the situation of Chinese citizens who were missing or trapped abroad. The public discourse in China also shifted – from initially viewing the individuals in the scam compounds as mere perpetrators – to recognising that many of them are human-trafficking victims.

All of this instigated a series of major developments. Chinese officials travelled to Thailand for high-level meetings, and soon after the Thai government announced it was cutting power to border scam areas, along with supplies of fuel and the provision of internet connectivity. Myanmar junta and militia forces scrambled to limit the fallout and quickly raided major compounds and released thousands, handing them to Thailand for repatriation to their home countries.

While such developments give rise to cautious optimism, the work of civil society groups, international organisations, and others to support rescues and provide aftercare for survivors remains crucial. Yet, at the time of writing, many of these groups are in crisis, with the Trump administration and its advisors dismantling the aid programs central to funding this work. Many of our peers and comrades continue to work unpaid, and we are as inspired by their determination as we are repulsed by the nihilism of the ideologues whose actions will surely lead to more death and misery. If nothing else, this brings home the urgent need for the global community to channel more resources towards tackling the scourge of human trafficking, modern slavery, and forced criminality, in all their various abhorrent manifestations.

February 2025

Acknowledgements

We are deeply grateful to the survivors and to people involved in efforts to support victims who generously spent their time discussing their experiences with us as we were researching and writing this book. While we cannot mention them by name due to the sensitivity of some of the topics discussed here, we also wish to thank all the friends, colleagues, and peers who commented on partial drafts at earlier stages of writing. We extend particularly heartfelt gratitude to Sijia Zhong for her invaluable assistance in researching sections of this book.

Part of Chapter 3 was originally published in *Critical Asian Studies* in 2023, under the title 'Compound Capitalism: A Political Economy of Southeast Asia's Scam Operation'. We reproduce it in a revised and updated form with the kind permission of the journal editor. The section on Global China's underbelly in the Introduction, the historical excursus about Sihanoukville in Chapter 1, and the discussion of the victim identification system in Chapter 5 also first appeared in a slightly different form in the journal *Global China Pulse* in 2023 and 2024, and are included here with permission. Finally, we thank our editor at Verso, Sebastian Budgen, for his support of this book project since its inception, Mark Martin and Natalie Hume for their work in getting the manuscript into shape for publication, and Daphne Lawless for the index.

Index

Entries in *italics* refer to figures.

14K triad, 93
58 Tongcheng, 137, 173–4

Along (blogger), 163
Angola, 6
animal lovers, scams targeting, 127–8
Anti–Human Trafficking (AHT), 186, 188
anti-trafficking groups, 9, 118
Anti-Trafficking in Persons Act 2008
    (Thailand), 180
Antonopoulos, Georgios, 26
Ariston Inc., 40
armed organisations, ethnic, 26, 50–2, 72, 198
artificial intelligence, 130, 135, 202
ASEAN, 29, 180, 197

Bai family, 145n27
Bai Suocheng, 53–4
Bali Process Regional Support Office, 12
Bamboo Union, *see* United Bamboo Gang
Bangladesh, 30
Bank, James, 38
Bavet, Cambodia, 41, 44; law enforcement
    impersonation in, 129; local support for
    scam compounds, 153, 155; online scam
    industry in, 70; recruitment to scam
    compounds in, 83, 99; scam compounds
    in, 77
Binance, 122
'black cat black', 96
blacklists of destinations, 49, 101
blockchain analysis, 120, 122

'blood slave' case, 33–4, 69, 79, 172–5
Bo, Mark, 30
Branches of Hope, 80
Brazil, 30
BRI (Belt and Road Initiative), 60, 141–2,
    156–8
Broken Tooth, *see* Wan Kuok-koi
Bun Rany, 150
Burawoy, Michael, 20

C4ADS, 157
cainong, 117
Cambodia: 2022 crackdown in, 11, 43–4,
    70, 146–7, 153, 186; Bokor Mountain,
    40; citizenship of, 140–1, 151; criminal
    groups in, 94–6, 156; elite support for
    scam industry, 18, 26, 72, 144–6, 149; fake
    kidnapping scams in, 128; gambling in,
    39–44, 50; gateway companies in, 120;
    human trafficking laws, 180–1; human
    trafficking to, 9–12, 97; immigration
    authorities in, 187; kidnappings to, 98–9;
    Koh Kong, 44, 139, 144, 146–8, 164;
    land and property owners, 151–2; law
    enforcement cooperation with China,
    197–8; law enforcement impersonation
    scams, 128–9; Long Bay, 139–41, 148,
    158n53, 164; Oddar Meanchey, 44; online
    scam industry in, 1–5, 8–10, 30, 42–4,
    57, 70–1; O'Smach, 41, 80; Otres Village,
    65, 69; Poipet, 41, 44, 70, 131, 134; Preah
    Sihanouk, 10–11, 41, 43, 64, 66–8, 67n122,
    157; Pursat, 11, 144, 146, 161; repatriation
    of victims from, 189–90; social media

Cambodia (*continued*) in, 80; travel to, 101,
    103–4; victim identification in, 182–6,
    185, 188; *see also* Bavet; Phnom Penh;
    Sihanoukville
Cambodia-China Charity Team, 165–76
Cambodian People's Party, 144
Cambodian police, 33, 77, 128, 166, 173, 177,
    184, 188, 204
Cambodian Red Cross, 44, 149–50
Cambodian scam compounds, 1–2, 5, 34,
    42–4, 68–70, 146; escape from, 163–4;
    labour regime in, 132–3; recruitment to,
    76–8, 84–9, 107; support for survivors,
    195
capital, illicit, 158
casinos, 31; in Cambodia, 39–44, 61, 98; in
    Myanmar, 50, 52, 140; in the Philippines,
    45
CCTV, 57
Chainalysis, 120
chainification, 38
chat groups, 31
ChatGPT, 130
Chau, Alvin, 142–3, 156
Chen Baorong, 166–9, 171–6
Chen Yanban, 51
Chen Yanyu, 119
Chiang Kai-shek, 92
Chin, Ko-lin, 24, 142
China, 145n27; Anxi province, 35–8;
    charity law, 195; civil society groups in,
    193–5; crackdown on scam industry,
    71, 199–202; dormitory labour regime,
    21–2; Fujian province, 35–6; Guangdong
    province, 105, 154; Guangxi province, 77,
    104, 173; human trafficking law in, 189;
    Jiangxi province, 75, 189; and Kokang
    crime families, 54, 145n27; mule bank
    accounts in, 121; online gambling in, 39;
    online scam industry in, 3–5, 7, 35–7;
    otherisation of, 27; recruitment to scam
    compounds from, 81–2, 92–3, 106–8;
    repatriation of victims to, 189–90; and
    scam compounds, 23–9; in Sihanoukville,
    59–60; survivors of scam compounds
    from, 13–14, 30; travel restrictions from,
    101–4; use of AI in scams in, 130; *see also*
    Global China
China Daily, 201
China–Cambodia Law Enforcement
    Cooperation Office, 197–8
Chinese civil society, 27, 165
Chinese Commerce in Cambodia
    Association, 165, 171–2
Chinese criminals, non-traditional, 142
Chinese embassies, 124–5, 155–6; in
    Cambodia, 62–3, 77, 166, 173, 176, 187,
    190; and escape from scam compounds,
    161; in Myanmar, 142; in the Philippines,
    49
Chinese Expeditionary Force, 92
Chinese language: proficiency in, 13–14;
    see also Chinese-speaking community;
    Sinophone world
Chinese nationals: in Cambodia, 31, 33, 61–4;
    cremation of, 169; and cryptocurrencies,
    122; involved in scam industry, 13, 37;
    in Laos, 56; in Myanmar, 51, 53–4, 152,
    198; and online gambling, 41–2, 49; in
    the Philippines, 47; and rescue from scam
    compounds, 165, 171–2, 176; restrictions
    on travel, 102; in scam compounds, 5–6,
    75–7; social media used by, 31
Chinese Party-State, 29, 141, 155–9
Chinese police, in Myanmar, 51
Chinese students, overseas, 124–5, 128
Chinese Unification Promotion Party, 97
Chinese-language media, 5; and Anxi, 36; and
    Cambodia, 33, 43–4; on Cambodia–China
    Charity Team, 165, 171; and cyber slavery,
    14; and Laos, 56; and online scams, 31,
    129; on scam compounds, 76, 88, 105–7,
    113, 132; and Sihanoukville, 62; *see also*
    social media
Chinese-speaking community, 37–8, 92, 204;
    as rescuers and survivors, 194–5; social
    media influencers, 92
Christie, Nils, 15–16
citizenships, acquiring, 26, 139–41, 151, 172
civil society, 30, 60n98, 184, 203; Chinese,
    27; lack of trust in, 193; and rescue from
    compounds, 79, 164–5, 184, 195
commissions, 36, 77, 80, 99, 124, 130–1
compound capitalism, 17–23
compulsion, evidence of, 182
Convention against Trafficking in Persons,
    Especially Women and Children, 180
core managers, 115, 131
corporatisation, 38
COVID-19 pandemic, 2, 5; in Cambodia,
    65–7; and Cambodia–China Charity
    Team, 171; Chinese policies against,
    101–3, 169; and gambling, 42–3, 47;
    and kidnappings, 98; and scam industry
    recruitment, 23, 75, 77, 79, 81, 108, 137,
    202
credit card details, 118, 127
criminal groups, 3–5; and Chinese Party-
    State, 155–6; ethnic Chinese, 24–7; in
    Myanmar, 53; and online scam industry,
    17–18, 34–5, 79, 139–43; recruitment to
    scam compounds by, 93–8; and *saohei
    chu'e*, 62n106; transplanting, 71; *see also*
    Taiwanese gangs; triads

criminal law, 15–16, 155, 189
Cross-Strait Joint Crime-Fighting and Mutual
    Legal Assistance Agreement, 36
Crouching Tiger Villa, 53
crypto wallets, 73, 119, 122, 200
cryptocurrencies, 13; and Cambodia–
    China Charity Team, 172; and illicit
    infrastructure, 119–20, 122; and organised
    crime, 95; scams involving, 8, 15, 48, 76,
    124–7
cyber slavery, 12, 14, 108, 129
cyberfraud, *see* online scam industry
cybersecurity, 17

daigou, 82–3
data extraction, 22–3
dating apps, 126
deception, 87
deep-fake technology, 22, 130
dehumanisation, 86, 123n29
Democratic Karen Buddhist Army, 50
depression, 178, 187, 195
digital evidence, erasure of, 183
dispossession, 23
distress messages, 81, 161, 163, 177
division of labour, 115, 135, 194
Documentation Centre of Cambodia, 58
Dong Lecheng, 140–1
Dota, 86
Douyin, 31, 90–1, 93
Dubai, 77–8, 137, 154, 172, 176, 199
Duterte, Rodrigo, 45–7, 71

e-commerce scam, 126
Elliptic, 120
employment documents, and human
    trafficking, 114, 182
English language, proficiency in, 13
ethnic Chinese people: and other scam
    workers, 134; role in scam industry, 23–4,
    26–7, 71, 139; as victims of scam industry,
    90, 93, 107
excellent-employee certificates, 133
exceptionality, 19

Facebook, 6, 31, 80, 163
feminine characteristics, 113
Feng Fei Sha Gang, 93
forced criminality, 3, 93, 107, 135, 180–2,
    193–4
forced labour, 10–12, 14, 129, 148–9, 204;
    compound survivors providing, 182, 184,
    189; in Sihanoukville, 62
'foreign hostile forces', 193
Four Families, 53
Four Seas Gang, 93
Franceschini, Ivan, 30

Fraser, Nancy, 23
freelance recruiters, 79, 88–91
Frontier Myanmar, 152
Fully Light Group, 52, 54

GASO (Global Anti-Scam Organization),
    179
Gatchalian, Sherwin, 48–9
gateway companies, 119–20
Gaza, 16
Georgia, 72, 203
Global China, 4, 27–9, 60
Golden Triangle, 25, 55–6, 77, 107, 203
Golden Triangle Special Economic Zone, *see*
    GTSEZ
grey industries, 95
GTSEZ (Golden Triangle Special Economic
    Zone), 56–7, 72–3, 154, 156

hacking community, 18
heavenly and earthly scams, 116
Henry Group, 93
Hong Kong, 30, 39, 130; criminal groups in,
    95–6; money laundering in, 121; survivors
    of scam compounds from, 30
Hontiveros, Risa, 186
hotlines, 163
Huangsha Casino, 100
human resources departments, 110–11, 114,
    137
human trafficking, 1–3; and BRI, 156; in
    Cambodia, 44, 62, 69–70, 144; and
    COVID-19, 47; criminal groups and,
    25, 94–5; establishing victimhood,
    114, 181–5, *185*, 188–9, 204; extortion
    from victims, 191–2; Interpol on, 73;
    legal framework on, 180–1, 197; in the
    Philippines, 47–8; scam compounds as, 6,
    8–14, 83–5; by social media influencers,
    91; training for operating in field, 194
Hun Sen, 11, 41–2, 64, 140, 144, 150

IASA (International Anti Scam and
    Trafficking Alliance), 178–9
ideal victims, 15–16
identity work, 135
illicit infrastructure, 18, 72, 118–22, 135
immigration authorities: complicity with
    scam industry, 88, 150; and compound
    survivors, 16, 147–8, 180, 186; exit bans,
    102
immigration detention, 177, 179, 186–8, 195
impunity, 18
India, 72, 77, 91–2, 127, 203
Indonesia, 106, 118, 126, 139, 152, 158; and
    BRI, 157–8; and ethnic Chinese criminal
    groups, 26

instant-messaging apps, 30, 80
internet, 3, 12; victims connected to outside
world through, 20, 135, 163
Interpol, 6, 73
intimate-partner violence, 15
investments, fake, 2, 78, 126
IOM (International Organization for
Migration), 191

Japanese actors, 139
Jiandanwang, 31, 172
Jingcheng Group, 141
job ads, deceptive, 79–84, 102, 203
job-advertisement websites, 30, 80

K99 Group, 149
Kaibo, 158n53
Kayin Border Guard Force, 50, 55, 73, 141–2,
152
Kennedy, Jacqueline, 58
Khmer Rouge, 40, 58–60
kidnappings, 33, 47, 62, 79, 98–9; fake, 128;
in Sihanoukville, 62, 67n122
KNLA (Karen National Liberation Army),
50
KNU (Karen National Union), 50
Kok An, 144
Kokang Border Guard Force, 52, 144
Kokang crime families, 54, 145n27
KTVs (karaoke parlours), 100, 117n10, 154
Kuaishou, 76
Kuoch Chamroeun, 10

labour disputes, 69, 182
Lam, Jack, 45
land routes, 103–4
language barriers, 134, 194
Laos: human trafficking to, 91, 98; laws on
human trafficking, 180–1; local support
for scam industry, 55–7; and online
gambling, 43; and online scam industry,
3–4, 30, 70, 72–3; recruitment to scam
compounds in, 77–8, 106–7; scam
compounds in, 70; travel to, 101, 103
laoxiang, 86
Law against Telecom and Online Fraud,
101–2
law enforcement, 14, 17; in Cambodia, 42,
47, 61, 70, 144–5; in China, 36–7, 155;
complicity with scam industry, 117,
146–51, 163–4; and cryptocurrencies,
122; global, 72–3, 178; impersonating,
109, 124–5, 128–9; in Laos, 56; lax,
37, 61, 138; and organised crime, 26;
and scam compound survivors, 184,
186–90; in Taiwan, 35, 97; training in
human trafficking, 194; transnational

cooperation, 197–9, 203–4; see also
Cambodian police; Chinese police
Lee, Ching Kwan, 27
Li Ling, 30
Li Jie, 170
Li Saigao, 92–3
Li Yayuanlun, 33–4, 69, 172–5
Line, 80
List of Dishonest People, 200
Liu family, 145n27
local elites, 138, 143–5; and criminal groups,
17–19, 23, 26; and scam industry, 9, 37,
72, 193
Locard, Henry, 59
Lu Xiangri, 176–7
Ly Yong Phat, 144, 146

Ma Zhonghong, 37–8
Macau, 26, 39, 45, 56, 142
mafia groups, see criminal groups
Malaysia: and ethnic Chinese criminal
groups, 26; fraudulent job ads in, 81; MoU
on human trafficking, 180; survivors of
scam compounds from, 30, 106
managing directors, 131
Manila, 46, 48–9
Manila Times, 48–9
Marcos, 'Bongbong', 47, 49, 72
Marcos, Ferdinand, 45
mental health care, 165
Mertha, Andrew, 59
Mexico, 6, 72, 203
migrant workers, 12, 21
Ming Xuechang, 53
minors, and the scam industry, 14, 106–7
Mirror Media, 97
modern slavery, 2, 6, 11–12; and cyber
slavery, 108; and POGOs, 47; scam
industry as, 135, 159; victim-offender
overlap in, 15
money laundering, 25, 38, 47–8, 93; criminal
groups and, 95; and cryptocurrencies,
122n25; and illicit infrastructure, 119; in
the Philippines, 47–8
motorcades, 119–20
Motorcycle Uncle, 169–70
mule bank accounts, 120–2
multi-level marketing, 172
Myanmar, 3–4, 9, 30; criminal groups in, 93;
Dongmei Park, 93, 143; ethnic armed
organisations in, 72; gambling in, 43, 47,
50; Kayin State, 50–1, 72, 75, 111; Kokang
Self-Administered Zone, 51–5, 92, 144–5,
198; Laukkai, 52–3; law enforcement
cooperation with China, 197–8; local
support for scam industry, 18–19, 26,
29, 50–5, 144–5, 154; MoU on human

trafficking, 180; repatriation of victims from, 190; scam industry in, 70–2; Shan State, 51; Shwe Kokko, 4, 26, 50, 55, 111, 141, 156; social media influencers in, 92; survivors of scam compounds from, 106; travel restrictions to, 101; Wa State, 51–2, 55, 132, 198; *see also* Myawaddy

Myanmar scam compounds, 50–4, 70, 75–6; labour regime in, 130; recruitment to, 78, 81–3, 89, 93, 106–7; rescue from, 165, 175, 192; transferring workers between, 99; travel to, 103–4

Myawaddy, 50–1, 54–5, 75, 141; and criminal groups, 95–6; operations of scam compounds in, 115, *116*

NagaWorld, 40
New York Times, 143, 146, 149
New Zealand, 128
NGOs (nongovernmental organisations), 30, 58, 136; in China, 193–4; and rescue from compounds, 164–5, 176, 179, 188, 195
Nigeria, 3n3, 6
Nikkei Asia, 64, 126
non-punishment principle, 180–2

office space, 151–2
online gambling, 3–4, 38–9; in Cambodia, 41–4, 61–6, 68, 77, 98; in China and Taiwan, 37; Chinese entrepreneurs in, 141, 143; and cryptocurrencies, 122; as euphemism, 9–10, 69–70; in Laos, 56–7; in Myanmar, 54; in the Philippines, 45–9, 152; places known for, 80
online scam industry, 2–4, 71; Chen Baorong and, 166; corporatisation of, 135; criminal groups in, 17–18; and ethnic Chinese, 24, 28–9; forced criminality in, 182, 193–4; and gambling, 38–49; and global law enforcement, 72–3; labourers in, 9, 12–15, 23, 75–8; and local power brokers, 19, 49–57; official data on, 6–8; origins of, 34–7; recruitment patterns, 90; root causes of, 202–3; *see also* scam compounds
organised crime, *see* criminal groups

PAGCOR (Philippine Amusement and Gaming Corporation), 45–7
parcel-delivery phishing scams, 118, 127
people smugglers, 5, 111, 132, 190
performance indicators, 22, 131, 133
Peru, 6, 72, 203
Philippines, 3; and BRI, 158; e-commerce scams in, 126; gambling in, 39, 45–9; land and property owners, 152; law enforcement in, 150–1; online scam

industry in, 71–2; Pasay City, 45, 48, 150; recruitment to scam compounds from, 87–8; scam compounds in, 47; survivors of scam compounds from, 30, 106, 186–7; travel restrictions, 101, 199
phishing, 130
Phnom Penh, 1–2, 61; Central Security Department, 184–6; Chinese business owners in, 169–70; gambling in, 40–2; immigration centres in, 186; recruitment to scam industry in, 87, 89–90
phone-brushing, 117
phones: confiscating, 65, 75, 78, 114, 137, 182–3; formatting, 110
pig-butchering scams, 2, 22, 75–6, 109, 111, 122–4, 123n29, 179
POGOs (Philippine offshore gambling operators), 45, 47–9, 72
police, *see* law enforcement
post-modernity, 12
predatory loan scams, 127
professional brokers, 79, 85–8, 99
proletarianisation, 23
property management fees, 138
property managers, 110, 117, 147
ProPublica, 149
prostitution, 25, 47, 133, 181; *see also* sex work
Pun Ngai, 21
punishments, in scam compounds, 112, 133, 163, 183
pyramid schemes, 15

QQ, 80, 115

ransom, 9, 22, 96, 114; extorting, 128; fees as part of, 111; negotiations on, 76; raising funds for, 162; recruitment as alternative to, 86
recruitment by scam compounds, 75–8; and diversity, 105–8; methods of, 78–100; profiles of victims, 12–14, 16, 23; routes of, 100–5; staff responsible for, 111
repatriation, 30, 54, 183–5, *185*, 193–4; hurdles to, 189–90; media and police reports of, 37, 51; NGOs organising, 165–9
rescue teams, 147, 161–2, 175–6, 187, 190, 192
rescuer-influencers, 192
retraumatisation, 188, 204
Reyes, Vicente Chua Jr, 45
Rithy Raksmei, 144
Rithy Samnang, 144
romance scams, 22, 48
running-points platforms, 120

San Guang Gang, 93
saohei chu'e, 62
Saw Chit Thu, 142
Saw Min Min Oo, 142
scam compound survivors, 30–1; aftercare, 195; establishing victimhood, 180–4; and immigration authorities, 186–9; narratives of, 1–2, 9–16, 33–4, 75–9, 109, 137–8, 161–2, 204–5; personal details, 194; punishment of, 201; repatriation of, 189–90; as rescuers, 176–9
scam compounds, 3–6; criminal groups running, 25–6; and data extraction, 22–3; entrepreneurs behind, 139–43; and ethnic Chinese, 29; and global law enforcement, 72–3; human resources departments, 110–14, 139; internal structure of, 109–10, 116; international mobility of, 138; labour regime of, 8–12, 20–2, 130–4; and local economies, 138–9, 151–5, 158–9; local elite support for, 17–20, 143–51; operations departments, 115–16; other units in, 117–18; paradoxes of, 135–6; precursors of, 36, 38; public knowledge of, 108; rescue from, 161–5, 191–6; sales of workers between, 79, 99–100, 114; see also Cambodian scam compounds; Myanmar scam compounds; recruitment by scam compounds; scam compound survivors
scam rooms, 109
scam techniques, 77, 123–30; training in, 111–13, 115
scam township, 36
scamdemic, 2, 34
sea routes, 104
security guards, 19, 68–9, 117, 144, 153
Serbia, 72, 203
sex trafficking, 15–16, 25
sex work, forced, 83
sexual exploitation, 15, 165
sexual services, in scam compounds, 117–18
sexual violence, 188, 204
SEZs (special economic zones), 4, 4n9, 19, 45, 49, 56–7, 60
shaming, public, 2, 201
She Zhijiang, 55, 141–2, 156
Sihanouk, Norodom, 58
Sihanoukville, 57–71; blood-slave case in, 33–4, 79, 172–4; boom period, 61–3; bust period, 64–7; Chen Baorong and, 167, 170; and the Chinese state, 156–7; criminal groups in, 95; early period, 58–60; gambling in, 40–2, 47; immigration centres in, 186; Jinshui compound, 140–1, 147, 158n53; and Kok An, 144; labour regime in scam

compounds, 132–4; law enforcement in, 146–7, 149; local economy of, 153–4; online scam industry in, 1–2, 5, 44, 68–71, 109–10; physical infrastructure of, 72; police raids in, 183; recruitment to scam industry in, 81, 89–91, 100, 107; Russian and former Soviet community in, 59; sea routes to, 104–5; structure of scam compounds, 109–10, 117; transferring workers between compounds, 99
Singapore, 7, 75, 91, 120n19, 127
Sinophone world, 5, 7, 123
Sister Pang, 170–1
slavery, modern, see modern slavery
Slobodian, Quinn, 19
Smith, Chris, 21
snakeheads, 103, 107, 190
social media: Chinese-language, 5; recruitment to scam compounds on, 30–2, 80, 104; scams using, 127; survivors' details on, 194
social media influencers, 79, 83, 91, 111; recruiting to scam compounds, 91–3; as rescuers, 192
SOEs (state-owned enterprises), 158
solidarity, between compound victims, 22, 134, 176
South Africa, apartheid labour regime, 20–2
South China Morning Post, 120
South Koreans, 54, 139
Southeast Asia: Chinese-language media in, 31; ethnic Chinese in, 23; and online gambling, 38; and online scam industry, 3–9, 13, 17–19, 37–8, 71; restrictions on travel to, 101–2; scam compounds in, 5–6, 13, 19, 30
spinach cities, 4, 57
spoofing software, 119
Sri Lanka, 30, 72, 203
SSEZ (Sihanoukville Special Economic Zone), 60, 60n98, 157
state actors, 20, 159, 168, 193, 203; local, 31, 145–51
suicides, 65, 69, 170
surveillance capitalism, 22

Taiwan: and China–Cambodia Charity Team, 171; crackdown on scam industry, 71; criminal collusion with bank workers in, 121–2; online scam industry in, 3, 5, 7, 34–6; recruitment to scam compounds from, 81–3, 93, 97; survivors of scam compounds from, 1, 30, 204–5; travel from, 102, 104, 199
Taiwanese gangs, 35, 37, 93–4, 96
task scams, 124
tea fees, 99

team leaders, 113, 115, 131–4, 192
technology parks, 4
Telegram, 31, 125; and illicit infrastructure, 118–19; information about scam compounds on, 112, 116
Tether cryptocurrency tokens, 94, 122n25
Thailand: border with Myanmar, 50–1, 54–5, 72, 131; and ethnic Chinese criminal groups, 26; human trafficking laws, 180–2, 190; mule bank accounts in, 121; online scam industry in, 7; survivors of scam compounds from, 30
Thento Union, 93
Three Brotherhood Alliance, 52, 198
'three lows', 13
TikTok, 31, 89, 192
TIP ('Trafficking in Persons') report, 181
torture, 9, 148, 183
tourism: Chinese, 61; and COVID-19, 66, 98; gambling, 43, 45–6; sex, 59
training, in scam compounds, 111–13
trauma, 165, 170, 188
triads, 24–6, 93, 96–7, 142
trust, lack of, 90, 193
Try Pheap, 144
Tu Cheng-che, 94
Turkey, 72, 203
TVBS News, 94

Uganda, 30, 77–8
United Arab Emirates, 6, 72, 138, 176
United Bamboo Gang, 93, 94n42, 97–8
United Kingdom, 73
United Nations: Office of the High Commissioner for Human Rights (OHCHR), 9, 78, 191; Office on Drugs and Crime (UNODC), 191
United States, 69, 73

Varese, Federico, 17
victim identification, 182–4, 188–90, 193–4
victim support, dark side of, 191–3

victim–offender overlap, 14–15
Vietnam, 30; border with Cambodia, 70, 77, 190; and ethnic Chinese criminal groups, 26; MoU on human trafficking, 180; and online scam industry, 7; recruitment to scam compounds from, 85–6, 106
Voice of Democracy (VoD), 66, 68, 97, 146–8, 164
volunteer groups, 165, 176, 178

Wan Kuok-koi, 93, 142–3, 155
websites, fake, 118, 124, 179
WeChat, 31, 65, 77, 141, 200; and China–Cambodia Charity Team, 169, 173; compound rescuers on, 192; recruitment on, 80–1, 86, 90; scam worker assigned to, 115; selling IDs on, 119
Wei family, 93n39, 145n27
Weibo, 113
Whittle, Joseph, 27
wildlife trading, illegal, 25
workers' movements, 21
workplace discipline, 20

Xiao Yankuai, 51–2
Xiao Zheng, 87
Xiaohongshu, 90
Xinchuang Network Technology, 48

Yamada, Teri Shaffer, 40
Yatai International Holding Group, 141–2
Yatai New City, see Myanmar, Shwe Kokko
Youk Chhang, 58
Yutang, 177

Zambia, 6
Zhang, Sheldon X., 24–5, 142
Zhang Anle, 97–8
Zhao Wei, 56–7, 155
Zhengheng Group, 139–40
Zhuang Hua, 37–8
Zun Yuan Technology, 150